THE PATTERN IN THE CARPET

The
PATTERN
in the
CARPET

◆◆◆

A Personal History
with Jigsaws

Margaret Drabble

HOUGHTON MIFFLIN HARCOURT
BOSTON   NEW YORK
2009

First U.S. edition

Copyright © 2009 by Margaret Drabble

ALL RIGHTS RESERVED

www.hmhbooks.com

First published in Great Britain in 2009 by Atlantic Books,
an imprint of Grove Atlantic Ltd.

Library of Congress Cataloging-in-Publication Data
Drabble, Margaret, date.
The pattern in the carpet : a personal history with
jigsaws / Margaret Drabble. — 1st U.S. ed.
p. cm.
Includes bibliographical references.
ISBN 978-0-547-24144-9
1. Jigsaw puzzles — History. 2. Jigsaw puzzles — Psychological aspects.
3. Drabble, Margaret, date. I. Title.
GV1507.J5D73 2009
793.73 — dc22   2009012214

Printed in the United States of America

DOC 10 9 8 7 6 5 4 3 2 1

For Phyllis Bloor

CONTENTS

FOREWORD

This book is not a memoir, although parts of it may look like a memoir. Nor is it a history of the jigsaw puzzle, although that is what it was once meant to be. It is a hybrid. I have always been more interested in content than in form, and I have never been a tidy writer. My short stories would sprawl into novels, and one of my novels spread into a trilogy. This book started off as a small history of the jigsaw, but it has spiralled off in other directions, and now I am not sure what it is.

I first thought of writing about jigsaws in the autumn of 2005, when my young friend Danny Hahn asked me to nominate an icon for a website. This government-sponsored project was collecting English icons to compose a 'Portrait of England', at a time when Englishness was the subject of much discussion. At random I chose the jigsaw, and if you click on 'Drabble' and 'jigsaw' and 'icon' you can find what I said. I knew little about jigsaws at this point, but soon discovered that they were indeed an English invention as well as a peculiarly English pastime. I then conceived the idea of writing a longer article on the subject, perhaps even a short book. This, I thought, would keep me busy for a while.

I had recently finished a novel, which I intended to be my last, in which I believed myself to have achieved a state of calm and equilibrium. I was pleased with *The Sea Lady* and at peace with the world. It had been well understood by those whose judgement I most value, and I had said what I wanted to say. I liked the idea of writing something that would take me away from fiction into a primary world of facts and pictures, and I envisaged a brightly coloured illustrated book, glinting temptingly from the shelves of gallery and museum shops amongst the greetings cards, mugs and calendars portraying images from Van Gogh and Monet. It would make a pleasing Christmas present, packed with gems of esoteric information that I would gather, magpie-like, from libraries and toy museums and conversations with strangers. I would become a jigsaw expert. It would fill my time pleasantly, inoffensively. I didn't think anyone had done it before. I would write a harmless little book that, unlike two of my later novels, would not upset or annoy anybody.

It didn't work out like that.

Not long after I conceived of this project, my husband Michael Holroyd was diagnosed with an advanced form of cancer and we entered a regime of radiotherapy and chemotherapy all too familiar to many of our age. He endured two major operations of hitherto unimagined horror, and our way of life changed. He dealt with this with his usual appearance of detachment and stoicism, but as the months went by I felt myself sinking deep into the paranoia and depression from which I thought I had at last, with the help of the sea lady, emerged. I was at the mercy of ill thoughts. Some of my usual resources for outwitting them, such as taking long solitary walks in the country, were not easily available. I couldn't concentrate much on reading, and television bored me, though DVDs, rented from a film club recommended by my sister Helen, were a help. We were more or less housebound, as we were told to avoid public places because Michael's immune system was weak, and I was afraid of poisoning him, for he was restricted to an unlikely diet consisting largely of white fish, white bread and mashed potato. I have always been a nervous cook, unduly conscious of dietary prohibitions and the plain dislikes of others, and the responsibility of providing food for someone in such a delicate state was a torment.

The jigsaw project came to my rescue. I bought myself a black lacquer table for my study, where I could pass a painless hour or two, assembling little pieces of cardboard into a preordained pattern, and thus regain an illusion of control. But as I sat there, in the large, dark, high-ceilinged London room, in the pool of lamplight, I found my thoughts returning to the evenings I used to spend with my aunt when I was a child. Then I started to think of her old age, and the jigsaws we did together when she was in her eighties. Conscious of my own ageing, I began to wonder whether I might weave these memories into a book, as I explored the nature of childhood.

This was dangerous terrain, and I should have been more wary about entering it, but my resistance was low. I told myself that there was nothing dangerous in my relationship with my aunt, and that my thoughts about her could offend nobody, but this was stupid of me. Any small thing may cause offence. My sister Susan, more widely known as the writer A. S. Byatt, said in an interview somewhere that she was distressed when she found that I had written (many decades ago) about a particular teaset that our family possessed, because she had always wanted to use it herself. She felt I had appropriated something that was not mine. And if a teapot may offend, so may an aunt or a jigsaw. Writers are territorial, and they resent intruders.

I fictionalized my family background in a novel titled *The Peppered Moth*, which is in part about genetic inheritance. I scrupulously excluded any mention of my two sisters and my brother, and

I suspect that, wisely, none of them read it, but I was made conscious of having trespassed. This made me very unhappy. I vowed then that I would not write about family matters again (a constraint which, for a writer of my age, constitutes a considerable loss) but as I sat at my dark table I began to think I could legitimately embark on a more limited project that would include memories of my aunt's house. These are on the whole happy memories, much happier than the material that became *The Peppered Moth*. I wanted to rescue them. Thinking about them cheered me up and recovered time past.

But my new plan posed difficulties. I could not truthfully present myself as an only child (as some writers of memoirs have misleadingly done) and I have had to fall back on a communal childhood 'we', which in the following text usually refers to my older sister Susan and my younger sister Helen. My brother Richard is considerably younger than me, and his childhood memories of my aunt are of a later period, although he did spend many holidays with her.

This book became my occupational therapy, and helped to pass the anxious months. I enjoyed reading about card games, board games and children's books, and all the ways in which human beings have ingeniously staved off boredom and death and despised one another for doing so. I enjoyed thinking about the nature of childhood and the history of education and play. For an hour or two a day, making a small discovery or an unexpected connection, I could escape from myself into a better place.

I don't mean in these pages to claim a special relationship with my aunt. My father once said to me, teasingly, 'Are you such a dutiful niece and daughter because you married into a Jewish family?' And I think that the Swifts may have played a part in my relationship with Auntie Phyl. I was captivated by the family of my first husband, Clive Swift. He was the first member of his generation to marry out, but despite this I was made welcome. I loved the Swifts' strong sense of mutual support and their demonstrative, affectionate generosity. They were a powerful antidote to the predominantly dour and depressive Yorkshire Drabbles and Staffordshire Bloors. It was a happy day that introduced me to Clive and the Swifts.

In *The Peppered Moth* I wrote brutally about my mother's depression, and I never wish to enter that terrain again. It is too near, too ready to engulf me as it engulfed her. Some readers have written to me, taking me to task for being hard on my mother, but more have written to thank me for expressing their complex feelings about their own mothers. I had hoped that writing about her would make me feel better about her. But it didn't. It made me feel worse.

Both my parents were depressive, though they dealt with this in different ways. My father took to gardening and walking with his dog, my mother to Radio 4 and long laments. He was largely silent, though Helen reminds me that he used to hum a lot. My mother could not stop talking. Her telephone calls, during which she complained about him bitterly for hour after hour, seemed never-ending. The last decades of their marriage were not happy, but when they were on speaking terms they would do the *Times* crossword together.

Doing jigsaws and writing about them has been one of my strategies to defeat melancholy and avoid laments. Boswell regretted that his friend Samuel Johnson did not play draughts after leaving college, 'for it would have afforded him an innocent soothing relief from the melancholy which distressed him so often'. Jigsaws have offered me and many others an innocent soothing relief, and this is where this book began and where it ends.

Margaret Drabble, 2008

As she went to bed that night, she said that she wished we had been able to finish the jigsaw. 'It's a pity,' she said, as she gave up. 'It's a pity.' It was the last evening of the last summer. We had tried to finish it. We sat up late, past midnight, struggling with patches of tree and fern and grass and sky. In the morning, we would have to drive away and leave it incomplete on its table, for others to finish another day. It was unsatisfactory. She knew she would never come back. She knew it was her last summer with us. It was Thursday, 7 August 1997, and she was eighty-eight. She was getting older, and I was getting older, and the journey back to her home was across country and very long. Next year, even if she were still alive, it would be too much for both of us. Neither of us mentioned this. There were many things we never mentioned. But she knew, and she knew I knew.

My aunt had been spending a week in West Somerset with us each summer for fifteen years. Her first visit was to a house I was renting from friends in Nettlecombe, not far beyond Taunton, and she drove herself all the way across England to us from the East Midlands in her Morris Minor. She didn't attempt the journey in one day; she stopped off for a night, with her bad little white dog, in a bed and breakfast, then drove on in the morning, arriving long before I expected her. She was a very determined old woman. That year, we finished our jigsaw.

In 1989, I bought a house at Porlock Weir, which was even further west. She had parted with her car and was no longer driving, so I used to go to collect her and her little white dog for her annual holiday. I drove north from London up the A1 to her house and then on south and west to Somerset in the day. I didn't want to stay the night with her; the house I had so loved as a child had become uninhabitable for anyone fastidious enough not to love dogs more than people. In later years, I learned to break my journey by overnighting discreetly in the neighbourhood at my favourite wayside inn, a roadhouse of which I have many good memories. She may have been surprised by how fresh and early I arrived to collect her, but if she was, she never let on. Maybe she knew I'd been lurking in the Ram Jam.

My earliest memories of jigsaws date back to Auntie Phyl. Auntie Phyl, as she was known to all our family and to my friends, was my mother's younger and only sister. In the village where she lived for the second half of her life, she was known as 'Miss Bloor', a form of address that honoured her status as schoolteacher. Homerton-trained in Cambridge, she taught small children, and she liked small children, and my sisters and I enjoyed going to stay with her during the war in her independent, semi-detached house in Dixon Crescent, Doncaster. She had been teaching in Woodfield Primary School from 1930, and would probably have remained in Doncaster, but when my grandfather fell ill just after the war she moved, as unmarried daughters did, to live with my disagreeable grandmother in Long Bennington, a village between Grantham and Newark on what was then the Great North Road, where she accepted a post in the village school. My grandfather died shortly after, in December 1947, but she stayed on to look after Grandma.

After Grandma's death she remained in Long Bennington for the rest of her active life. She is remembered in the village. 'If you had a loose tooth, Miss Bloor would pull it out for you.'

My grandmother was bad-tempered but her home, a small red-brick pantiled Georgian farmhouse called Bryn, was wonderful to a suburban city child, and Auntie Phyl was an excellent aunt. (Bryn means 'hill' in Welsh, and Long Bennington is one of the longest and flattest villages in England; the farm a few hundred yards along the road is slightly more appropriately called Valley Farm.) She taught us to peg rugs, and to sew, and to do French knitting, and to make lavender bags, and to thread bead necklaces, and to bake rock cakes and coconut fingers, and to play patience. She let us run wild in the field at the back of the house during the day, and in the evenings she played card and board games with us, or sat with us, hour after hour, as we did jigsaws on the gate-leg table in the front room. Bryn, as she grew older, became so cluttered with objects from the distant past and from more recent car boot sales that it was hard to find a clear surface, but for a jigsaw she could make room. The dark cubbyhole under the back stairs was stuffed with all manner of junk and treasures, including dozens of old jigsaws, piled up in their battered cardboard boxes. I inherited some of them, and brought them to Somerset, but they are all gone now, to their own car boot sales.

For two or three decades, while I was an undergraduate, and then as a young mother trying to work in all the spare hours I could find, I was too busy for puzzles and games and pastimes. There wasn't space, there wasn't time, and in the evenings I was too tired. We sometimes played cards on family holidays, but I thought I had put childish games behind me for ever. I don't recall that I did any jigsaws during those middle years, but maybe my memory betrays me here, for it has recently been pointed out to me by Danny Hahn that I mention jigsaws very specifically, in my novel

The Millstone, which was published in 1965, and written while I was expecting my third child, Joe. Danny claims that he first read this novel in the Australian Outback by candlelight in 2007, which is odd, because that is where son Joe claims to have read it too, two decades earlier in 1987. Maybe the Australian Outback is full of old copies of *The Millstone*.

It is true that there is an extended reference in the novel to this motif, as narrator Rosamund takes to jigsaws in the later stages of pregnancy, and describes them as therapeutic:

> One can, if one tries, buy extremely complicated jigsaw
> puzzles with a thousand interlocking pieces, and pictures by
> old masters, or of ships at sea, and heaven knows what:
> also puzzles in the shape of maps of Europe, square puzzles,
> circular puzzles, star-shaped puzzles, reversible puzzles, anything
> one can imagine in the way of puzzles...when I went to
> bed I would dream not of George, nor of babies locked away
> from me where I couldn't feed them, nor even of childbirth,
> but of pieces of blue sky edged with bits of tree, or small
> blue irregular shapes composing the cloak of the Virgin Mary.

There is also, I note, some attempt to contrast the 'jigsaw puzzle mind' of the narrator, who is writing a doctoral thesis, with the carefree, creative pretensions of her friend Lydia, who is trying to write a novel. I must have been wondering which of these characters I wanted to be.

Many jigsaw puzzlers reveal a degree of anxiety about their hobby, fearing it reveals a neurosis that might expose them to hostile analysis. Do they do puzzles because they are lonely, like the orphaned heroine of Elizabeth Bowen's *The Death of the Heart*, who dutifully works on pictures of aeroplanes given to her by an equally lonely and much older family friend? Or because they are dyslexic or autistic and no good at fireside conversation? Or because they are timid, uncreative and imitative, satisfied with reconstructing the ready-made, like would-be artists who prefer to paint by numbers? Or because they know that jigsaws are designed to waste time, and that the killing of time is, as Daniel Defoe said, the worst of murders?

I had completely forgotten that I had written about the subject until Danny reminded me. It must be an old obsession.

According to their chronicler Anna Funder, the 'puzzle women' at Nuremberg who work on the shredded security files of the East German Stasi claim that they took on this task because they have always enjoyed doing jigsaws. They say they still go home to do jigsaws in their spare time, after a grim day's work piecing together thousands of scraps of torn paper detailing ruined lives. This, one could claim, is obsessional behaviour, but it is a useful obsession, harnessed to a higher purpose.

Maybe I did purchase the odd jigsaw when I was in my twenties and thirties, but I think that I took to them seriously when Auntie Phyl began her annual Somerset visits, when I was in my forties and she in her seventies. Together we rediscovered the jigsaw.

Auntie Phyl was not wholly easy to entertain on holiday. She was so used to living alone that she was slightly uncomfortable with the concept of conversation. My mother talked incessantly, but Auntie Phyl lacked small talk, and had to be encouraged. She was not interested in any of the television programmes that might have interested the rest of us, although she consented to watch the news. Once, watching images at Bryn of famine or genocide in Africa, she said to me, more in enquiry and bewilderment than with anger or resentment, 'What are these people to us?' At home, she occupied herself with crochet, and needlepoint, and stitching yards and yards of decorative trimming round the edges of pillowcases, and holding amorous or teasing conversations with her dog, or playing games of patience. But with us she was clearly in need of some other form of diversion. The summer days in Somerset were straightforward, for she loved an outing, a picnic, a cream tea, a visit to Ilfracombe or Minehead, a flower show, a dog show, even a tour of a church. She was surprisingly knowledgeable about churches and antiques. The evenings were more difficult, until we thought of the jigsaw.

Why do I say 'surprisingly' knowledgeable? Because she set so little store by her own knowledge. Her bossy and manipulative big sister had staked her claim as the clever one and the pretty one, and Auntie Phyl always had to make do with second place. Her family tended to take her on her sister's estimate. My mother's attitude to her sister, both socially and intellectually, was offensively patronizing.

Doing a jigsaw can be a solitary time killer, a way of getting quietly through life until death, an oblique confrontation with the absence of meaning, but it can also be a companionable pastime. In a family group you can talk, you can work silently at your corner, you can discuss other matters, you can engage in minor spats about intrusive elbows or pieces wrongly placed. I met a man recently at a friend's wake, a distinguished-looking man with a white moustache, who became quite fierce about his mother-in-law's contributions to the family Christmas jigsaw; she would force pieces into the wrong place, he said, and he had to creep down in the night when she was asleep to prise them out.

When I do jigsaws now I can hear my aunt's urgings and admonishments, and hear the click and suck of her teeth as she concentrated on her task. She is present with me as I sit alone. She had good teeth, much better than mine, and much less expensively maintained. I have spent as much on dentistry as Martin Amis, with whose problems I have great sympathy. Auntie Phyl's teeth, well coated and preserved by nature's protection of plaque, lasted her very well.

She it was who taught us that we must always sort out the edge and construct the frame of the puzzle first. This, she assured us, was the only correct procedure. Only once you had formed a complete rectangle (or, more rarely, a complete circle or oval) were you allowed to embark on filling it in.

So strong was this directive that I experienced one of the most intense panics of my early life when I was asked to do a jigsaw with an incomplete edge. I remember the occasion with vivid humiliation. I must have been five or six years old, and my mother had taken me for an 'interview' at the Girls' Public Day School Trust school in Sheffield, known as Sheffield Girls' High, the junior department of which I was shortly to attend. I am not sure who was interviewing whom, but I was sent off to sit in a corner at a low, undignified, nursery table with a box with jigsaw pieces in it, and told to play with them. I must have regarded this as an intelligence test (a notion that my mother would have encouraged) because, while my mother and the Junior Head conversed, I struggled seriously with the task. It was impossible. The pieces were too large and easy for a child of my age, and some of the edge was missing. How could I be expected to tackle a baby jigsaw that was so incomplete? Was it a trick? I was indignant and confused. It was an intensely distressing quarter of an hour. I cannot remember whether or not I protested; if I did, my mother would have turned my protest into a story that went: 'Margaret was so clever that she complained about the missing pieces.' She was always telling everyone how clever I was. This made me much hated in some quarters. Even today, I get letters from women my own age telling me how much they hated me, even though they had never met me. They sometimes say they don't hate me any more, but if so, why do they bother to tell me about it now?

What I remember from this episode of the little Goldilocks table is the feeling of bewildered inadequacy, of knowing that I would never fit into this new school. I had loved my old village school in East Hardwick just outside Pontefract, where we lived as evacuees from Sheffield during the war. I had attended this school from the age of three and a half, travelling to it by bus with several other children, and I felt at home there. From the bus stop, just outside our house, Mr Turton would pick us up and drive us all to school. There were two classes, one for big children and one for little children, and I have not forgotten the two teachers, Miss Cooper and Miss Royston, though I have not seen them for well over sixty years. I fancy I can still see their grave and friendly maiden faces, their neat blouses, their coils of hair. Miss Cooper's hair was brown, Miss Royston's grey. I met a woman in Norwich recently who had been at this little school at the same time as me, and she reminded me of Mr Turton's name, and of the brightly coloured pictures of Biblical scenes that Miss Cooper used to show us. I liked them very much. She also had some striking pictures of fields of tulips in Holland, tended by women in Dutch bonnets. They must have been part of a geography lesson. Teaching by pictures is a centuries-old tradition.

I had liked East Hardwick, and I knew this new superior Sheffield school would be no good. I never liked it. It never liked me. I never fitted in.

A child psychotherapist whom I consulted tells me that children who come from a disorganized, chaotic background may have difficulty in putting jigsaws together because they don't know how to start with the frame. 'They don't seem to see the straight line round the edge of the jigsaw.' That was not a problem from which I suffered.

II

We always started with the frame. Auntie Phyl taught my sisters and me how to pick out all the straight-edged pieces of jigsaw first, to find the corners, and to build up the four sides. Then we would begin to sort the colours, and to construct areas of the picture. Unlike some people, we did not have a set procedure for this stage of the puzzle, and we were never of the wilfully austere school that does not look at the picture on the box. Looking at the picture for us was part of the pleasure. Doing a jigsaw was not an intelligence test, or a personality assessment programme; it was a pursuit that lay somewhere between creation and imitation and discovery and reverie. And it was not, for us, a form of competition.

As we progressed from easy children's puzzles to more compli-cated adult puzzles (willow pattern plate, Dutch skating scenes, a Fra Angelico nativity, the birds of Britain) we would sometimes reach a stage when Auntie Phyl would say, 'Well, I can't see by the colours any more, we've done all the bright ones, so I'm going to have to go by the shapes now.' (I have just reached that stage with Uccello's *The Hunt in the Forest* from the Ashmolean; I've done all the bright-coated hunters, the horizontal leaping hounds and the vertical tree trunks, and am left with the brown canopy of foliage.)

I don't think that we ever did trick jigsaws, cut without identifiable edges. I have encountered them recently, in the course of research, and have found that they do indeed induce a mild degree of panic. But with Auntie Phyl, there was always the safety of the edge.

I have another memory of early panic, this time connected with a maypole. I must have been very small as I was still at the East Hardwick school. I and a group of other children were taken by coach to a neighbouring village and issued with maypole ribbons of red and blue and white and asked to dance around a maypole with strange children from other schools. It must have been May Day, or was it a celebration of the end of the war? Nobody had rehearsed us or told us which way to go round, and we and the ribbons became hopelessly muddled and entangled as we all went in different and wrong directions. The teachers were cross and we were upset. I think what upset me most was the knowledge that the ribbons could and should have made a beautiful and intricate pattern, if we had been taught properly how to interweave them. Instead, there was this guilty muddle. I don't think I was prematurely mourning the death of village life and rural England; I was simply distressed by the lack of clear direction. This, strangely, is my only unhappy memory of East Hardwick. It was a happy school, where I felt at home, where our days were a joy, and our paths through flowers.

Children need order, and the knowledge that a problem can be resolved. I don't know whether I, as a child, needed this more than most and, if so, why. But I suspect that my liking for jigsaws and my enduring affection for Auntie Phyl are connected with the fact that she was such a good teacher.

At the very end of a large and difficult jigsaw, when there were just a few irregular bald patches left, Auntie Phyl might embark philosophically on the topic of 'the missing piece'. For at this late stage in a puzzle's life, it has become clear to all participants, sometimes over several nights of struggle, that certain pieces are, almost without question, missing. Sometimes there is one particular space, a distinct and obvious space, and the piece that should occupy the space cannot be found. If it could, it would have declared itself. The floor has been searched, and sometimes it is suggested that the bag of the vacuum cleaner be emptied. Occasionally pieces are retrieved by these methods, though often not the ones you are looking for. It is at this moment that Auntie Phyl might say, 'Now's the time when we could count the spaces, and see if we've got the right number of pieces left to fill them.' This is always a controversial moment, for the depression cast by an incontrovertibly missing and irrecoverable piece is considerable, so in a way it is as well to delay this disturbing realization for as long as possible. On the other hand, if you confront the problem, and bravely count the spaces, and find that you have the precise numbers to fit them, there is an increased satisfaction in staring at these recalcitrant remainders, knowing that, implausibly, impossibly, they will eventually be made to supply the gaps and complete the image.

One of the strangest and most unsettling cognitive experiences of a difficult jigsaw (say, a Jackson Pollock) occurs when a piece that has eluded intensive search over hours and days and weeks suddenly makes itself known, and fits itself into its home. At once, the piece loses its profoundly unknown quality, and becomes so much a part of the pattern that within seconds you cannot remember where the gap was. What Freudian denial had concealed its identity for so long? Once it has been seen and placed, it is impossible to recall its previous invisibility.

One night, while writing an early draft of this book, and in honour of Auntie Phyl, I took the risk and counted the last pieces of Henri Rousseau's *Tiger in a Tropical Storm (Surprised!)* with which I was then engaged. There were thirty-two spaces left, and thirty-two pieces. They would have to go in. And they did, although I had difficulty in placing even the last four. I am not very good at jigsaws. That is one of the reasons why I like them so much. I had been working on this striped beast of the forests for months, albeit very intermittently, with a little help from my daughter Becky and other visitors, and I was pleased to finish it off, and to resume serious work on this book, in which I had hoped to explore the nature, satisfactions, history and imagery of this curious activity.

I like to think that my aunt was happy, as I was, during those summer evenings in Somerset. I always anticipated her visits with a mixture of pleasure and apprehension, because she could be a very rude and demanding guest. Graciousness was not her forte. She belonged to a generation that expected younger people, even younger people in their fifties, to behave with deference. Once, driving back towards Porlock Weir over Exmoor from an excursion, my daughter, my daughter's friend and I engaged in a lively dispute about which route to take back. All were beautiful, so which to choose? Should we take the coast road, or drive inland over the moor via Simonsbath? After a few minutes of this banter, my aunt said, and not as a joke, 'Oh, do shut up about it, you're making me feel sick.' We fell silent at once, but when we got back home my daughter's friend confided to me that she had never heard an adult speak to another adult in that tone.

(This elegant friend, Guyanese-born and educated in England, now lives in Johannesburg, whence she sent me a jigsaw of camouflaged African animals that at first sight looked easy, but was far more difficult to complete than Rousseau's tiger. I emailed her to say, 'The African jigsaw is impossible,' and she responded, 'The African jigsaw is difficult, but not impossible.' I think that is still her view of the situation in South Africa.)

Auntie Phyl's eating preferences were also a little tricky. She was not a good cook, but when we were little she had cooked for us what I remember as delicious snack meals, like Welsh Rabbit (sic) and Scotch pancakes and drop scones and omelettes (a word that she pronounced, as I do, with three good syllables). She was not keen on anything continental. Late in her life she came round in a big way to the notion of the pub lunch, but she considered herself allergic to mushrooms, and it was surprising how many pub menus on Exmoor seemed to feature mushrooms in almost everything. I remember one potentially disastrous meal in the Notley Arms in Monksilver when she was presented with some dark dish (perhaps an omelette?) covered in mushrooms, but luckily the lighting in the pub was so dim that she didn't see them. She ate them all, and there were no ill effects.

I maintain (though she queried this) that it was I who usefully introduced her to scampi and chips, at an excellent but now defunct castellated hostelry overlooking the Bristol Channel at Linton. On a fine summer day, as wasps circled the cider, the view was as glorious as the French Riviera, and we felt on top of the world. She took to scampi very well once she had got over the shock of the novelty. Fish and chips wrapped in newspaper she had always enjoyed, and she used to go out to get them from the van at Long Bennington when it did its weekly round of the villages.

She always insisted that she deeply disliked mayonnaise, but one day, making egg sandwiches for our picnic, I thought, what the hell, and mashed in a generous spoonful of Hellman's while she wasn't looking. We ate our sandwiches in a green sloping field beneath an azure sky, surrounded by the surreal pink sheep of Somerset, as happy as can be, and she devoured every morsel. That evening she rang my sister Helen and I heard her say that she had had a lovely day out, and that Maggie's egg sandwiches were 'out of this world'.

I wasn't as nice as I should have been to her succession of dogs. I didn't pat them or speak to them, and when I took them for walks I was silently morose. Auntie Phyl used to tell them, 'Now, be good for your Auntie Maggie, she doesn't like it when you make a mess on the carpet.' And she was right, I didn't. The first little white dog – a rescue dog called Kelly, whose original owner was in gaol – metamorphosed at some point into a slightly smaller and slightly better-behaved but otherwise almost identical West Highland terrier called Daisy. These were part of the summer deal, and they did alarm the rabbits, which since their visits ended have become completely out of control. When I was a small child, I had loved her large collie dog, Chum, but in my recollection Chum was a much better-trained dog.

A friend of mine once suggested that the later dogs became so naughty because my aunt had de-trained them, and that, by allowing them to pee on the carpet, lick her face and feet, masturbate against her ankles, jump at visitors, and bounce on beds, she was expressing the bad behaviour that had been pent up in her by a lifetime of schoolmistressy propriety and younger-sister, maiden-aunt syndrome. I think there is truth in that.

My aunt preferred animals and birds to people. In general, despite the condoned anarchy of Kelly and Daisy, she was good with animals. In Doncaster, she had had a green budgerigar called Skippy who used to be able to say, 'Auntie go to school,' as she set off for her day's work at Woodfield Primary. She wore a little green Skippy feather in her hatband, which I thought was stylish. His death in the hard winter of 1946 was a sad loss to all of us, and the subject of eloquent letters of condolence from her nieces, which she preserved for the rest of her life.

Creatures accepted her. Cats would come to sit on her lap, and calves offered their noses to her for a scratch. Birds flocked into her back garden, and sometimes came right into her large farmhouse kitchen. She called them 'her little dicks', an unselfconscious abbreviation of the already curious phrase 'dicky bird'. Pheasants often visited her, flaunting their handsome plumage amongst the motley assembly of potted plants in her yard, and for a long while a little free-range hen, escaped from a neighbouring flock, came to peck about beneath her kitchen window. She was very distressed when a fox got it, leaving nothing but feathers.

Bryn was full of pot plants on windowsills – geraniums, cactuses, African violets, streptocarpus – not all of them in perfect health. In the summer, she would put most of them out in the yard, by the stone trough full of the sturdy grey-green rosettes of stonecrop and houseleeks. 'If they thrive, they thrive,' she said. 'If they give up, well, that's it, they've had their chance.' One of these plants she called a 'hot water plant', and she watered it direct from the boiling kettle. It seemed to like this treatment and responded with a small purple flower. She gave me a pot of little hot water plant pups, and they did quite well for a few years in London. I don't know what their botanical name was.

I still have in London a fine orange lily, a clivia, which I bought for her one Christmas, and reclaimed when she had to leave Bryn. It blossoms unexpectedly, I think every other year. I am pleased that it continues to flower.

In Somerset, she enjoyed a visit to Home Farm at Blue Anchor with her great-great-nephews and nieces, to look at the sheep and the goats and the ducks and the piglets. She had no fear of animals, nor they of her. The only animal I saw her take against was a very large sow at Home Farm, who was lying on her side in her straw, exposing a vast, bald, yellowish underbelly of teats, over which various piglets squabbled and fought. The sow's expression was one of bored contempt. She was an unpleasant heap of flesh – 'Not a pretty sight,' said Auntie Phyl, with a slight shudder. I think the sow reminded my aunt of her mother, who was not a pretty sight either. Grandma Bloor was a stout, grim and unyielding woman.

Auntie Phyl, in old age, was not pretty, though this did not prevent her from criticizing the appearance of others. 'Not very attractive, is she?' she once said, bluntly, of one of the new girl-friends of one of her great-nephews, to which the proper retort, the retort she would best have understood, would have been, 'Look who's talking!' But in fact, as a girl, she had been bonny: slim, with fair hair, fair skin, and blue eyes. Most of the Bloor women were slim as children and adolescents; it was in middle age that their figures thickened, their waists spread, their bosoms swelled and drooped. I used to look at these women and hope I wouldn't get like that, but of course it was the genes that did it, not the diet or the lack of exercise. A waistless stoutness lay in wait for all of us. A piggish, balding, bristling yellowish pinkness was our genetic fate.

My mother disliked exercise and became agoraphobic, but my aunt enjoyed walking through the village with her dog.

We used to think the Bloors had Dutch blood, because many of them were potters, and because of their Dutch-doll colouring, but in fact Bloor (or Bloore or Blore) is an old English name. The Bloors (like the Drabbles) were English through and through. There is a little village in Staffordshire called Blore, which I once went to visit when doing family research for the background of *The Peppered Moth*. Our car got stuck in the deep damp unmown grass of the churchyard, and we had to ask some funeral mourners for a shove. They were more than happy to oblige. Helping hapless strangers was more fun than burying the dead.

Auntie Phyl had little vanity, though she was proud of her yellow hair, and even in her eighties fancied that it kept a golden tint. (It did, but it was the tarnish of age, not the bright flax of youth.) As far as I know, she never had a boyfriend or a love affair. When I was a small child her single status seemed natural and desirable to me, for it enabled her to concentrate her affections on her nieces and her nephew. Later, I wondered whether she had lesbian leanings. She had several close female friendships, some dating from her college days when she did her teacher training course at Homerton, but none of them seemed to me to have a sexual component. (One Homerton couple lived together, but I doubt whether they were practising lesbians. Sexual abstinence, like sexual ignorance, was far more common then than it is now.)

Born in 1909, she was too young to be considered a member of the tragic generation that lost its fiancés and lovers to the Great War, so I assume she lived alone by choice. She had several male friends, some of them connected with the trade that my grand-parents had plied at Bryn, which they bought when it was already established as a bed and breakfast and tea garden. These friends included the toffee boys, as we called them, who drove a lorry full of confectionery up and down the Great North Road; another couple called Len and Arthur; and a young man who worked at a gentleman's outfitters in Grantham. I think now that maybe these men were what we would now call gay.

I do not think my aunt had any sexual interest in men, although she liked children, and in my mother's view would have liked to have had a baby. Maybe she was asexual.

In the late 1960s and 70s she and my parents came every year to stay with me in Hampstead for a few days over Christmas, and Arnold and Dusty Wesker, then living in Highgate, adopted a kindly habit of dropping in for a smoked-salmon high tea on Christmas Eve. I think they felt sorry for me, coping alone with such an intense and loaded domestic celebration. And, indeed, I sometimes felt sorry for myself. It was exhausting, for my first husband Clive and I had by this time separated, and it was a lot of work for one person. I don't know how it happened that I became the daughter who always did Christmas, and when I suggested that it was somebody else's turn, I was met with a blunt refusal. 'They wouldn't want to go anywhere else' was the miserable excuse I was given. This was disingenuous, to say the least.

Arnold closely observed the bickerings and manoeuvrings of the elderly trio (these became so fractious that eventually my father used to sleep in a friend's house over the road) and speculated at one point that maybe Auntie Phyl had been in love with my father when young. Arnold is a writer, and he saw a plot. Two sisters, both in love with the same handsome, eligible, upwardly mobile bachelor in Mexborough: one wins the man, marries him and has children, the other stays single all her life. An Arnold Bennett story. (My aunt's middle name was Bennett and, as we are from the Potteries, we claim some as yet unverified connection with the great man.) But I don't think Arnold Wesker can have been right. Arnold is strong on family and aunts, but his imagination is (or in those days was) inexorably heterosexual. I do not believe that my aunt loved and lost. It was not like that. I don't know how it was, but it was not like that.

My aunt survived both my parents by nearly ten years, and that is one of the reasons why I now think of her so often. She lies more recently in my memory. And my memories of her are less painful than my memories of my parents. It is true that she could be rude, cutting, ungrateful, demanding, even offensive, but her insults or rejections were not wounding. One Christmas, she examined her newly opened gifts with some scorn, and complained that the book she had been given would be too big for her bookshelf, and that the chocolates were very near their sell-by date. I think the rest of the family just found this funny, whereas my mother's criticisms of presents I gave her wound me to this day. I remember them word for word.

I cherish Auntie Phyl's remark about the queen's corgis. I arrived at Bryn one year from my hideout on the A1, furnished with a newspaper I had acquired at the Ram Jam: it was a tabloid, bearing a banner headline proclaiming CORGI BITES QUEEN. Auntie Phyl read the item with interest, and a naughty, girlish, sideways little smile lit up her face.

'Good!' she said.

She preferred animals.

I tried to write about her and my mother in my novel *The Peppered Moth*, where she became dressmaker Auntie Dora, and her white dog Daisy became a marmalade cat called Minton. (My grandmother, before her marriage, had been a dressmaker, and I think one of my Wadsworth great-aunts, Auntie Lizzie, was a wigmaker.) I caught some of her eccentricities and mannerisms, but in fictionalizing her I moved her into a dark territory that was not her natural habitat. It was my mother's, but it was not my aunt's. By writing this book I would like to rescue her (and thereby a part of myself) from that contamination, to show her in plainer, brighter and more cheerful colours and in simpler prose. Many of the happier times of my childhood I owe to her, and although I often tried to tell her this, she was not much of a one for compliments or emotional declarations. She did not know how to deal with them.

I see some of those childhood scenes at Bryn in bright colours and clear blocks, like the large pieces of a child's wooden jigsaw. I see the house with its red-tiled roof and its Virginia creeper and its front door set squarely in the middle, as a door should be. (The Virginia creeper was of a great age, and I think Bryn, a century earlier, had been called Ivy House.) I see the sash windows with their small square panes, the apple loft that served as a bedroom for us children, the stone pump in the back yard, the shallow muddy pond in the field, where once I thought I saw a fish. I see the greengage tree, the Victoria plum, the apple orchard, the bonfire, the deep gulley of the hedge bottom, the stone slab over the dangerous cesspit. I see and smell the cool larder, with its perforated zinc window and its rows of bottling jars and its pre-war tins of corned beef and its leaning towers of tea plates and its shelves of little cracked cream jugs.

I see the rhubarb rearing up through an upside-down tin bucket in the yard, and the houseleeks growing in the stone trough and on the outhouse roof.

The deep hedge bottom reminded me of the poetry of John Clare. Or, more chronologically, I should say that when years later I came to read the poetry of John Clare, I was reminded of the hedge bottom. He had a ground-level, tree-root view of the natural world, not a prospect view. I knew in my bones that the hedge bottom dated back to the enclosures of 1796.

It was an old house, and it smelled of old England, and it seemed full of folk memory. But it wasn't a family house, an inherited house. My grandparents bought it in the 1930s. My grandfather gave up his job as an electrician in Mexborough in industrial South Yorkshire and bought it as a going concern. He borrowed some of my aunt's teacher's savings to help him to do so, or so she later claimed. She did not resent this, or not much. She might have resented it a little, or she would not have told me. But she thought he had pluck to take a chance in middle age with a new life. That was the word she used. 'Pluck'.

My grandparents came from a background of northern urban streets. My grandmother, who was born a Wadsworth, came from the nineteenth-century, densely terraced housing of Leeds, now occupied by students, and my grandfather Bloor from the Potteries. Photographs of now unidentifiable young women standing on well-scrubbed, white-edged doorsteps on bleak pavements suggest a life of hard-working respectability. Neither of my grandparents was country born, but they chose to escape the coal mines and pot banks to move to a not particularly picturesque Midlands village, to an old house on an ancient thoroughfare. Was this a sort of Mr Polly-ish, Wellsian escape to a cleaner, happier world? I wonder whether they had any sense of returning to a way of life that their grandparents, before the industrial revolution, might have known. The towns and cities of the North of England and of the Midlands, which had expanded with such rapidity during the industrial revolution, were still informed with a sense of the nearness of a countryside that was felt to be a common birthright. Novelists of the North and of the Midlands, from Elizabeth Gaskell to D. H. Lawrence, J. B. Priestley and Alan Sillitoe, have described these Arcadian longings, these strangely intermingled neighbourhoods where fields and paddocks and quarries pock the haphazard housing developments. I have always felt an affinity with these landscapes.

Sillitoe, a writer who emerged from a red-brick estate of council housing on the outskirts of Nottingham, and whose working life began in a factory at the age of fourteen, writes that he lived in 'a street with houses behind and fields in front'. As a boy he could walk, carrying a stick and a sandwich, through nettles, Queen Anne's Lace and elderberries the mile or so to his blacksmith grandfather's cottage. This cottage had neither gas nor electricity and smelled, in his view wholesomely, of stale lavender, lamp oil, strong soap and turpentine. His grandfather Burton was granted the gleaning rights to the wheat that grew too close to the hedges to be harvested by the combine harvester, a right that now sounds medieval. This was a life on the edges of two worlds, in which the memory of the old country ways persisted, and Sillitoe, a self-educated scholar, in his novels consciously evokes the pastoral idyll and Virgil's *Eclogues*. Working men spent their days in the factory and at the weekends bicycled, hiked and fished by canals. The countryside was penetrable and close.

The Easter visit of a men's cycling club was one of the big

annual events at Bryn, and it made my dour grandmother almost girlish. She loved the bicycle boys and spoke of them flirtatiously. She liked to cook them their eggs and bacon.

Long Bennington is not far from Laxton, a village in Nottinghamshire that boasts the only surviving open-field system of medieval strip farming in England. Children of my generation used to spend a good deal of time in history lessons colouring in maps showing strip farming, though I don't think we really understood what it was. In my fifties I was seized with a desire to see the Laxton system and try to read its meaning for myself. I suggested to Auntie Phyl that I could drive her there on my next visit – we could make it the destination for our pub lunch, I said. Unwisely, I mentioned the field system. She was not taken with the idea. 'I don't fancy wandering round fields to get at my lunch,' she said. I gave in instantly, for I was fond of the Wheatsheaf and the Staunton Arms, our regulars, but from time to time I am still visited by the picture of myself and Auntie Phyl, straying through cornfields or along strips of swedes or potatoes on our way to our scampi and chips.

Sillitoe's Grandfather Burton was one of the last of the blacksmiths. In the Nottinghamshire village of Scarrington there is a pile of horseshoes, which Auntie Phyl used to take us to see as children when we were staying at Bryn. It is a fine phallic monument, seventeen feet high, weighing about ten tons, and it is said to have been built by blacksmith George Flinders, the village's last farrier, between 1945 and 1965. It is still there. What was once work is now labelled heritage. A bid was made to purchase this tower and transport it to America, but it was saved for the village by Nottinghamshire County Council. The village is very neat and trim now, with some grand houses and expensive new buildings amongst the old. I suppose it is a dormitory village for Nottingham. It doesn't look as 'real' as Long Bennington, but it is very pretty.

I don't know whether my grandparents had any sense of return-ing to a countryside in which they had never lived. They, too, must have had uncles or great-uncles or grandfathers who had been blacksmiths or ploughmen or farm labourers. Maybe the old way of life called to them. But it is more likely that they thought they were making a fresh start, and moving up in the world into the era of the genteel, 1930s, middle-class, Hovis tearoom.

As a child, I never thought much of these matters, though I was aware of the difference between the professional aspirations of my parents and those of the household at Bryn. I have no personal memory of my Drabble grandparents, as they both died when I was too small to notice. Auntie Phyl was not particularly interested in social history and local history, but her friend Joyce Bainbridge was, and still is. Joyce's house and garden in Long Bennington have an unbroken history. The village has spread around them, with many new houses built in the last twenty years, but the house where Joyce lives is unchanged, and its carefully tended cottage garden is a garden of earthly delights. She grows flowers and vegetables through the seasons — crocuses, daffodils, tulips, dahlias, begonias, scarlet runners, courgettes, carrots, broad beans, beet-roots, potatoes, tomatoes. The flowers blossom colourfully and clamber amidst a miniature landscape of stone animals, birds and figurines.

People give Joyce garden ornaments, and there they cluster in their magic village, which like Bosch's painting has its own random scale, with giant rabbits, large shoes, tiny manikins, middling-sized elves, little cottages, drinking birds, stone bird-baths. And there stand old agricultural implements that her husband Eddie salvaged, collected and treasured. Eddie had worked as a ploughman for the local farmer and he knew these objects and their history well. They are authentic. Eddie, like John Clare, appreciated and loved the landscape that he worked. He was saddened when the Lincolnshire potato went out of fashion. He regretted the dominion of the continental supermarket potato. He gave me some fossils that had been turned up by the plough, and he told me that village people called them 'the devil's toenails'. I put them in a novel once, these coiled and wrinkled twists of stone, and I keep them in my study.

III

My rediscovery of jigsaws belongs largely to the years after my parents' death, to the last decade of Auntie Phyl's life, when she was the senior surviving member of the family. It was, in a way, a second childhood, though she never lost any of her wits. She was all her life, at heart and in part, a child, with an ability to enjoy childhood things. This is a rare gift, and it was important to us.

Watching the news on television with her one evening, when she was in her eighties, we were exposed to one of those regularly recurring items about poor conditions and abuse in homes for the elderly. I was distressed by the sight of old people dumped in recliner chairs, and by interviews with defensive staff, and I worried that it would distress her, but it was too late to switch off without drawing more attention to the subject. So we sat through it. Auntie Phyl listened in silence, but all she said when it was over was, 'I'd always rather work with children, I don't know why people take on jobs like that.' She still saw herself as a worker, not as a victim, as the helper, not the helped. She never identified with the old.

The death of my parents in the early 1980s left me with many unanswerable questions, which I have tried to work through in my own way, and now that I am old I recognize that I may be condemned to live with an unresolved story and an incomplete picture. I may never fully know why my mother was so unhappy and so angry, or whether there was any way in which I could have made her life (and therefore mine) less painful. But I cannot resist continuing to try to piece things together, although I know it is a doomed pursuit and has in the past made me profoundly unhappy. Maybe through the story of Auntie Phyl I see some hope of another chapter, a less despairing coda, a more gracious farewell.

When campaigning for the NHS funding of child psychotherapists, I have presented myself to the world as a 'depressed child'. But I was not continuously depressed. Sometimes I was quite happy. I had periods of intense misery, but maybe they were no worse than those of many children. I claim no singular status. My mother was seriously depressed for much of her later life, and her depression oppressed and infected me, or so I have come to believe. She was fond of the very word, which she applied to herself with some pride. 'I suffer from endogenous depression,' she would tell people, whether they wanted to know or not.

Many writers have suffered from childhood depression. Harriet Martineau and Edith Wharton, women from very different social backgrounds, both appear to have had a keen sense of unallocated guilt when very young, which both managed to outgrow through lives of exceptional activity and productivity. My mother succumbed, in part, I believe, because she felt action was not available to her. As, in many ways, it was not.

Auntie Phyl was free, or had freed herself, from this congenital burden, and her company was therefore less burdensome. She was not an imaginative woman, in the conventional sense of the world, but she dreamed a great deal, and she liked to recount her dreams. It was during her last summer visit to Somerset, the year of the unfinished jigsaw, that she told me one morning over breakfast that she had had a very vivid dream. She had dreamed that she was going to die that night, in her bedroom at Porlock Weir, overlooking the sea. And, she said, the dream was not at all frightening. On the contrary, it was reassuring. Because, she said, she knew that it was all going to be all right. She had her little suitcase with her, ready packed, so there was nothing to worry about. It would be quite safe to die here in the night, with me in my room just along the corridor, and her suitcase by her bed.

Would, in so many ways, that she had done so. She would have been spared her last two years in a care home, years that were not good. I did not foresee all of this when she told me over breakfast of her dream, but I guessed that her dream was saying that she would prefer not to die alone, and in a strange place. She would have liked to finish the jigsaw, and then to die safely under my roof.

Her health eventually deteriorated, although she struggled bravely to remain independent, with the help of some admirable neighbours. She then moved into a care home in Newark, which, as care homes go, was acceptable, but she did not take well to institutional life. Most of her nieces and nephews and great-nieces and great-nephews were attentive, and a kind and dog-loving friend took Daisy once or twice a week to sit on her bed. But she said that if she could get up, she would go out into the road and let a bus roll over her. At times she was delirious, I think due to heavy medication rather than senile dementia. Her medical report diagnosed 'florid paranoia'. She thought she could hear voices calling 'Phyllis! Phyllis!' (She probably could; Phyllis was a name of the period, and there was more than one old woman called Phyllis in the home.) She disliked being called 'Phyllis' by the nurses, although they insisted, against any evidence, that she really preferred it. She had always been 'Miss Bloor' to strangers and acquaintances. She was still 'Miss Bloor' to her friend Joyce, who had known her nearly all her life.

She celebrated her ninetieth birthday in the home, with a large family gathering, and she nursed the latest baby on her lap, coaxing a smile from it. The baby, too small to see that Auntie Phyl was very old and alarming of aspect, responded to her eyes, her smile and her clucking noises.

Auntie Phyl kept her eye on the birthday cake and reported to us, very angrily, on the phone the next day that pieces of her cake had been distributed, without her consent, to other inmates. This was clearly common practice, for how was one ninety-year-old to get through so much complimentary confectionery? But she was right. They should have asked for her approval.

She died on 20 May 2001, after a long last struggle, during which visits became distressing both to her and to her visitors. She died as I was walking round the National Botanical Garden of Wales, which seemed appropriate, in view of all the gardens and stately homes we had over the years toured together. It has been claimed that her last word was 'Daisy!' and certain it is that Daisy was one of her last visitors.

The funeral service was held at the crematorium in Grantham. We were a small congregation for, as Joyce said, she had reached a good age and most of her contemporaries in the village were dead. We sang 'The day thou gavest, Lord, is ended', and the Reverend Tony Pick of the Grantham and Vale of Belvoir Methodist Circuit gave the address. He had never met Auntie Phyl, whose church and chapel attendances were confined to bring and buy sales. (The car boot sale has largely replaced religion in rural England.) Nevertheless, Reverend Pick spoke well of Auntie Phyl's life as a schoolteacher, and he spoke well of Joyce, who had first got to know Auntie Phyl when she was the lollipop lady policing the school crossing over what had then been the Great North Road. The minister had done his homework.

He also gave a reading that brought tears to my eyes. Unlike

Lawrence's poem 'The Ship of Death', it cannot claim to be great literature, but as an elegy it worked well. It comes from the thoughts of Bishop C. H. Brent, and here is his version of the ship of death.

What is dying? I am standing on the sea shore. A ship sails and spreads her white sails to the morning breeze and starts for the ocean. She is an object of beauty and I stand watching her till at last she fades on the horizon and someone at my side says 'She is gone.' Gone where? Gone from my sight, that is all; she is just as large in the masts, hull and spars as she was when I saw her...The diminished size and loss of sight is in me, not in her, and just at that moment when someone at my side says 'She is gone', there are others who are watching her coming, and other voices take up a glad shout, 'There she comes'...

And so I saw the great beached hulk of Auntie Phyl's body, stranded on her hard, high, care-home bed, launching off from its moorings, free again, sailing into another world.

After the service, we all repaired to the Marriott Hotel for funeral baked meats and a glass or two of wine, and then Joyce took us to see my grandfather's grave in Long Bennington church-yard, which she has tended and we have neglected all these long years. Auntie Phyl has a memorial plaque there now, thanks to Joyce and not to us. Auntie Phyl had been worried that her life would be left without record and voiced this anxiety not infre-quently, which may be one of the reasons why I am writing this. 'If you're cremated, there's nothing to show you ever lived,' she used to say. We used to talk about names inscribed in the crematorium Book of Remembrance, about the planting of memorial roses. But these ruses did not satisfy her.

The day after the funeral, my son Adam, his two children and I went to Sherwood Forest to see the Major Oak. This is another of the many outings on which Auntie Phyl used to take us when we were children. The mysterious phrase 'Major Oak' had thrilled me when I was little, because I did not know what it meant. This aged tree is said to have been a hiding place for Robin Hood, but I don't think I found that aspect of it particularly interesting. It was more its girth and seniority that appealed to me. There it was, there it is, ancient, hollow, perhaps a thousand years old, with its great spreading boughs propped up by many sticks and stakes, but growing still, with leaves of green. It has been cordoned off now, and children can no longer play inside it, as we did. But it stands.

IV

We worked at many jigsaws at Bryn, but we also played card games and board games, games that we never played at home in sombre, silent, bookish Sheffield, where we lived in a suburb called Nether Edge and were always being told to shut up. My father worked at his briefs in the evening on the dining-room table, for the house was too small for a study, and we children had to be quiet. (Insomniac in middle age, I invented a mantra that went, 'Shut up and go to sleep, shut up and go to sleep,' which I repeated to myself, and which I think echoed my mother's admonitory voice. For a while, this directive worked quite well, although I have recently replaced it with something more calming.)

One of our favourites at Bryn was an improbable card game called Belisha, created, as I now see, with the aim of promoting road safety. The little pictures in the top right-hand corner denoted sets of traffic signals, and the large pictures illustrating each individual card portrayed stages on a car journey from Oban in Scotland to London. The aim was to collect sequences of signals, as one collects suits in other card games. I salvaged the pack of cards when Auntie Phyl was in the Oaks care home in Newark, and Bryn was in the process of being sold. For a long time, superstitiously, I did not like to check to see whether it was complete, but it is. It has no missing pieces and, mysteriously, it even has one extra card. *Guards at Buckingham Palace: Stop at Red Traffic Lights* is in duplicate, I assume unintentionally. (It's not designated as a joker, as there is a special card labelled Joker, portraying a Scotsman wearing tartan and a beret, driving an open-topped, tartan-painted car with the number plate OCH1. I loved that.) This game was published by Castell Brothers Ltd, of Pepys Stationery, Covent Garden and Glasgow, and the road signs featured are Traffic Lights, Crossroads, Bends, Level Crossings, Road Narrows, Steep Hill, Slow Major Road Ahead, Halt at Major Road Ahead, School, Please Cross Here, and the Belisha beacon itself. These signs signal, for my generation, nostalgia.

(I used to think 'road narrows' was a double noun, like the narrows of a strait or a river, but looking at it again I see that it is probably a short sentence of warning, consisting of a noun and a verb.)

Our well-thumbed pack is undated. Belisha beacons were introduced in 1934 by the Minister of Transport, Leslie Hore-Belisha, and I think our set must date from the 1940s. (The beacons are Hore-Belisha's most lasting memorial; strange that a long and not wholly successful political career should have entered the dictionary in this context.) The pictures on the cards are mostly of well-known beauty spots, and I found them enticing. I longed to visit all these places. An interest in topography and travel guides (amateur and intermittent but persistent) and a love of aimless touring were born as I hoarded my pictures of Loch Lomond, Loch Awe, Carlisle and Catterick. The place names are engraved in my memory, and I have by now checked off most of these beauty spots, though I remain baffled by one labelled 'Clock-a-Druid, Paisley', which shows a giant potato or a small asteroid standing in a bright green field, dwarfing a row of trees and a trio of tiny sightseers – a woman in a red dress, accompanied at a slightly eerie distance by a small child and a man pointing with a walking stick. It has some of the unsettling magic of a Magritte.

I could not and cannot think what this large object was meant to be. There are 'druid stones' and Neolithic carvings in this part of Scotland, and ancient monuments with folk names like 'The Auld Wives' Lift', 'The Witch's Stone', 'Rob Roy's Bonnet' and 'King Cole's Grave', but none of them for which I can find records looks anything like the asteroid. Was it a fantasy of the artist? Is it (or was it) a local name for the famous Cochno Stone, discovered in 1888?

I looked up the Cochno Stone, which I am told is one of the largest and most impressive ancient petroglyphs of Scotland, and almost certainly of astrological significance. But it doesn't in any way resemble the picture on my Clock-a-Druid card. The Cochno Stone is large, and flattish, and covered with cup-and-ring markings, and now it lies under three feet of earth, deposited on it by the Department of the Environment to keep the vandals away. So I couldn't go to see it even if I tried. Like the caves of Lascaux, it may never be seen again by human eyes.

The caves of Lascaux with their prehistoric cave paintings have also been sealed, but they have been reproduced in replica. They have become part of the simulated world.

I've never been to Paisley. It is a treat in store. An unsolved mystery perhaps awaits me there.

But the most significant of all the cards in the Belisha pack, for us, were those that illustrated staging posts on the Great North Road itself. This was the legendary route of the legions, and on it stood Ferrybridge, Wetherby, Doncaster, Grantham, Newark, Stamford, Biggleswade, Sandy, and Mill Hill. We felt a particular and personal attachment to this road, because Bryn was situated right upon it, hence its positional role as a tea garden and bed and breakfast stopover. Long Bennington has now been bypassed, but in those days the road flowed right through the whole length of the village. There was a very wide grass verge separating the road from the pavement, but we could see and feel the traffic pouring unceasingly northwards towards Scotland, and southwards towards London.

It seemed important to us to be there, in that very place, on this major route. Lorries, cars and coaches swished past rhythmically, endlessly. All night long they journeyed, and I would lie in bed listening to the swish and the boom, the swish and the boom, as they came and they went, as they came and they went. I loved that sound. (Is it the sound of what is called a slipstream? It is a word I have never used before.) It was like a cradle, endlessly rocking: it was like a lullaby, it was like a river pouring past, it was like the incessant movement of the Earth. You were a child in bed, trying to sleep, but the road was awake and alive with travellers, and therefore you were not alone, and life had not come to a grim halt. The blood coursed through the body, and the traffic along the road. Your heart would not seize up and stop if you fell asleep. It would beat on until the morning.

You can still hear the roar of the road, very faintly, in the Ram Jam Inn, through the double glazing, and that is one of the reasons why I like to stay there. As I lie there listening to the trucks of night, I think that the gates of memory will open, and I will be able to step back into childhood and discover what has been lost from that early world.

Not everybody found the sound so soothing; in Bryn's visitors' book one family's remark stood out. Instead of the anodyne formula of 'A Home from Home', or 'See you Next Year', one couple had irritably noted, 'How can you stand the din?'

The bypass put an end to all that.

George, in Tom Stoppard's *Jumpers*, pays tribute to the spirit of the A1 as an affirmation of the existence of God:

And yet I tell you that, now and again, not necessarily in the contemplation of rainbows or newborn babes, nor in the extremities of pain or joy, but more probably ambushed by some quite trivial moment – say the exchange of signals between two long-distance lorry drivers in the black sleet of a god-awful night on the old A1 – then, in that dip-flash, dip-flash of headlights in the rain that seems to affirm some common ground that is not animal and not long-distance lorry-driving – then I tell you I *know*...

I don't think Auntie Phyl ever saw any Stoppard, and I do not think she had any interest in God, but she might have recognized this sentiment.

As children, we were issued the strictest of warnings about this major road, for it was a fearsome force. We must never, ever try to cross it alone. We must never even walk on its grass verge. We must never go to the village shop opposite without an accompanying adult. Crossing to the shop was like crossing a perilous torrent. I can't remember now whether there were many proper crossings in the village where lorries had to stop for pedestrians; I suppose there must have been. I remember well Joyce's crossing, which she policed for the school in her smart yellow fluorescent uniform, but there must have been others. We were far too docile to try anything risky, but I think we were impressed by the danger on the doorstep. It made life more exciting.

The romance of the Great North Road had appealed to Auntie Phyl since her girlhood, years before her parents moved to live by it. She had written an essay on it at Mexborough School, which she treasured and which I have piously preserved. (It was Joyce who told me to look for it when the house was being emptied: 'Miss Bloor set great store by that essay,' she told me, and I found it in the little wooden chest in the hall.) In this twenty-two-page document, still tethered by its original rusting paper clip, Phyllis Bloor of VIC summons up the Roman days of Ermine Street (the Romans were interested in straight lines, not beautiful scenery), of toll roads (according to my aunt, initially manned by hermits and 'false hermits'), and of mail coaches, tarmac, motor cars and bicycle clubs. She describes the market gardens of Biggleswade, the fate of the young University of Stamford (which was 'strangled out' in 1463 by threats from Oxford and Cambridge), Cromwell's victory at the battle of Gonerby Hill, and the travels of Nicholas Nickleby. It is a well-researched narrative, enlivened by strong personal feeling. She abandons the story at Ferrybridge (where one of her aunts lived) with the words: 'The Great North Road proceeds into Scotland to Edinburgh but we will not trace its course now.'

Auntie Phyl was not as clever as my mother, but she was not as stupid as my mother liked to suggest.

It is 450 miles from Edinburgh to London, and Long Bennington is strategically placed en route, just under two-thirds of the way south. (Grantham is 111 miles from London, a symmetrical signpost that I always note with respect as I pass.) One summer afternoon, in my grandmother Clara's dour reign, a car pulled into the drive, and a woman knocked on the door, requesting not tea and bread and butter, or accommodation for the night, but asking whether she could use the toilet. Her excuse was that they'd come all the way from Scotch Corner. 'Well, you should have stopped earlier,' said Grandma, and sent her on her way. I can't remember whether I witnessed this incident, or whether Grandma told me about it. I often think of it when driving long distances.

Bryn, as I now know, was one of the few houses in the village to boast two flush toilets. It had these long before it had electricity, which was not installed until 1946; before that, we used to go to bed by torch and Kelly lamp. One of these toilets was outdoors, whitewashed and full of spiders; the other was indoors, in the communal bathroom, which served family and guests alike. This bathroom, like the bathrooms of many old houses, had two doors, an arrangement that was disquieting, and which may be the source of the recurrent dream in which I am interrupted by an intruder while in the act of lowering myself onto a lavatory seat.

The drinking water at Bryn came from a well, and was pumped into large white chipped blue-rimmed enamel jugs. It was soft, tasteless water, unlike the water in Sheffield, which had a mineral limestone tang. I did not like it; this was one of the few aspects of Bryn that I did not like. But I liked the pump, and I enjoyed filling the jugs. The building was AA registered on a 'Farmhouse Agreement Form' at some point in the 1930s, and it was licensed to sell liquor and tobacco, though I don't think it ever did so in my day. What it did sell was hand embroidery, which consisted largely of piles of tablecloths and cushion covers embroidered with floral motifs by my grandmother and aunt. They despised crinoline ladies, which appeared on many embroidery transfers at that time; I never knew why they held them in contempt. Secretly I rather liked them, but I knew better than to say so. They despised cross-stitch, too. Again, I could not guess their reasons. Perhaps they thought it a childish stitch, fit only for samplers.

I used to get very bored, in the covered market in Newark, waiting while my aunt interminably inspected those thin, papery, grey-and-blue transfers, looking for attractive designs to iron onto tablecloths.

V

The sources of the aesthetic preferences of the Bloor and Drabble families intrigue me. They were formed in industrial South Yorkshire, a region not best known for its natural beauty or its artistic discrimination. The images of high art would have reached them through calendar art, jigsaw art, biscuit tin art, tea caddy art. The Brontës, intellectually isolated in their small moorland parish, were well acquainted with high art through periodicals, prints, engravings and Bewick's woodcuts, but I do not think my ancestors had access to this kind of material. The Brontës lived in a bleak and unspoiled landscape, which they perceived and dignified as romantic, whereas the Bloors and the Drabbles lived in a debased and despoiled landscape, amidst the decor and mass-produced artefacts of the machine age, which were directed at a popular taste without much education or aspiration. Some of these artefacts are, to us, attractive and have now become collectors' items. Many of them were in themselves freely adapted reproductions of earlier works by Romney, Reynolds, Landseer, Lancret, George Morland, and other popular and easily sentimentalized artists. Some of these artefacts are now reproduced, a century and a half later, as newly manufactured specimens of Victoriana, to be sold in shops with names like Past Times. But they are not art. They are nostalgic kitsch.

The Bloors, it is true, were sightseers, interested in natural wonders – waterfalls, rocks, boulders, mountains, minerals, caves – and, perhaps to a lesser degree, in stately homes, with their artificially contrived waterfalls, rocks, boulders, mountains, minerals and caves. But it would never have occurred to them or to anyone they knew to buy a painting. They might perhaps think to embroider a painting; one of the great-aunts embroidered in fine unfading silks a bluebell wood, which hung in its pale wooden frame on a wall at Bryn. And Grandma Bloor once won a watercolour of a harbour scene at a whist drive. But they did not think that the world of art galleries or paintings had anything to do with them.

Hanging in the kitchen at Bryn was a large framed reproduction of a work by the children's illustrator, Margaret Tarrant. It showed an elf instructing a circle of small woodland animals – a mouse, a blackbird, a squirrel, perhaps a frog. I think there was a blackboard involved in this Goody Two-Shoes scene, on which the elf was inscribing a lesson. It belonged to Auntie Phyl, not Grandma, and I took it to be a tribute to her profession as an infants' teacher. I liked this work of art, and I used to enjoy discussing with Auntie Phyl the relative merits of Margaret Tempest, creator of Little Grey Rabbit as we knew her, and Margaret Tarrant, who specialized in wild flowers and fairies. We liked them both. I remember trying to get my mother to agree with me that *The Woodland Class* was a fine work of art, but she would not. She knew what she didn't like, and she didn't like elves. I suspected she was in the right, as she usually was. I recognized that in her eyes elves were as bad as crinolines or horse brasses. But I was quite tenacious and stood up for Margaret Tarrant. I liked that painting, and I wasn't going to say I didn't. And my mother wasn't going to say that she did.

Auntie Phyl's taste in clothes and furnishings was of its time, and stayed in that time. Furniture didn't require choice; chairs, tables, beds, wardrobes were inherited and lasted for generations, so you never had to buy new ones. She had some cheerful crockery that I now know to have been Art Deco, and she favoured 1920s *chinoiserie*, likings that went back to her college days. I also associate her with Chinese lanterns (*Physalis alkekengi*, known to some but not to us as winter cherry), which grew in Bryn's garden and stood gathered in a vase in her sitting room. (I could never persuade these charming plants to grow for me, though I did succeed with Bryn's Solomon's seal.) But it was generally considered that the artistic taste of my parents was superior to hers. So I was shocked and impressed when she took against a new armchair that my father had bought. I remember it fairly clearly: it was a large Parker Knoll upholstered in strawberry crushed velvet and had some fancy golden fringing attached to its parts. He was very proud of it, and it was comfortable, as Parker Knoll chairs are. (I have invested in several, including an electronically operated recliner more suitable to a care home than a study. Small children love going for rides in it.) My father's new chair was uncharacteristically showy, even opulent. Auntie Phyl confided to me one day, 'I don't really *like* it.' She was scornful about it, her face wearing a look of Bloor disapproval. I was intrigued by this declaration of independence, all the more because I secretly agreed with her. It was a bit vulgar, that chair. Not like my father.

VI

Crafts were familiar to the Bloors and the Drabbles. These 'half-arts' (*Halbkünste*), as Goethe called them, were part of their daily lives, and they occupied a halfway territory between idle diversion and domestic economy. They filled the winter evenings.

In later years, Auntie Phyl took to sewing a kind of ready-made trim called 'rickrack' round the edges of pillowcases. She sold these pillowcases to bed-and-breakfast guests. They were a popular line. I used to possess many of these value-added pillowcases, but the last ones are now beginning to unravel.

A Teas-with-Hovis sign hung for many years on the tall elm tree that stood in the front garden, advertising Bryn to passing travellers. I don't recall that Hovis was ever served. The bread we and the guests ate was always square and white and certainly not home-made. I think it came from the village bakery just down the road. My grandparents owned a Teas-with-Hovis teaset with square plates that portrayed a tea garden not unlike Bryn itself. I do not know where they acquired it; maybe it came with the house, or maybe a travelling salesman presented it to them as a promotional gift. The tea house in the picture is red-brick, like Bryn, and has a red-tiled roof, like Bryn, and it has a Teas-with-Hovis sign hanging from a tree, like Bryn, but it is not as good-looking a house as Bryn and, unlike Bryn, it is not thickly covered in romantic Virginia creeper. The painted house is a modern house, of the 1920s or 30s, and looks as though it stands in suburbia, near somewhere like Bournemouth. Bryn was clearly superior and senior, and the painted house on the plates was paying homage to Bryn. Or that was how I saw it.

Years later, the elm tree at Bryn caught Dutch elm disease and was chopped down, and thus this well-known landmark on the Great North Road vanished for ever. Most of the Hovis plates are chipped, but some have survived time and the dishwasher.

The Bryn menu featured 'Tea – Bread and Butter – Jam – Cakes, All Home-Made' for a shilling, 'Tea and Cakes' for eightpence, boiled eggs at fourpence each, and poached eggs at fivepence. You could also have Fruit and Cream (I think this would have been tinned fruit and tinned cream) and Coffee and Biscuits, combinations that are not priced on the handwritten card that I retain. The card is adorned by a prancing elf that Auntie Phyl had made out of coloured gummed paper. She probably learned how to make gummed elves at Homerton.

One of Auntie Phyl's specialities was whipped evaporated milk. I don't think the guests were ever lucky enough to be offered this, but my sisters and I loved it. You whisked a tin of evaporated milk in a large jug or bowl with a rotary hand whisk until it became stiff and frothy. On jelly, it was delicious. The combination of textures was out of this world. When, a few years after the war, I first knowingly sampled fresh double cream, I did not like it at all. I think many war babies had the same initial recoil from its mild and tasteless fatty blandness. We favoured harsher, more metallic, more synthetic, more warlike flavours.

Hovis in 2006 listed its ingredients as wheat flour, water, wheatgerm, yeast, salt, wheat protein, vinegar, vegetable fat, soya flour, barley fibre, emulsifier E472e and flour treatment agent 300. I don't know what its ingredients were in 1946. Maybe they were even less authentic, more artificial, more ersatz. I think it is in part coincidental that the word Hovis came to represent a nationwide sense of nostalgia, through the famous Hovis advertisement by Ridley Scott, which featured a boy pushing a bike loaded with loaves up what purports to be a cobbled Northern street to the strains of Dvořák adapted for a brass band. (The street, I am told, is in fact in Dorset.) This TV commercial was first shown in 1973, and had no connection with my Bryn and Hovis associations, or with my concept of being Northern, which did not include the cliché of the brass band. To me, Hovis was genteel.

The brass-band notion of the North used to puzzle me. I never knowingly saw such a band when I was a child, and I was surprised when director Richard Marquand, when making a BBC television documentary about me in the 1960s, saw fit to include a misleading sequence showing me watching a Salvation Army band on a street corner in Sheffield. I may have protested against appearing in this context, but he overruled me. He wanted to film the Salvation Army, whether it had any connection with his subject or not. He didn't mind faking it, just as Ridley Scott was to do. Richard was a film-maker; he was using me to practise his art, and he had his eye on the big time. He made it, with a Second World War thriller called *The Eye of the Needle*, and went on to make *The Return of the Jedi*. Richard was a good friend of mine and the most handsome undergraduate in Cambridge, on whom King's College and E. M. Forster smiled in vain. He died of a stroke in 1987. He was only forty-nine.

Clive Swift knew a lot more about brass bands than either Richard or me, and he co-wrote a very good play about one called *All Together Now*, which was performed with great aplomb at the Leicester Haymarket in 1979. It ought to be revived, but I suppose it's hard to find a cast of actors all of whom can act and play brass instruments, as the script required. Clive used to be good on the trombone and still plays it from time to time.

VII

When I was at Bryn as a child, I felt proud to be part of the traditional life of the road. Wayfarers came and had their tea and bread and butter, or they stayed the night and had their bacon and eggs and toast in the morning, and then on they went, south towards Stamford, north towards Ferrybridge. Sometimes they came back another year; sometimes they disappeared without trace. I felt that Bryn had a connection with all the hundreds of roadhouses and inns and staging posts, known and unknown, along the hundreds of miles of the Great North Road. The combination of a sense of old-fashioned security and continuity with the promise of incessant change and movement was profoundly reassuring to me. The life of the road has been the source of innumerable stories, legends, dreams, novels, poems and movies, and my heart warmed to Princess Anne who, when asked in an interview long ago what she would like to be if she wasn't a princess, replied, 'A long-distance lorry driver.' What an elegant answer! America created the road movie, but surely the Great North Road or the Great West Road inspired Princess Anne.

My aunt stopped doing teas, but she went on doing bed and breakfast for a long while after Grandma's death. There was less trade after the village bypass was built in 1965, but some travellers remembered their old stopping place and turned off the A1 to stay the night. It remained very traditional, though there were small innovations, and at some point in the 1950s guests began to be offered a very small glass of tinned Del Monte orange juice with their tea or coffee. My aunt had to get to school to teach in the mornings, so occasionally she would instruct trusted guests who wished to linger to lock the door after them when they left. One summer, when our children were very young, Clive and I took over the business for a week or two while she was on holiday, and I felt grown up as I cooked the breakfasts, although I was frightened of breaking the yolks of the fried eggs. Eggs were still precious, to be treated with respect, and one could not present a paying guest with a broken yolk. (Clive claims he was a dab hand at frying eggs, a skill he learned at prep school.) We were allowed to pocket the 12s 6d per person per night that was then the going rate. Auntie Phyl had said we could keep any money that we made.

When we were little, visitors would occasionally and unpredictably give us a sixpence. This was very exciting. There was a little low wooden gate separating the kitchen from the narrow hallway and the guests' dining room. It was painted a thick glossy globby milk-chocolate brown, and it was just the height of a small child. I used to hang around behind this gate, peering over it and hoping for a tip. I don't think my parents would have approved of this, but Grandma and Auntie Phyl didn't mind.

I remain a little nervous about frying eggs, and watch with apprehension as chefs in breakfast buffets in hotels nonchalantly crack them and sizzle them and occasionally discard those that go wrong. We weren't allowed to be so casual during the war or in the years of austerity after the war. Dried eggs were not pleasant (although dried mashed potato was delicious) and a fresh egg was a treasure. I remember being enthralled, as a small child, by a riddle about an egg that appeared in one of Alison Uttley's story books. I thought it was in one of the Sam Pig or Tim Rabbit series, but I can't find it there, though I came to know it by heart.

In marble walls as white as milk,
Lined with a skin as soft as silk,
Within a fountain crystal clear,
A golden apple doth appear.
No doors there are to this stronghold,
Yet thieves break in and steal the gold.

I loved this rhyme and thought for many years that Alison Uttley had written it herself, but I now discover that it is what is called 'traditional' or 'anonymous'. I still think it enchanting and am full of admiration for the way it manages to transform the unpleasant, mucous texture of egg white into something pure, clear and wondrous. And when did I last pause to look at that 'skin as soft as silk'? Maybe it was thicker and stronger in the old days, before battery farming, when hens were better fed.

One of the pleasures of visiting Bryn was the opportunity to reread my way through the store of children's books that Auntie Phyl owned. I could not read them often enough. She had sets of Alison Uttley and Helen Bannerman, some Enid Blyton and many annuals – but no Noddy, and no Beatrix Potter, or none that I can remember. Little Grey Rabbit, Sam Pig, Little Black Sambo, Little Black Quasha, Epaminondas – these were my friends at Bryn, and some of them as I now see were charged with a racist innuendo that at the time escaped me completely.

Epaminondas is a little black boy, a character created in 1911 by American author Sara Cone Bryant, but the version we had was an English adaptation by Constance Egan, illustrated by A. E. Kennedy (who also illustrated Uttley's *Sam Pig*) and published by

Collins. The story I loved best was 'Epaminondas and His Mammy's Umbrella', which turns on the little boy's over-literal interpretation of his mother's instructions to go to find the umbrella she had left beside the grandfather clock at his grandmother's house. He finds it, but fails to bring it home, as his mother had not explicitly told him to do so. She greets his mistake with, 'Sakes alive! Epaminondas, you ain't got the sense you was born with,' a reproach that I seem to have internalized, as I often say it to myself when I do something particularly stupid. But it is a reproach that does not destroy, uttered in what I hear as a benign voice. The Mammy of Epaminondas is a fat and kindly figure who loves her foolish little boy, and who knows he means well.

One of the most Epaminondas-like things I did was to come home from school in Sheffield one day wearing odd shoes, one of my own, and one that belonged to the girl with the next peg in the cloakroom. I was about nine years old at the time. My mother and the mother of the other girl (I can remember her name but dare not write it down) were extraordinarily angry about this. I could not see why, for the two pairs of brown Clarks lace-ups were almost identical and to me interchangeable. Who cared? My mother cared, and the other mother cared, and their wrath was annihilating. I think the Mammy of Epaminondas would have been more forgiving.

A. E. Kennedy's illustrations now look grotesque, but the story still seems harmlessly engaging, and the Mammy still smiles.

For some reason we despised Larry the Lamb from Toytown, as we despised crinoline ladies, but, again, I don't know why. Maybe we despised Larry, or failed to find him amusing, because he, like me, had a stammer. 'Mr M-m-m-mayor...,' he used to bleat. But I don't think I took that personally when I was a child, any more than I noticed the black racial stereotypes.

It could be that Auntie Phyl noticed Larry's stammer for me, for she was personally and professionally sensitive to the way children were treated. I remember she told us off for teaching our very little brother, when he was aged two or three, to parrot: 'Tomorrow and tomorrow and tomorrow/Creeps in this petty pace...' The way he pronounced these words was so sweet, and we loved to hear him say them, and we got him to repeat them again and again as we sheltered from the rain in the beach hut on our summer holiday at Minehead. But Auntie Phyl was quite right, it wasn't at all the thing. We were nasty teenage sisters, and we should have known better.

At Christmas one year Auntie Phyl was given a new biography of Alison Uttley, with which at the time she professed herself pleased, but when she had read it she told me that she had not really enjoyed it. It was too sad and not what she had expected. Not having read it myself, I did not know what had disappointed her and was not particularly interested in why she had disliked it. Now, many years later, trying to track down the causes of her disturbance, I find I cannot even be sure which biography she read, for there are two candidates. The first, by Elizabeth Saintsbury, published in 1980, seems chronologically the most probable, but it is hard to see what aspect of it could have upset her. It cannot have been solely the perfunctory nature of the author's narrative and research. The first three-quarters of this work are largely a paraphrase of Uttley's own many diffuse and scattered autobiographical writings, drawing most heavily on her classic childhood memoir *The Country Child* (1931), and it adds little to what was already known. But there are darker elements suggesting that the ending of the story was sadder than the author could say, and Auntie Phyl may have found it threatening.

It now seems to me much more probable that she must have read Denis Judd's fuller and franker account, published in 1986, though I am slightly surprised that she had tackled it in her late seventies, when her eyesight was beginning to deteriorate. This biography would indeed have shocked her, as it shocked me.

The childhood of Alison Uttley was different from that of my aunt's in Mexborough, and mine in Pontefract and Sheffield, but it had some similar features. Unlike us, she was a true country child, born in an isolated and ancient farmhouse near Cromford in Derbyshire, and she wrote about her childhood years and her family with acute recall, passionate intensity, some partiality and not a little censorship. (Her brother is edited out of most of her recollections, although he was close to her in age, and she usually presents herself as an only child.) Bryn was old, but Castle Top Farm was ancient, with foundations dating back many centuries, and a supply of four-poster beds, seventeenth-century oak chests, eighteenth-century hangings and gilded wallpapers, Victorian china, knick-knacks and whatnots, and a great kitchen full of polished pewter and brass, and a copper warming-pan. 'Everything shone, everything held a tiny red flame in its heart, but the shiniest, most important thing was the grandfather clock which ticked solemnly in its corner, where it had stood for two hundred years...' From the village school, Uttley went to Bakewell Grammar School (a trajectory not too dissimilar from that of the Bloors and Drabbles) and then on to read physics at Manchester, to study at a teachers' training college in Cambridge, and to teach in London.

There was much in her life with which Auntie Phyl would have identified – her educational rites of passage, her love of animals, her interest in crafts, her understanding of children's games, her liking for miniature objects, her succession of Scottie dogs – but the biography revealed a personality very far removed from the homely sweetness and reassuring goodness of Little Grey Rabbit. Manipulative, appropriative, self-centred, possessive, she ruined the lives of her husband and her son, and drove both of them to suicide. She also quarrelled fiercely with her illustrator Margaret

Tempest about copyright. She deeply resented any suggestion that Margaret Tempest had played an important part in creating the characters of Little Grey Rabbit, Hare, Squirrel, Moldywarp and Fuzzypeg, just as she hated any suggestion that her inspiration owed anything to Beatrix Potter. And she loathed her Beaconsfield neighbour Enid Blyton, because her books sold better.

In old age, her house became more and more cluttered, just like Bryn, with little figurines on every surface, and she got fatter and fatter, just like the Bloors. She dressed eccentrically, with a ribbon in her hair.

Auntie Phyl may well have found in her life a fearsome, mocking echo, and a travesty of the innocence of the books we had all enjoyed so much. Auntie Phyl, in her seventies, took at one point to wearing her hair in a plait tied with a ribbon. My mother ridiculed this regression, and I think she abandoned it, though whether this was in deference to her older sister I do not know.

As a Christmas present, Auntie Phyl preferred *Snookered* by Donald Trelford, which one of the family gave her — I can't remember who, but I know it wasn't me. This was a most successful gift. She loved watching snooker on television. I don't know what Alison Uttley would have made of that. I never learned to follow the snooker, but I enjoyed hearing Auntie Phyl describe how she had had to sit up till midnight to watch Jimmy White. This seemed a good hold on happiness, and I wish I had acquired it.

VIII

I have found rereading Alison Uttley's autobiographical works, as an adult, unsettling, as Auntie Phyl and I both found her biography. Uttley takes the reader back, past the dead cow in the ditch, into the dark wood of the suicides, and she fills these places with whispers and eyes and monsters. When she was little, she endowed inanimate objects with life; animals and trees spoke to her, as did jugs and plates and knives and buttons and pebbles and stones and fragments of quartz and mica, and what they said was not always pleasant. The buttons talked in 'tiny metallic sounds' from 'pursed-up button mouths', which does not sound agreeable, and the enormous 'fat green body' of the heavy pincushion that sat on the kitchen dresser, bristling with hatpins and broken darning needles like an aged porcupine, is not a wholly friendly object.

All children, according to Swiss psychologist Jean Piaget, have this capacity (or this misapprehension), and the animated object is a commonplace motif in stories for children. *The Adventures of a Pincushion* by Mary Jane Kilner, published in the 1780s, is a striking early example, with an undercurrent of violence, for the poor, downwardly mobile narrator ends very sadly. Uttley had this talent of animation to an exceptional extent, carrying the memory of it, as well as the power to revive it, throughout her life. She also believed she had a gift for predictive dreaming, and her accounts of her experiences of this are uncomfortably plausible. She found it easy to put herself into a trance.

The ability to 'receive' rather than to 'invent' has been claimed by other celebrated writers for children. P. L. Travers was another disturbing and difficult character with a penchant for the occult and a tendency to wish to dominate her illustrator. She was an admirer of Gurdjieff, whom she met in the 1920s, and of Jung and Ouspensky. She said, enigmatically, that she 'never for one moment' believed that she had invented Mary Poppins, who came to her while she was recovering from an illness; perhaps, she said, Mary Poppins invented *her*, 'and that is why I find it so difficult to write autobiographical notes'. Enid Blyton claimed that, while composing, she would shut her eyes for a few minutes, with her portable typewriter on her knees, and make her mind go blank, whereupon real children would appear and stand before her, and take on movement, and talk, and laugh, as though they were on a cinema screen. All she had to do was to watch and listen, and then to transcribe their words and actions. Uttley, Travers and Blyton had strong visual memories and imaginations, and all three seemed to have had something of the medium about them. They received and transcribed stories and messages from some source of childhood experience that is closed to most adults.

Why do I find these accounts uncomfortable? Is it merely a natural scepticism that protests? Not quite. For, as an adult, Uttley continued (like Conan Doyle) to believe in fairies, and that is enough to make most people feel uncomfortable. The mixing of the power of childhood animism with a self-deluding sense of arrested development suggests that something went wrong with her progress towards what we call maturity. A touch of J. M. Barrie crept into her patchwork-quilt recollections. The animism threatened to tip over into fanciful embroidery, the acute recall into whimsy. The elves invaded. The revered historic rural objects – the pincushion, the button box, the grandfather clock, the spinning top, the fivestones – became copies of themselves, end-lessly celebrated, endlessly reproduced, like a picture on a calendar or a biscuit tin, their authenticity debased by repetition. She reworked her material too often. Maybe her talent was arrested at a certain point and then devoured itself. She was imprisoned in what poet and critic Susan Stewart calls in her book *On Longing* 'the childhood of the self'. The memories sickened and became nauseating, though they never (except in her books for very young children) became sentimental or sweet. She was too clever for that.

IX

Alison Uttley was indisputably an authentic country child, so it is strange that her version of the pastoral seems, at times, so unconvincing. The question of authenticity and artificiality has attached itself to the pastoral since the form was invented over two thousand years ago; indeed, the form is itself a question, forever playing the real against the unreal, the brutal against the idyllic, the true country against the town's idea of the country.

These queries are raised even by the work of John Clare, who was indisputably an authentic countryman. Clare at one point proposed the title *The Midsummer Cushion* for a volume of his poetry, although it was never adopted. It was, he hoped, an attractive title, and referred to an old custom among villagers in summer time of sticking 'a piece of greensward full of field flowers and place it as an ornament in their cottages, which ornaments are called Midsummer Cushions'. Such a pretty custom might well have been recorded with approval by Alison Uttley as a cottage survival. But Clare's upper-class patron Eliza Emmerson needed to have the phrase explained to her, and although she at first liked it, she began to have doubts about it, and the volume was eventually, and less quaintly, published as *The Rural Muse.* The real was becoming unreal even during its own lifespan.

There was a pronounced, nostalgic, Georgian strain in Uttley's writing. (She was an admirer and later a friend of Walter de la Mare, one of the best-known writers of the group that flourished during the reign of George V; it included John Drinkwater, John Masefield, Lascelles Abercrombie, Edmund Blunden and W. H. Davies.) Some critics have dismissed the whole Georgian pastoral movement as one of infantile regression and a denial of the onward march of urban life and industry. (In fact, in her London youth, somewhat improbably, Uttley had been influenced and befriended by Ramsay MacDonald and his wife Margaret, but with age her views became more conservative, though not necessarily, as we have seen, more orthodox.) The Georgian poets connected the countryside with childhood, and their work prompted in some quarters a suspicion that being interested in childhood, or writing for and about children, is in itself childish. T. S. Eliot, writing in *The Dial* in 1927 on a book by Blunden about the Metaphysical poet Henry Vaughan, produces what is intended to be a devastating condemnation of the concept of Vaughan's 'angel infancy'.

Eliot writes:

> It does not occur to Mr Blunden that the love of one's childhood, a passion which he appears to share with Lamb and Vaughan, is anything but a token of greatness. We all know the mood; and we can, if we choose to relax to that extent, indulge in the luxury of the reminiscence of childhood; but if we are at all mature or conscious, we refuse to indulge this weakness to the point of writing or poetizing about it. We know that it is something to be buried and done with, though its corpse will from time to time find its way up to the surface.

Eliot continues in this vein for some paragraphs, accusing Blunden of attempting to re-create Vaughan in his own image as 'a mild pastoral poet – that is to say, a poet who, enjoying fresh air and green hillsides, occupies himself in plastering nature with his own fancies'. Blunden's praise for Vaughan's religious sense of 'solar, personal, flower-whispering, rainbow-browed, ubiquitous, magnanimous Love' understandably gets short shrift in Eliot's critique, but Vaughan himself, now considered one of the greatest poets of the seventeenth century, does not emerge with much more credit; the emotion in his poetry is described by Eliot as 'vague, adolescent, fitful, and retrogressive'. These are harsh words. That word 'retrogressive' is particularly damaging, coming as it does from the Modernist who did so much to reinstate the Metaphysical poets. One would have thought that Eliot would have responded more warmly to Vaughan's religious verse, and his description of childhood as a corpse is, to say the least, startling. I don't know what Wordsworth and Freud would have made of that.

Eliot had no children, though he had godchildren, and it is said he could entertain them when he needed to. He wrote *Old Possum's Book of Practical Cats* in part for them. He is also said to have liked practical jokes, but I choose to consider that a sign of arrested development.

X

Liking children and 'being good with children' are gifts that seem to be somewhat randomly distributed. I do not know whether there is any literature on the subject of the child-friendly personality. I suppose there must be, but I have not been able to find a word for it. (The word 'normotic', coined by psychoanalyst Christopher Bollas, was suggested to me as a possibility by a friend, but, as she says, this seems to pathologize the very normality I am trying to describe.)

Certainly not all parents possess these gifts naturally. We were lucky in Auntie Phyl. You could argue that being a good aunt was for her, as it was for Jane Austen, a strategic move, one that earned value in the family, but I trust there was more to it than that and, as she chose to be an infants' teacher, I think there must have been. (Not that there was much career choice, for women of her generation.) I have occasionally wondered whether she really enjoyed playing simple, childish games like Belisha with her little nieces and her nephew. At the time, I assumed she loved these diversions as much as we did. It did not occur to me that she was faking it for our sake until I had children of my own and found myself less than enthusiastic about playing endless games of Monopoly and

Snakes and Ladders and Snap with them. Then I began to wonder whether she had not, after all, been more possessed of great patience and generosity than of great childishness. I hope she enjoyed Belisha. I know she enjoyed the jigsaws.

I am suspiciously loyal to the pleasure and purpose of jigsaws, which seem to me to belong to a higher category of activity than card games.

When my father was near death, in a hospital in Amsterdam, I found myself asking him whether he had enjoyed our seaside family holidays at Filey on the Yorkshire coast. They had been happy times for me, on the whole, and I needed to know whether he had been happy too. I was worried, then, so near the end, that he had been pretending, all those years ago. But he smiled, and he said, as though I should not have doubted, 'Oh Maggie, I *loved* Filey.' That meant a great deal to me. I was glad I had dared to ask.

My father worked very hard all his adult life and had little time for play, except during those long official summer vacations. Gardening, in his retirement, was his refuge from himself, from the dullness of time, and from my mother in the house. My father dreaded boredom. He admitted this openly, as few dare to do. Admitting to a fear of boredom is usually considered a sign of weakness. Some make a point of boasting that they are never bored. 'Oh, I've always known how to occupy myself, I've never known a day's boredom in my life!' are lines often spoken by those bores who do not fear boring others.

Elizabeth Bowen's novel, *The Last September*, set in Ireland between the wars, describes a life of idleness under threat, of tennis, flower arranging, teas, dances, wasting lives. Discontented Hugo arrests his wife's gossip with the words, 'life is too short for all this,' but what he is thinking is that life is too long. The young are allowed to complain about the slowness of time; it is sadder when the old do so.

My mother did not much like 'amusements'. I cannot blame her for that, for as an adult I did not like them very much myself. After my father's death, she said to me one day, 'I don't know what I'm expected to do with my time. I can't read all day, can I?' Auntie Phyl alleged that she gave up reading towards the end of her life, but I'm not sure that was true. My mother was in the middle of James Clavell's *Shōgun* when she died. It was open on her bedside table. This was lowbrow reading, for her, and I was surprised to see it there. The night before, on 3 April 1984, she had managed to see the last episode of *The Jewel in the Crown*. I have always been pleased that she got to the end of the story. She died unexpectedly in the early morning of 4 April, and she was not alone in the house, because her daily housekeeper and good friend Mrs Cattermole had arranged to spend the night with her. I don't think this was because my mother was feeling ill – I think they'd decided to watch telly together, as a little treat, with their supper on a tray. This knowledge was a comfort. She had a much better death than her sister. Although a self-confessed hypochondriac all her life, she died without a murmur.

Some adults have a natural and uninhibited capacity for play. The detective fiction I used to read as a moody fourteen-year-old during the long dull school holidays featured house parties that frequently involved games like charades. As I never knew anyone who gave such house parties, I attempted to despise them as the diversions of the upper classes and the idle rich, but in fact they could not be dismissed on a class basis. H. G. Wells, who was nei-ther upper class nor idle, threw himself boyishly into floor games, war games, hide-and-seek and charades. He liked organizing house parties full of boisterous fun. His literary heir, J. B. Priestley, wrote with a similar gusto about riotous, lower-middle-class assemblies, and was a gifted entertainer of grandchildren. Some families never grow out of play. I watch them with wonder, excluded, unwilling and unable to join in. I would like to be able to play games, but I can't.

But, I sometimes ask myself, was there not something a bit *odd* about Wells? That's rather a T. S. Eliot kind of thought. Was there not something *not quite grown up* about Wells? He remained boyishly irresponsible both in his private and public life, reacting petulantly to criticisms, quarrelling over trifles, never quite accepting adult liabilities. Was this a necessary part of his capacity for play?

I have realized that, at Bryn, I felt both protected and included. I felt able to be a child, and to enjoy childish things. They were ordinary and undemanding. We sat round a little, low, oblong table in the front room (we didn't call them coffee tables in those days, although as we grew older we were allowed mugs of milky Nescafé) and we played cards, or a board game called Millionaire, or we cut wool, or pegged rugs from scraps of old clothes. (Alison Uttley, of course, had pegged rugs.) Or we sat up at the gateleg table, doing a jigsaw. I don't think we could hear the passing lorries from the front room – it was from the apple-loft bedroom upstairs that we heard the incessant, pouring sound of the slipstream – but we were aware of the proximity of the Roman road, leading north to Scotland, south to London. I can't remember how old or young I was when I began to plan my own travels, to long to see the sights, to desire to conquer territory and to tick off cities. But Bryn, from the beginning of my life, was a calm fixed point in a restlessly ambitious world. It wasn't a backwater, but it was safe.

XI

The romance of the road, as I recently discovered, was the inspiration for the first known English table or board game, which pre-dates Belisha by nearly two hundred years. The connection between dreams of travel and sedentary evenings spent round a lamp-lit table is an old one. You sit secure at home in your family circle or in the parlour of the inn, but at the same time you may toss your dice or spin your teetotum, and you may move freely through unknown lands. Manufacturers from early days knew how to attract what they called 'tarry-at-home' or 'parlour' travellers.

Now we explore the unknown world through watching television programmes or feature films made in exotic locations, but in my childhood we learned at school through geography lessons, and unofficially through games or jigsaws, or through holiday slide shows of varying degrees of sophistication projected by holiday-makers keen to share their experiences with a captive family audience. In the late 1950s and 60s, even Auntie Phyl took colour slides. She could never remember what they were of, but we enjoyed watching her jumbled images of Denmark and Norway, East Germany and Scotland, Ireland and the Shetlands. Home entertainment has been connected with the virtual journey for a very long time. A correspondent in Alberta writes that she spent many winter evenings 'in my hometown in Saskatchewan doing jigsaws and they were for me, along with my books, windows on the world'.

I had never heard of the mother of all modern table track games until I set off on this jigsaw journey. I now know more about it than I need to. The earliest track board game, the most ancient of tracks, is called the Royal Game of the Goose, and it dates from the Renaissance. Its invention is sometimes attributed to Francesco de Medici, one of the later and more decadent Medici, who was Grand Duke of Tuscany from 1574 to 1587, and who presented a copy of the game to Philip II of Spain. It was mentioned by Pietro Carrera in *Il Gioco degli scacchi* in 1617 in connection with Francesco, whose mother Eleanora of Toledo was Spanish. Francesco cultivated the Spanish alliance by gifts, and this game was amongst them

Francesco de Medici was a discriminating patron of alchemy, craftsmanship and the decorative arts, was better renowned for these pursuits than for high statesmanship. He was passionately interested in chemistry and cosmography, as well as being a skilled and innovative jeweller 'adept at making vases from molten rock crystal and precious metals', according to historian Christopher Hibbert. By the time he came to power in Florence, the Medici family was in vigorous and scandalous decline, and Francesco's eccentric trajectory was exploited in England some thirty years after his death by John Webster and Thomas Middleton, in whose Jacobean tragedies he appears as a murderous, lecherous villain.

Francesco was famous for his melancholy, and for keeping goldfish and Swedish reindeer as well as mistresses. Wealthy and beleaguered, he invented many curious devices for killing time. Most of the Medici of this period played cards and chess, and gambled for high stakes. (Chess was a game more favoured in Spain and Italy than in England, a point stressed by Jacobean dramatists, several of whom used chess as a theatrical device to reveal court intrigue. The English tended to regard chess as Machiavellian.) The Medici were also given to more inventive and extravagant entertainments, such as water ballets on the river Arno and sixty-five-course feasts, parades and pageants, literary experiments, and the commissioning of villas, palaces, gardens and murals. In his dark and secret *studiolo* in the Palazzo Vecchio in Florence, designed by Vasari, Francesco created an arcane cabinet of mythological and alchemical paintings, surveyed by portraits of his father Cosimo and his Spanish mother Eleanora. He was the prince of dark staircases and ornate display. But the board game he is said to have originated was cheap and easy to reproduce, thus becoming part of the daily lives of ordinary people who could never have afforded any of the precious stones, thickly clustered paintings, or curious scientific objects that crowded his cabinet.

The Gioco dell'Oca, or Le Jeu de l'Oie, is a very simple game, much simpler than chess, and it soon caught on throughout Europe. It reached England by the end of the sixteenth century, for there is a reference to it in the Stationers' Register on 16 June 1597, where John Wolfe entered 'the newe and most pleasant game of the Goose'. Shakespeare might have played it, as might Queen Elizabeth who, like most kings, queens and princes, was fond of a game of cards. Shakespeare never mentions it, which is a pity. Nor does Robert Burton, in his list of winter aids to ward off melancholy. He includes 'cards, tables and dice, shovelboard, chess-play, the philosopher's game, small trunks, shuttlecock, billiards, music, masks, singing, dancing, Yule-games, frolics, jests, riddles, catches, purposes, questions and commands, merry tales of errant knights, queens, lovers, lords, ladies, giants, dwarfs, thieves, cheaters, witches, fairies, goblins, friars', but he omits the goose game.

Nine men's morris, which Shakespeare does mention, was a more ancient and primitive board game, an elaborate form of noughts and crosses that could be played indoors with pegs or pins, or outdoors on a pitch carved out in the turf. It seems to have become a well-known village game by his day, as Titania's reference in *A Midsummer Night's Dream* reveals, but some form of it had once been played at court, where it was known as 'merells'. Games, as historian Philip Ariès was to tell us, had a tendency to slide down the social scale. John Clare, who called it 'peg morris' or 'ninepeg morris', certainly knew it as an outdoor game, 'nicked upon the green'. I don't think this game is played anywhere in Britain now, though there may be some 'heritage' reconstructions of it in heritage-conscious villages, but it has been revived as a board game by the National Trust. I bought it at the National Trust shop at Heddon Mouth in Devon, and gave it to my grandson Stanley at a lunch party in Hackney in June 2008; he and his uncle Adam attempted to play it, but found the instructions confusing. Stanley, an enterprising boy, looked it up on the internet, where he found a better explanation of the rules, and uncle and nephew proceeded to do battle. I don't know who won. They are both by nature persistent.

The Royal Game of the Goose is a game of luck, like Snakes and Ladders. Unlike many later board games, it has no moral or intellectual content, although some later variants have tried to introduce one. The players begin at a given starting point, throw dice for the number of moves, and work their way gradually with a token round a spiral track of sixty-three places towards the centre of the board, advancing, missing a turn or going back if they land on certain spaces – a bridge, an inn, a dungeon, a well, a maze. Space 58 is particularly unlucky; sometimes it portrays a death's head, sometimes a cooked or dead goose, or some other symbol of ill luck, and it always sends the player right back to the beginning. There are so many versions of this type of board game now that it is hard to imagine a world before it was invented. How did people get through time without it?

Irving Finkel, the colourful curator of the Department of the Ancient Near East at the British Museum, is an expert on the games of the ancient world. All games, he claims, fit into groups – race games, all-in-a-row games, hunt games, position games, counting games and war games. The Royal Game of Ur dates back to 2600 BC, whilst chess, a 'war game of pure skill' of Indian origin, appeared about 500 BC. Pachisi, also an Indian game, mutated into Ludo in modern times, and the goose game, another derivative, is also a race game.

The human capacity for and fear of boredom must have an evolutionary significance. Animals in nature do not seem to get bored, even when (like gorged lions) they have plenty of time for boredom. Domestic animals have caught the habit from us, and caged animals clearly and visibly suffer from it. So do horses in small wet fields. It has been experimentally demonstrated that laboratory rats, given stimulating activities such as a treadmill, retain their *joie de vivre* much longer than those deprived of these entertainments, and also retain a capacity for neurogenesis. Jigsaws and treadmills renew the brain cells. Activity is good for you, lethargy is bad for you. So the human intolerance of very long periods of lethargy is in itself an evolutionary stimulus towards invention, creativity, discovery. Playing games to pass the time is connected with intellectual development, just as funerary rites are connected with an apprehension of mortality. Palaeolithic children may not have played board games, but they must have played in the dirt with pebbles and shells.

I read about the Royal Game of the Goose, unwittingly, long before I thought to ask what it was, and what its provenance. It is mentioned in Oliver Goldsmith's pastoral lament, *The Deserted Village* (1770), a poem with which any student of English Literature of my age must be familiar, and which I have certainly read several times over the past fifty years. Indeed, I had often thought of this poem in connection with the changing life of Long Bennington, the only English village I have known throughout my life. In my middle years I became very interested, for reasons that are not yet clear to me, in the subject of the pastoral as a literary and (to a lesser extent) as an artistic form, and spent a good deal of time reading the poetry of Thomson, Crabbe and John Clare, as well as following the discussions and revisionist analyses of writers such as Raymond Williams, John Berger, John Barrell and, more recently, Matthew Johnson. (John Barrell's analysis of George Morland's painting *The Alehouse Door*, in *The dark side of the landscape*, is a masterpiece of sympathetic and revelatory interpretation.) My liking for wild and empty romantic landscape was easy enough to explain, and its literary sources obvious, for the Brontës were dear to many English, middle-class schoolgirls who loved Heathcliff, Mr Rochester and desolate moorland with an erotic and ideological passion. My interest in the pastoral was more unaccountable, and is in some way connected with my feelings for Bryn and with the flat fields and mild beasts around it.

The fate of Long Bennington does not much resemble that of Goldsmith's 'Sweet Auburn, Loveliest Village of the Plain'. Auburn is taken to be in part a description of Lissoy, the village of the Irish Midlands where Goldsmith was reared. Both Long Bennington and Lissoy are Midlands villages, but Long Bennington has grown and prospered rather than dwindled and declined. Its several public houses have done good business in the past five decades, despite the bypass. For years Auntie Phyl enjoyed her bargain pensioner's lunch at the Wheatsheaf, where the child of the house would often join her to chat to her on her banquette as she ate her fish and chips or gammon, egg and chips. Her gift for entertaining children did not fade with age.

Nevertheless, despite Long Bennington's successful adaptation to the twentieth and twenty-first centuries, one can glimpse in its living present the traces of a pastoral way of life that has been a long time dying. These traces link us to Goldsmith's sense of a not-quite-lost Golden Age, a Golden Age that lives on in our bones and flickers through the imagery of our collective memory, a Golden Age in which we are not utterly alienated from the earth.

Long Bennington retains its authenticity. It is not yet a facsimile, a virtual village. Although housing developments built from the 1960s onwards have considerably increased the size of its population, the community still has a strongly agricultural feel to it. Local businesses deal in animal feeds, agricultural engineering and ironwork, and not all the children at the village school want to be footballers or firemen or policemen. Some still want to farm, or to drive a tractor, or to become a vet.

The elm tree is gone, and the Teas-with-Hovis sign has gone. In Goldsmith's depopulated Auburn, the thorn tree survived, but the signpost near it that 'caught the passing eye' and directed the traveller to the ale house had vanished.

Here is Goldsmith's description (lines 226–36) of what was once the alehouse of Auburn:

> Imagination fondly stoops to trace
> The parlour splendours of that festive place;
> The whitewash'd wall, the nicely sanded floor,
> The varnish'd clock that click'd behind the door,
> The chest, contrived a double debt to pay,
> A bed by night, a chest of drawers by day,
> The pictures placed for ornament and use,
> The twelve good rules, the royal game of goose,
> The hearth, except when winter chill'd the day,
> With aspen boughs, and flowers, and fennel gay;–
> While broken tea-cups, wisely kept for show,
> Ranged o'er the chimney, glisten'd in a row.

I used to read this passage, taking in the generalized sense of regret and loss, without having any notion of what the 'royal game of goose' was, and without stopping to enquire. Nor did I recognize 'the twelve good rules', which have nothing to do with the goose game, as I (and others) have ignorantly assumed; the phrase appears to refer to a list of rules of conduct fancifully ascribed to King Charles I, which were produced as popular broadside sheets illustrated with woodcuts and hung on the walls of inns, alehouses and taverns. The rules included advice not to pick quarrels, not to make comparisons or keep bad company, not to lay wagers, and not to make long meals.

Bryn did not display the twelve good rules, but it had those very teacups described by Goldsmith, kept for show on the mahogany sideboard in the dining room and imprisoned within a glass-fronted china cabinet in the parlour. (We didn't call it the parlour; we called it the front room.) The cabinet also contained a selection of Coronation cups and mugs, as well as some alabaster eggs and small glass animals of more recent date, many of them Christmas presents and souvenirs. Some very miscellaneous, old, painted plates and tiles were suspended on brackets from the walls or hung from a picture rail. On twin oblong plaques, two bulbous green ceramic monks in habits drank ale from tankards, suggesting alehouse conviviality. A decorative round plate with a green-and-gilt edge portrayed a rose-crowned woman in a flimsy pink-and-white garment perched on a thorny precipice. A blue-and-white tile framed in gilded wood displayed a couple of ragged black 'piccaninny' children, a boy and a girl, sitting on the branch of a tree above a river in a Deep Southern landscape, kissing one another; their features are exaggerated and caricatured in a manner that would now be considered profoundly offensive, and the work of art is signed with the initials ABB. I never liked this image, which even as a small child I found crude, ugly and disturbing.

These piccaninnies, unlike Epaminondas, were unacceptable.

Was this tile a Bloor piece, by a Bloor potter? It is too embarrassing to show to an expert, too strange an heirloom to discard. It remains hidden in a spare bedroom. The vogue for such artwork now seems inexplicable.

The Bloors, as I have noted, were potters. A Robert Bloor had once owned the Old Derby China Works, in the early nineteenth century, though the quality of its products is said by some to have deteriorated under his management.

Grandma Bloor collected brass and copper ornaments, and the mantelpiece in the public dining room was crowded with small brass and copper knick-knacks of varying value and charm – a fine, smoothly sculpted hare, two Oriental oxen pulling a cart, many little bowls and ashtrays, some figurines, assorted candlesticks, a miniature set of fire-irons, a tiny kettle. I don't think there were any horse brasses. These objects were a talking point with guests, who liked to remark that they must take a lot of cleaning. Her collection was very useful to her grandchildren, who always knew what to buy her for Christmas. I used to enjoy hunting around in junk shops for bits and pieces for her. I was told, perhaps wrongly, that one can distinguish copper from brass by the colour of their glow and lustre; copper is yellow-gold, whereas brass has a more reddish, metallic, fiery tint. I prefer the yellow copper. I don't think any of us knew anything about the quality of these pieces, though my father thought the ox cart might be valuable.

Bryn, like Auburn's alehouse and Alison Uttley's farmhouse, had a varnished grandfather clock that had once clicked behind the door. I think I can remember the weights of its pendulum, which hung down obscenely like dirty sausages. Grandpa Bloor used to wind it up, once a week, but after his death it stood silent.

Bryn also housed some cracked and crazed old oil paintings – a portrait of an eighteenth-century gentleman in a red jacket and a cap, a Scottish landscape with pine trees and a torrent, which had a small tear in the canvas. Auntie Phyl gave these away for nothing to an itinerant antique dealer, because he assured her they were 'worthless'. I think she felt slightly shifty about this, as well she might have done. I don't know where those paintings came from, or how old they were, and I don't know where they went. They looked pretty damn old to me, even when I was quite grown up. Maybe they'd been hanging there since the house was built. Maybe Oliver Goldsmith himself had seen them on his travels. Maybe Samuel Johnson had passed by Bryn, and called in, and supped or taken tea before those very paintings, in the summer of 1773, on his way to Scotland and the Western Isles.

In fact, Dr Johnson must have been driven through Long Bennington and therefore past Bryn, although the house wasn't called that then. Everybody who went along the high road to and from Scotland passed by Bryn. Dr Johnson passed by in a post-chaise with his friend and travelling companion, the lawyer Robert Chambers, on his way to meet Boswell in Edinburgh. (Chambers was on his way to Bengal, via a lengthy detour to bid farewell to his family in his home town of Newcastle-upon-Tyne.) Boswell records that Johnson enjoyed his journey: 'I choose to mention that he travelled in post-chaises, of which the rapid movement was one of his most favourite amusements.' Elsewhere, Johnson is recorded as 'doating' on a coach, and declaring that life had not 'many better things than being driven rapidly along'. His friend Mrs Piozzi remembered that he 'loved indeed the very act of travelling, and I cannot tell how far one might have taken him in a carriage before he would have wished for refreshment. He was therefore, in some respects, an admirable companion on the road, as he piqued himself upon feeling no inconvenience, and on despising no accommodations.'

He enjoyed a captive audience in a carriage. His captives were not always so content. A drive through Scotland that pleased Johnson ('we were satisfied with the company of each other, as well riding in the chaise as sitting at an inn') was described by Boswell as 'tedious' and 'drowsy'.

Johnson's view of the Great North Road is well known: 'The noblest prospect which a Scotsman ever sees, is the high road that leads him to England.' But he relished both the notion and the act of movement.

At one point I began to hope that my grandfather's grandfather clock might be nearly as old as the house (which would have made it both more valuable and more authentic) but I discovered an invoice indicating that my grandfather had bought it on 2 October 1905, at Arthur Cook's in Leeds, for £3 5s. So it had started its life with the Bloor family in a terraced house in Mexborough, before it moved to its more appropriate rural setting in the corner of the dining room in Bryn.

The mahogany sideboard, the second most expensive single item in the sale list, had cost £5 10s. The most expensive was a brass bedstead, which was bought for £8 10s, and on which my grandmother died.

I don't know when my grandparents acquired the warming-pan that I rescued from Bryn, and which I keep in my study in London. I don't know whether it was ever used. I remember the cream-and-brown stone hot-water bottles, as does everyone of my age, but not the warming-pan. It may have been bought in Leeds in 1905, along with the brass bedstead, although it isn't listed in the inventory. But that would not in itself have confirmed it as an item of inauthentic retro-chic.

Can a horse brass ever be authentic? A warming-pan may be, but I'm not sure whether a horse brass can. Antique, yes, though not many are; authentic, no.

Samuel Johnson loved an inn as well as a post-chaise, and he claimed that good inns contributed greatly to human happiness. But he is very unlikely to have supped in Bryn, for it was not then a public house. He might well have stopped at the George in Stamford, or at the Angel in Grantham, or at the White Hart in Newark, and seen a group of fellow travellers or locals playing cards or the goose game. The Great North Road is lined with famous coaching inns with long pedigrees. The upper dining room of the Angel in Grantham, with its three fine, deep oriel windows, is one of the most handsome public dining rooms in England. King John and Richard III both knew this inn, so why not Dr Johnson?

There is no evidence that Johnson ever played the goose game. As we have seen, Boswell regretted that his friend did not play draughts after leaving college, 'for it would have afforded him an innocent soothing relief from the melancholy which distressed him so often…there is a composure and gravity in draughts… which insensibly tranquillises the mind.'

That's what I feel about jigsaws.

XII

Once you start looking for a motif like the Royal Game of the Goose, you find that it pops up in unexpected places. It has now been forgotten in England, but it had its day of fashion here. In the mid-eighteenth century in England, the Duchess of Norfolk planted an outsize goose game of hornbeam in the grounds of her vast mansion at Worksop, which Horace Walpole saw on his visit in 1758. Unfortunately the manor, its five hundred apartments, and all its paintings and *objets de vertu* were destroyed by fire three years later in 1761, and we hear no more of the hornbeams. A generation later, Byron knew about the goose game and refers to it in *Don Juan*: 'For good society is but a game / The royal game of goose, as I may say.' And the game lives on in the popular culture of Europe. French and Italian children still play it, as we play Snakes and Ladders. It surfaced recently in Spain and Italy as a game show. A human form of it, claiming to be more ancient than the board game, is played in the square in Mirano, near Padua.

In France, the game flourished from its first introduction. Many pretty, fragile and delicately coloured versions of it survive in the Print Room of the British Museum, with variants embracing journeys through the street vendors of Paris (a penalty is exacted for a stay at the vintner's), the myths of Greece, Roman history (a penalty for landing on the space representing the Emperor Commodus), the military campaigns of Napoleon, and even the lives of famous actors and actresses. Most of these spin-offs have vanished, but the classic board game is well remembered in France, and cheap and cheerful plastic mass-produced versions of it are still on sale in French toyshops. I bought one in Nice in 2005. Its images are of an old-world, bucolic, farmyard prettiness.

I had assumed that it was on the way out in Italy, its birthplace, as my attempts to buy it there in the spring of 2007 were unsuccessful. But my requests for it in newsagents and toyshops were met not with blank indifference but with a smile of happy, nostalgic recognition, the same kind of smile that often greets a query about jigsaws in England. Oh yes, of course they knew the Gioco dell'Oca, they didn't happen to have it in stock, but of course they knew it. And finally I found it, in the autumn, in a newsagent's in Sorrento, where the proprietor who sold it to me told me it was 'un gioco classico'. The board I bought is made by Clementoni, one of the most famous of contemporary jigsaw manufacturers, and the counters are in the form of little wooden geese. They are pleasanter to handle than the French plastic pieces. The scene portrayed is in the Italian Alps, with a mountainous backdrop, a chalet-style farmhouse, an old-fashioned well, cows, a goat, a pig, a rabbit, a tortoise, a butterfly and other designators of rustic life, and the game is described as suitable for players aged from five to ninety-nine. The description doesn't conceal the fact that it is a game of chance, but magnificently insists that the journey along the spiral track also symbolizes 'una vicenda, un'avventura, lo scorrere del tempo, la vita stessa'. (An event, an adventure, the flowing of time, life itself.) We need to justify our diversions.

Why the goose game survived on the continent and not in England is a mystery. Why did we go for Snakes and Ladders and

Ludo instead? It was clearly well known in Zembla, that northern realm created by the arch-cryptographer and games-player Vladimir Nabokov in *Pale Fire*, where his royal narrator alludes to a version 'played with little airplanes of painted tin'.

Games and manias come and go – board games, card games, collecting crazes. One year the playgrounds and streets are full of mini-scooters, or hula hoops, or yo-yos, or Frisbees, or skateboards, or roller skates, or children wearing bouncy antlers or springy tiaras on their heads, and the next year these objects vanish, or go underground for a while. Pokémon succeeds cigarette cards, and tamagotchi pets succeed Pokémon, while sudoku and kakuro chase the crossword. Some seemingly classic pursuits veer towards extinction or linger on with a small cult of practitioners. Diabolo, a juggling game played with two sticks and a spinning top, and once considered wickedly addictive, is rarely mentioned now, but it was once immensely popular. It is said to have been imported from China to England in the 1790s, round about the same time as the emergence of the jigsaw, and it caught on throughout Europe. Unlike gambling, it wasn't a social evil, but it was a real time-waster and, unlike the hula hoop two hundred years later, it could not be convincingly claimed that its aim was to provide bodily exercise. Dexterity, perhaps, like fivestones, but not good health.

One of the most bizarre tributes to the Royal Game of the Goose appears in a little-read novel by Jules Verne titled *Le Testament d'un excentrique*, published in 1899. I came across this very recently, but as a child I read and re-read Verne's more popular stories. I loved *Journey to the Centre of the Earth*, to which I owe an enduring interest in volcanoes and a character in my novel *The Realms of Gold*. I treasure a copy of *Twenty Thousand Leagues Under the Sea*, given to me by my parents for Christmas 1948, which I reread with intense pleasure and renewed admiration as part of the research for my most recent novel, *The Sea Lady*. The edition is an attractive Rainbow Classic, published in Cleveland, Ohio, by the World Publishing Company, and edited by May Lamberton Becker, who, I now find, was a distinguished Anglophile American scholar and journalist. (There was a room dedicated to her memory in the National Book League at 7 Albemarle Street; it was opened in 1960 by none other than T. S. Eliot.) My copy has good illustrations by a German-born and widely travelled artist, Kurt Wiese. As a nine-year-old, I liked best the pictures of the narwhal and the submarine forest. As an adult, I was pleased and astonished to find the narrator and his manservant Conseil portrayed in handsome (though not full-frontal) nakedness.

Verne has long been the darling of armchair parlour travellers. He had an interest in scientific discovery and experiment, and an extravagant love of all forms of locomotion and communication, coupled with a childlike eagerness for geological 'wonders'. The travel industry is greatly indebted to his novels. He preceded mass tourism and globalization, but he was a prophet of both.

I used to feel slightly embarrassed by my juvenile liking for Verne's work, and was both surprised and relieved to discover that he is one of the heroes of Oulipo, that 1960s games-playing and cryptogram-loving movement of the French avant-garde. (Oulipo stands for '**Ou**vroir de **litt**érature **po**tentielle'.) Verne is a frequent point of reference for Oulipian Georges Perec, author of the classic jigsaw novel, *La Vie: Mode d'Emploi*, of which we shall read more later. Raymond Roussel, the rich man's Proust, considered Verne one of the greatest of French novelists. His bold and adventurous imagination, his passion for puzzles, challenges, wagers and scientific marvels, appealed to a ludic and fantastic strain in French artists and writers, who took him more seriously than we have taken his English counterpart and literary descendant, H. G. Wells. Long after his death, his fictions continue to create new forms.

In May 2006, an astonishing piece of public art, in the form of a vast mechanical elephant five storeys high, appeared in the streets of London. The elephant walked through Trafalgar Square and along the Haymarket, seeking a giant wooden maiden. The spectacle was based on Verne's travel-quest story, The Sultan's Elephant, and children and adults gathered from far and wide to see it, summoned by word of mouth, mobile phones and glimpses on the television news. Both of my sons saw it, independently, as did two of my grandchildren, who reported to me that the elephant was 'bigger than a house'. I have a photograph of nine-year-old Stanley Swift, sitting on a bollard just inside the crowd barrier, holding up a copy of the specially printed Elephant Echo, with its headline FOUR MAGIC DAYS IN MAY. His seven-year-old sister Constance Swift, who was with another group, was one of the children who climbed up onto the arm of the giant girl to be scooped up by her and swung into the air.

I like the thought of these members of my family, unknown to each other, being drawn together in a huge crowd in central London by a magical elephant. And Jules Verne would have liked this evidence of the durability and adaptability of his fantasies, living on into another medium, another millennium.

Le Testament d'un excentrique has not been revived or much reprinted, but it is not without interest, particularly to one trying to distract herself by puzzles and travel games. In this novel, translated as The Will of an Eccentric, Verne converts the traditional goose game into 'the Noble Game of the United States of America'. Like its more famous predecessor, Around the World in Eighty Days, published a quarter of a century earlier, this is a race game, involving wagers made in a gentleman's club, large sums of money, and an eccentric millionaire. (Wagers in gentleman's clubs are a staple ingredient in the fiction of adventure writers such as Verne and John Buchan; as a Yorkshire schoolgirl, I didn't know what a gentleman's club was, but I liked the conceit.)

The story begins in Chicago, at the vast and festive funeral celebrations ('funérailles à la fois pompeuses et joyeuses') of William J. Hypperbone at Oakwood Cemetery. This character had been a well-known bachelor member of the Eccentric Club in Mohawk Street, where he had been a devotee of

> the Royal Game of Goose, the noble form that has come down to us in a more or less altered form from the Ancient Greeks. It would be impossible to say how passionately he was fond of it…great was his excitement in leaping from one division to another at the caprice of the dice, hurling himself from goose to goose to reach the last of these denizens of the poultry yard, walking on 'the bridge', resting in 'the inn', falling down 'the well', losing himself in 'the maze', casting himself into 'the prison', stumbling against 'the death's head', visiting the compartments of 'the sailor', 'the fisherman', 'the harbour', 'the stag', 'the mill', 'the snake', 'the sun', 'the helmet', 'the lion', 'the rabbit', 'the flower-pot', etc.

This breathless encomium, which credits the game with greater antiquity than Irving Finkel would grant it, provides the spring of the action. Hypperbone, apparently dying suddenly and mysteriously in his club, in mid-game, has left a will that selects by lot six random citizens of Chicago, who are expected to chase his fortune through the States of the Union at the dictates of the throw of the dice. (The novel incorporates a pull-out spiral track printed on thin paper and based on the original goose track, showing the fifty states with their heraldic devices.) The first contender to arrive at number 63, back in the home base of Chicago, inherits a fortune of sixty million, and the runner-up wins the sum of the fines and losses of all the other players.

The reading of the will created a frenzy of excitement in the press. Bets were taken on each of the players, and the chase took place largely by rail, though some contestants resorted to steamer, cariole, schooner, motor car, horse and bicycle as they made their way through the hazards of coyotes, stampedes, shipwrecks, storms and armed robbers. (The threat of 'Red Indians' has vanished from the scenario since the days of Phileas Fogg and Passepartout.) The chief delight of the book lies in its role as a vehicle for highly coloured travelogue, and its appeal to railroad enthusiasts. The beauty spots of America – Yellowstone National Park, Colorado, the Mammoth Caves of Kentucky – are described in purple prose, and the complex connections and timetables of the iron network of the railways are explored with the scholarly and pedantic enthusiasm of a railroad fanatic. The Mammoth Caves held a particular fascination for Verne; he invokes them in many of his works, including his bizarre and moving tale of life underground, *Les Indes noires*, published in 1877, which is improbably set in a Scottish coal mine beneath Lake Katrine. Maybe I owe my liking for caves to Jules Verne, or maybe we both drew from the same source – prehistoric folk memory, perhaps?

The story of *The Will of an Eccentric* is racy, and it is inconspicuously educational, for it teaches the reader the names of the States of the Union, which may or may not have been part of Verne's agenda. When I reread Nabokov's *Lolita* recently, it occurred to me that this notorious and brilliant novel of the road is like a pornographic parody of Verne – a vast travelogue of the United States, with a guide to all the motels, hotels and historic tourist sites that might appeal to a dissatisfied teenager. It is a Belisha route darkened by a ghastly combination of boredom and lust, a wild-goose chase that can end only in death.

Verne's novel, unlike Nabokov's, makes the reader long to buy a rail pass and set off at once across America on Amtrak. I did that very thing in 1974, travelling from San Francisco to New York with my three young children, courtesy of the E. M. Forster Award of the American Academy of Arts and Letters. I don't think Forster would have approved of his money being given to a woman writer encumbered by children, but he was dead by then – not long dead, but dead. Ours was an epic, a memorable journey. We didn't mean to go all the way by train, having booked our passage on a Greyhound bus, but the bus system was in chaos because of a random bomber (this was way back in the mid-1970s, and I can't remember why he was bombing the buses) so we switched to Amtrak. We arrived a mere nine hours late in New York, and just in time to catch the *QE2* home. I wouldn't fly in those days. Crossing the continent was exhilarating, and the railway staff were kind to the children.

Angus Wilson, a novelist much given in his prime to travelling abroad, liked to tick off the names of the American states that he had visited. He had an innocently childish desire to see them all, which he almost fulfilled. According to his partner Tony Garrett, the only ones he missed were Colorado, Oklahoma and Alaska, although Tony wonders whether he ever actually set foot in Wisconsin – he sent Tony to put a foot over the border (in much the same manner as I once put a foot over the 39th parallel into North Korea) but Angus may not have followed him over.

Michael, in most respects a man with adult interests, proved surprisingly eager to tick off all of the Canary Islands. This he achieved, with the exceptions of a few inconsiderable rocks, but not without much persistence and some hazardous journeys.

Like Perec's tragic protagonist, Bartlebooth, in *La Vie: Mode d'Emploi*, we invent arbitrary goals. We tick off states and islands. We make wagers with ourselves. We spot aeroplanes, and thereby risk being imprisoned as spies. We stand on stations or crowd by level crossings in the middle of the countryside, wearing thick glasses and anoraks, sporting binoculars and spotting trains. We collect stamps or coins or cigarette cards or jigsaws of the American Depression or Victorian and Edwardian biscuit tins or moustache cups or Sylvanian families or plastic toys from cereal or crisp packets. According to a visitors' book on display in the Victoria and Albert Museum, we collect elastic bands and chocolate coin wrappers and fridge magnets and bottle caps and sick bags and dead bees. And worse, unmentionably worse.

We collect objects that have no purpose other than to be collected, and we call them 'collectibles'. If we are very rich, like Elgin or Arundel or the Farnese family, we collect marbles. If we are less rich, we collect micromosaics or first editions or snuff-boxes. My father, as a barrister practising in Sheffield, collected Sheffield plate. (I worry about polishing the valuable pieces I inherited, as he said he knew I would. I polish them, spasmodically, irregularly, for his sake.) Twelve-year-old Rémi Plassaert, living on the top floor of the apartment block where Bartlebooth struggles with his self-appointed jigsaw labours, collects promotional blotters, with the help of the concierge, Madame Nochère. Perec itemizes these blotters in characteristically evocative detail: a singing toreador stands for Diamond Enamel toothpaste; *The Fox and the Slork* (sic), a print by Jean-Baptiste Oudry, advertises Marquise Stationery, Stencils and Reprographics; The Four Musketeers of Tennis (Cochet, Borotra, Lacoste and Brugnon) represent the Aspro series of Great Champions of the Past.

I don't think promotional blotters are made any more, though they were clearly still abundant in 1975, the year in which Perec's novel is set.

Jean Baudrillard, in his essay on the 'Non-Functional System of Objects' (1968), notes that the taste for collecting is at its height between the ages of seven and twelve; it tends to disappear with puberty and reappears most frequently in men over forty. In this essay he also discourses at length on the inauthenticity of the warming-pan. Its presence in a modern home, he claims, is 'strictly mythological'. It is unwarranted, vain and perfectly useless. The warming-pan standing in my study, he suggests, is 'like a splinter of the True Cross', 'something like a talisman, like a fragment of absolute reality which would be at the heart of the real, and enshrined in the real. Such is the bygone object.'

Yes, that is fair enough.

According to William James in *The Principles of Psychology*, 'the hoarding instinct prevails widely among animals as well as among men.' He quotes a description of the hoard of a Californian wood rat, made in the stove of an empty house, of which the outside was composed of spikes,

> all laid with *symmetry*, so as to present the points of the nails outward…Interlaced with the spikes were the following: about two dozen knives, forks and spoons…several large plugs of tobacco…an old purse containing some silver, matches and tobacco; nearly all the small tools from the tool-closets, with several large augers…The outside casing of a silver watch was disposed of in one part of the pile, the glass of the same watch in another, and the works in still another.

James suggests that rats are like misers, and that they don't have a plan. They collect for the sake of collecting. But that wood rat's collection sounds very deliberate to me and demonstrated a fairly sophisticated degree of classification.

Howard Hardiman is a collector who collects stray jigsaw pieces, found in the street. He has strict rules about his collection, rules that provide what Oulipo would call 'constraints'. He is a sign-language interpreter by profession, which implies that he is interested in signs. He doesn't actually do jigsaw puzzles; he just collects pieces. 'They have to be on their own, rather than several pieces at once.' So far he has collected about twenty-five to thirty pieces. One day he may be going to turn them into a work of art. This is clearly a metaphysical, perhaps even a metaphysical-topographical project, or perhaps, as he puts it, just 'a little bit of madness'. While brooding on his strange habit, I encountered a soggy spread of jigsaw pieces on the edge of a muddy car park in Taunton. I don't know what he would have made of that. Would any of these pieces have been eligible? I don't think they would. And they were very wet.

Raymond Queneau, one of the founder members of Oulipo, spoke at a meeting in 1961 of 'rats who construct the labyrinth from which they plan to escape'. Baudrillard, in his 1968 essay quoted above, told us that 'the organisation of the collection is itself a substitute for time'.

Auntie Phyl and I collected car numbers on car number plates. This was the game: you had to begin at the beginning, with a single 1, and then note a single 2, and then a single 3, and so on, in strict sequence. We too had rules. You were not allowed to hoard or bank a spotted number, even for a couple of minutes. We used to report on progress during our weekly Sunday-morning telephone conversations, when we had finished with the exploits of Jimmy White or the early flowering of the aconites. It gave us something to talk about. I think I went through two or three rounds of this game, giving up each time round about 294 or 295. I don't think I have ever reached 300.

And the strange thing was that she was always ahead of me. Although in later years she led a fairly local village life, enlivened by shopping trips on the bus to Newark or Grantham, she spotted more car numbers than I did. I, in the thick of the thickest of London traffic, surrounded by number plates, always busy and always on the move, lagged behind. This was not because I was not concentrating. I was. It was because she lived on the Great North

Road. Even with a bypass, it provided a good vantage point from which to see the world go by.

Once, years ago, on a lecture tour of Mississippi and Alabama, I was put up for a night or two in a motel just outside Hattiesburg near the University of Southern Mississippi. It was on one of those American strips, lined on both sides by gas stations and Tex-Mex diners and Baskin Robbins and small superstores. As I remember it, the motel had a wooden veranda on which were lined up some wooden rocking chairs. Sitting on one of these chairs, rocking myself gently and watching the polluting traffic pass noisily by, I was at peace. It is a surprisingly pleasant memory. I think the motel reminded me of Bryn. It is one of the best recollections I have of all those book tours and lecture tours, where time was divided between frenzied anxiety at airports and imprisoned restlessness in hotel rooms waiting for the next interview. Sitting in the slipstream, rocking, watching the world go by.

XIII

Auntie Phyl was trained as a teacher at Homerton College in an era when the pedagogical concept of learning through play was well established. Learning through terror or by rote was well out of fashion by the time Auntie Phyl taught us to sew and encouraged us to do jigsaws and sat down with us to play Belisha and to learn, subliminally, our road safety signs. When my children were little, in the 1960s, 'learning by doing' and Galt toys (products of a long-established manufacturer of educational supplies) were in fashion, and their children benefited from toys made by the Early Learning Centre, which began trading in the 1970s. The progressive ideas of Pestalozzi and Montessori and Rudolph Steiner have long infiltrated the mainstream. But it is nevertheless claimed that games manufactured and marketed for and dedicated to children are of surprisingly recent origin.

Jigsaw puzzles have led me to explore concepts of childhood that had not much interested me when I was bringing up my own family. As a 1960s mother, I had consulted the reassuringly liberal Dr Spock, and worried about the 'separation theory' of John Bowlby, and espoused the principles of comprehensive state education, but I had never been particularly interested in childhood as a subject, nor had I been much drawn to write about children in my fiction. I didn't consciously share T. S. Eliot's view of childhood as a rotting corpse best left buried; I just hadn't bothered to think about it much, in the abstract. Flashbacks and formative memories had featured in my novels, but I'd never tried to re-create a sustained childhood sequence – no imitations of *The Mill on the Floss*, or *David Copperfield*, or *The Shrimp and the Anemone*. I'd succeeded in forgetting much of my childhood, and was surprised by the powers of recall of some of my friends and colleagues. My novels began and ended in mid-career. I was interested in the contemporary world and enjoyed tracking events as they happened, or as they were about to happen. (I guessed right about several topics, including the privatization of public utilities.) Age has given me a different timespan and a different agenda. *The Sea Lady* is largely a retrospective narrative, looking back over five decades of social change and scientific discovery. I wouldn't have been able to write that kind of novel when I was in my twenties, and I wouldn't have wanted to.

Early images of children at play have, over the last fifty years, been intensively analysed. The French social historian Philippe Ariès, in *Centuries of Childhood: A Social History of Family Life* (1962) – first published in 1960 as *L'Enfant et la vie familiale sous L'Ancien Régime* – initiated a growing interest in what had been a surprisingly neglected subject and inspired a host of scholars in various disciplines. I had left university and completed my formal education just before this important book was published, and when I look back to what I absorbed at school and college about children and educational theory, I recognize that most of it came from commentaries on Blake (whom I revered) and Wordsworth (whose work I learned to enjoy somewhat later). I also knew a fair amount about schooling in the days of Jane Austen and George Eliot, and must have registered, without any particular interest or sense of recognition, the presence of an early jigsaw in Austen's *Mansfield Park,* just as my eyes had moved unseeingly over the Royal Game of the Goose in Goldsmith.

Ariès, in his fourth chapter, 'A Modest Contribution to the History of Games and Pastimes', briefly outlines the history of games and the changing attitudes to childhood and children's amusements. He argues that adult games and children's games were much less sharply differentiated in the Middle Ages and the Renaissance than in later periods, and he harks back, somewhat in the spirit of Goldsmith or Clare, to 'an old community of games', when music, festivals, carnivals, maypoles, snowballs and skating united old and young, peasants and gentry. The names of traditional games, such as hot cockles, sweet knight, Blind Man's Buff, the love-pot, the knife-in-the-water-jug, and the little man who doesn't laugh (*main chaude, chevalier gentil, colin-maillard, le pot d'amour, le couteau dans le pot à eau, le petit bonhomme sans rire*), are listed by him with relish and regret. John Clare, in his poetry, provides a similar compendium of traditional, eighteenth-century, English-village games, some of which must have been played for many centuries: ducks and drakes, dancing the maze, town of Troy, pitch and toss, duck neath water, taw and hollows, lost love letter, hunt the slipper, crookhorn, nine men's morris…Perhaps inevitably, these phrases are imbued with an overwhelming sense of loss: of childhood itself, of a bucolic past, of a lost harmony. Clare mourned the death of the commons as well as the loss of love, and in 'Remembrances' he mourned his own boyhood:

> Dear heart and can it be that such raptures meet decay
> I thought them all eternal when by Langley bush I lay
> I thought them joys eternal when I used to sit and play
> On its banks at clink and bandy chock and taw and ducking
>   stone

Where silence sitteth now on the wild heath as her own
Like a ruin of the past all alone.

When I used to lye and sing by old eastwells boiling spring
When I used to tie the willow boughs together for a swing
And fish with crooked pins and thread and never catch
  a thing...

In the work of Philippe Ariès we find a similar, prevailing sense of loss and falling from grace, though it occurs at the other end of the social spectrum from that experienced by Clare. Later historians have associated his backward glance with his political affiliations with Vichy France and Action Française, for Ariès was a romantic royalist. He gives much space to the well-documented infancy and education of Louis XIII – indeed, this seems to have been the starting point of his intellectual journey. Louis graduated from dolls, toy soldiers, clockwork pigeons, crambo, playing charades, cutting paper with scissors, hide-and-seek, and other childish diversions, to the manly pursuits of hunting, riding, fencing, archery, tennis, hockey and bowls. Ariès notes that at this period games of chance using dice were played by both adults and children alike (Louis XIII, Louis XIV and his mother, Richelieu and Mazarin were all keen gamblers), and that these games attracted no censure except from those sections of the clergy who disapproved indiscriminately of all amusements. (Little Louis XIII was applauded for winning a turquoise in a raffle.) The notion that dice games were in themselves wicked had not yet been widely disseminated.

Incessant moralizing about 'good' games and 'bad' games came later, but it crept in inescapably and in some ways imperceptibly. The Dutch historian Johan Huizinga, writing in 1938 ostensibly in praise of 'homo ludens' (as his book of 1944 was to be titled), understandably condemned the 'puerilism' of the culture of boys' clubs and badges, marching, rallies and boy scouts that were shortly to lead to the closing of the University of Leiden and his detention by the Nazis, but in passing he also condemns playing bridge as a 'sterile' activity. Underlying this casual criticism lay the view that play should be educational or culturally rewarding, and that an immense expenditure of intellectual effort on playing card games for pleasure or money was disproportionate. John Locke, one of the most influential of all educational theorists, thought the time-less sport of knucklebones (or 'dibstones', as they were known to him) a time-waster, and wished that all the practice that children put into it could be applied to something more useful: in *Some Thoughts Concerning Education*, he wrote: 'I have seen little Girls exercise whole Hours together, and take an abundance of pains to be expert at *Dibstones*, as they call it: Whilst I have been looking on, I have thought that it wanted only some good Contrivance to make them employ all that Industry about something that might be more useful to them.'

Knucklebones, or fivestones, or dibstones, were still played in Alison Uttley's childhood, and in mine. The game is probably prehistoric, and its materials are free for all. But Locke is right: it has no information content, and apart from improving manual dexterity and co-ordination it cannot be described as educational. Marbles, usually associated with boys rather than girls, are not very educational either, and are moreover surrounded by an aura of *Just William* anarchy. Coveted, quarrelled over, embattled, scarred and confiscated, marbles are individual, capricious and subversive. Teachers and policemen disapprove of marbles, because they constitute an alternative economy, a different set of values. Teachers prefer games that teach.

Ariès does not mention the goose game specifically, either in praise or blame, but we know that French children as well as adults played it. A lost painting by Jean-Siméon Chardin, first exhibited in

1743 and surviving in an engraving, shows three young people, one of them still a child, grouped round a goose track laid out on a card table, solemnly intent on the next move. The engraving is accompanied by the obligatory sanctimonious little verse, at once trite and cynical, which claims that the game represents the risks and perils of adult life (*Que de risques à craindre et d'Eceuils à franchir*), but Chardin's art, as so often, escapes the subsequent superimposed interpretation. He painted children, not homilies.

(In the National Gallery, a luminously beautiful and affectionate painting by Chardin titled *The Young Schoolmistress*, showing an older girl teaching a younger child to read, is accompanied by an offensive tag that was attached to Lépicié's 1740 engraving. It says: 'If this charming child takes on so well the serious air and imposing manner of a schoolmistress, may one not think that pretence and artfulness come to the fair sex no later than birth?' This misinterpretation of childhood is deeply, revealingly shocking. We don't have a word for the attitude it represents. The comment is sexist, but it is also contemptuous of children.)

Games designed specifically for children are of recent origin, and the invention of the jigsaw puzzle proves to have been much more closely connected with education than with play. I would never have guessed this, and it comes as a surprise to most people to whom I've spoken. But, as historians such as Ariès like to insist, childhood was not invented until long after the Renaissance. Infant mortality rates were so high in earlier centuries that less attention and affection were invested in young children than in our child-centred and medically reliable era – or so one plausible theory goes. Even Simon Schama, who persuasively queries the theory in his account of Dutch family life in *The Embarrassment of Riches*, appears to accept that there may be some truth in it.

XIV

The most famous early illustration of children at play is Brueghel's *Children's Games* (*Kinderspieler*) of 1560, which has of course been made into a jigsaw, and which appears in most discussions on the evolution of the concept of childhood. It shows a scene of various and, in places, extremely vigorous outdoor activity in a very public space in front of a town hall, with children playing Blind Man's Buff and doing headstands and inflating bladders, playing at leapfrog and tug of war and king of the castle, climbing trees and building sandcastles and whipping tops and rolling hoops and riding on barrels and playing shop and blowing bubbles. The most peaceful and sedentary activity portrayed is a game of knucklebones, and the only artistic pursuit appears to be the playing of a flute. Scholars claim to have identified more than ninety different games in this painting, and to have counted 246 children, of whom 168 are male and 78 female.

Its iconography has been submitted to much controversial analysis. Is it a satire on human folly, and are the children miniature adults representing adult follies? Is an alchemical reading possible? Is the blue of the cloaks used in the 'blinding' and 'hiding' games the colour of deception or of truth? Are the naked swimming children emblems of false trust, and the boy on stilts of false pride? Is the game of Blind Man's Buff a tope for the blind choice of marriage? Why is nobody flying a kite? Are these children to be seen as ugly, gnomelike, miniature peasants, full of original sin, or are they innocents at play? Does Brueghel intend them to look like squat, diminutive, imitation adults, in their trousers and clumsy shoes and aprons, or is he deliberately distancing himself from the Renaissance tradition that portrays infants as naked, airborne putti?

The painting may be seen as an encyclopaedia or compendium of games, a successor to the famous list by Rabelais, in Chapter XXII of *Gargantua*. Published some thirty years earlier than the Brueghel was painted, this enumerated 217 Gargantuan games (a list to which Rabelais's English translator Thomas Urquhart generously added various English examples), including lottery, nivinivinack, the squares, the lurch, the madge-owlet, the gunshot crack and bo-peep. (Rabelais, Urquhart, John Clare and Ariès all relish such evocative words.) Many of these games were played with cards (*chartes*), dice (*dez*), and chequers and chessboards (*renfort de tabliers*), to the accompaniment of 'wenches thereabouts, with little small banquets, intermixed with collations and reer-suppers'. This large-scale panoramic sense of play is well illustrated by Brueghel, although it is to be noted that none of his children is eating or drinking. They are too busy for that. Maybe there is a moral significance to the absence of food. And, then again, maybe not.

My own feelings about this work, which I have come to know much better through its jigsaw format, changed very considerably during the course of my study. At first, I saw it as a satirical view, not of adult folly, but of childish cruelty, for some of the children did seem to be engaged in actively tormenting one another. There is a game of what seems to be hair-pulling, and another that shows a boy being stretched over a log as though about to be sawn in half by his captors. The small cowled boy whipping his top, and the hooded figures playing Blind Man's Buff, powerfully suggest flag-ellation and the activities of the Inquisition, with which Brueghel and his contemporaries were all too familiar. Moreover, my jigsaw had an odour of hell. It smelled very odd. I could not for some time locate the source of this unpleasant stink in my study, and kept wondering whether there was a dead mouse under the armchair, or dog shit on the carpet. But no, it was the pervasive smell of the cardboard, recycled from God knows what source, that filled my workroom. Was this odour in itself a commentary, a message from Brueghel and the dark and troubled times he lived through?

I decided not, and in time (for it took me a long time to complete this easy puzzle) the smell diminished, and I found that I was learning to like the children, or at least some of the children, more and more. Their unsupervised but contained freedom, their involvement with one another, the intensity of their concentration on their pursuits, their fertility of invention began to remind me of the playground of the school at East Hardwick, where we had played games as laborious, as delightful, as timeless as these. I no longer saw the children as images of futility and cruelty. I saw them as images of friendship and of hope.

I missed the little children when I finished the puzzle. They had become my companions. I could feel their little hands in mine. I did not like putting them back in their dark box. I delayed for days, gazing at them as they played on the black lacquer table.

Putting a jigsaw away can be a sad moment. Some people glue their finished jigsaws to a background and mount them on the wall, but this seems a curious perversion of what is intended to be an ephemeral activity. Some, more creatively, turn them into collages. In one of her many lives, my friend Gus Skidelsky taught mathematics for years to prisoners in Lewes Gaol and was able to alleviate the loneliness and boredom of one isolated, non-English-speaking, French inmate by responding to his request for 'un puzzle'. At first she didn't know what kind of 'puzzle' he was suggesting, but when she worked out that he meant a jigsaw, she took him one from her store. (She is an expert at games and puzzles.) It had taken her many hours to complete, but he did it very quickly, over the weekend (well, he wasn't as busy as she was, was he?) and then he glued it together to show to her, somewhat to her surprise. Why had he done that?

She kept him supplied with puzzles from Age Concern and Oxfam, until he was moved on to the next gaol.

Prisoners and royals and convalescents are fond of jigsaws.

I didn't glue the *Kinderspieler* together, but Michael took its photograph, so I have a memento. A photograph of a jigsaw of an oil painting is an odd treasure, but I am fond of it. I now think that I have come to associate this painting with my first school. I find it strange that I have no unhappy memories of East Hardwick, apart from the maypole episode, which involved transport to another school. I see us all in the playground, little moon-faced, country children, perhaps wearing home-knitted pixie hoods in winter, as children in those days did. The Girls and Boys outdoor toilets in the yard consisted of a row of wooden seats over a row of buckets, but I don't think I minded this, which is odd, as I was brought up to be fastidious and frightened of lavatories. My mother was very fastidious, and I suspect that she was fierce about toilet training, but the overriding sense of security and good intentions at school must have negated fear of the unhygienic buckets.

No photographs record this era to jog the memory, for no film was available in wartime. I remember once trying to emulate the bigger children by doing a somersault over an iron railing. I lost my grip and fell hard on my head. But this is not an unpleasant recollection. It hurt, but not very much, and nobody was cross with me. It was at the next school, at the Sheffield school with the defective, infantile jigsaw, that I lost much of my physical confidence.

The Brueghel children are confident, egalitarian, experimental, and the large space in which they play is their kingdom. I no longer see them as cruel brats or neglected ragamuffins. They are well dressed, well shod, well tended, yet happily free from supervision.

I was aided in this growing appreciation of *Children's Games* by reading two commentaries with a sharply contrasted outlook. One writer insisted on seeing every image in terms of its emblematic meaning, and found a message of folly and vanity in every image and every act. When she insisted, in an analysis of Pieter de Hooch's *The Linen Chest*, that the two women putting neatly folded linen into a cupboard were a symbol of miserliness, I parted company from her altogether. No, no, they were women putting away the washing, not women hoarding worldly goods, and the little child playing in the background was not an abused or neglected or naughty child, but a child in a happy and orderly household contentedly playing with a ball and a stick. And the chequered tiles and the painted basketwork are of a ravishing beauty, such a celebration of pattern! How could this painting be a satire on hoarding? It isn't even a satire on the embarrassment of riches, though of course we know what Simon Schama means by the phrase. But this painting is a salutation, not a condemnation.

I have always liked black-and-white chequered tiles. One of the pictures in our Sheffield home was a de Hooch reproduction showing an alleyway in Delft, with a mother and a daughter and a broom and some red-and-white brickwork. This didn't have black-and-white chequered flooring, but it might have done, and in my memory it did. Maybe this painting trained me to admire de Hooch's tiled interiors, for they sank deep into my psyche. (I used to tell myself that this liking was connected with my Dutch ancestry, but this ancestry proved, as I have said, to be a myth.) In the Somerset house, I inherited a corridor of black-and-white lino floor tiles, which gives me much pleasure. I sit and gaze at them with pride, even though they are not as spotlessly polished as they would have been in Holland. Perhaps a photograph of me admiring these tiles could be taken to represent worldly greed, the pride of ownership and domestic complacency. I plead guilty.

I have bid in an auction only once in my life, for an oil painting of an interior with a corridor of black-and-white tiles. I had never heard of the artist, and I can remember nothing about this work but the pattern of the tiles. I dropped out of the bidding, cautiously, when it reached £1,000. I have often regretted this failure of nerve. I could have hung it at the end of my own corridor.

The critic who led me towards a more sympathetic attention to Brueghel's children is the writer Edward Snow, who appears to have devoted some of his life to translating Rilke and some to writing about Shakespeare. Not, then, a professional art historian either, or an iconographer, or an iconologist, though far more scholarly in these fields than me. In his book *Inside Brueghel*, Snow responds to the children's activities with a warm attention, pointing to a happy face here, an absorbed concentration there. To him, the little swimmers in the upper-left passage of the painting are naked and natural and happy in the water, not emblems of the precariousness of life. Even the hair-pullers are condoned by him. If you look more closely, he urges, the child at the centre of the group doesn't look victimized. He looks as though he is sharing in the fun. I'm not so sure about this, myself, but I admire his latitude.

('Fun', wrote Huizinga, is an English word, for which most languages have no equivalent.)

So I learned to love my Brueghel, and to read it differently. Its bad smell diminished. But it retained another disconcerting aspect. The jigsaw of this masterpiece is printed in reverse, left to right. Many jigsaws are misleading in this way, and every time I see this painting in reproduction in a book I have to do a quick mental reorientation. (I have never seen the original.) This adjustment is at once stimulating and curiously unnerving. It must be affecting the neurons, and maybe usefully.

Brueghel's painting shows several objects (a hobby-horse, dolls, whipping tops, hoops) that have been designed specifically for children, but much of the activity consists of improvisation, mimic games and body games, which needed no capital investment or special materials. (The most touching toy is a red brick tethered to a table leg, in the lower-left corner; is this brick somebody's imaginary pet?) Perhaps, as a war baby, I came to identify with the lack of purpose-made and lavish toys on display. We didn't have many elaborate toys, and we didn't miss them because nobody else had them either.

I can't remember any of the toys I had before the age of five, though I can remember very clearly the books with which I learned to read – *The Radiant Way*, *Tot and the Cat* – and the books I was allowed to take out of East Hardwick library, which included a wonderful volume titled *The Curious Lobster*, by an American author named Richard W. Hatch. This instilled in me a passionate longing to see what was called 'the Ocean' and to explore the marine world. I didn't realize that the story was set in America, near Boston, and I suppose I thought the English coastline might also be provided with bears and bandicoots, and its waters with giant clams and sculpins, just as I thought Epaminondas inhabited some part of rural England as yet unvisited by me. I recall my joy when I found that this volume had a sequel, *The Curious Lobster's Island*, through which I could prolong my delight. I was a precocious reader.

One of my very early childish possessions was a red-glass mouse with white-glass whiskers, which my father brought back from Italy when he was demobbed from the RAF. (I think that's how the story went.) He brought glass toys for all of us, and I could not believe that I was allowed to have the mouse for my own. My father said its curly tail made the letter M for Margaret, so it must be mine. My older sister was not pleased, as it was much the most attractive of the objects. I think I felt a little frightened and guilty and could not believe my luck. I suspected it boded ill, and I was right, but I loved my mouse. I cannot remember the tears with which I must have greeted the demise of this delicate little creature. But I remember its transparent ruby glass and the sense of privilege it gave me.

My mother made a virtue of necessity, and taught us that it was not desirable to have expensive and fragile toys. (She did audibly sigh, though, over the poor-quality paper of wartime books, and the lack of illustrations. I did not know what she was talking about. *Tot and the Cat*, with its grey cover and black-and-white drawings, was good enough for me.) Large dolls, like big prams, were in her view common, and only foolish people saved up for them. Her moralizing about such matters (which I have tended to share, though I did once long ago recklessly buy one of my sons a Johnny Seven Gun) has a very long history. The Dutch iconographers would have approved of our middle-class condemnation of fragile, frivolous, clockwork gadgets and frilly dolls. The clockwork pigeon from Italy and the baubles from Nuremberg that were presented to the three-year-old Louis XIII would not have been considered admirable or edifying gifts by my mother.

The trade in expensive novelties for royal or aristocratic children was not new when Brueghel painted his *Kinderspieler* in 1560. Two years earlier, in 1558, Duke Albrecht had commissioned for his daughter what is widely regarded as the first doll's house, or 'baby house', as such objects came to be known in England. This was a little cabinet full of diminutive treasures, made by the master craftsmen of Nuremberg, and it helped to create a vogue for well-furnished miniature rooms and houses. But these elaborate objects, and their middle-class replicas, were scorned by serious pedagogues. John Locke and, a little later, Maria Edgeworth disapproved of frivolous toys such as doll's houses, rocking horses and squeaky pigs, whilst Rousseau disapproved of fancy apparatus like 'armillary spheres' for the teaching of cosmography to children. He thought their confused circles and strange figures might suggest witchcraft.

In the section on 'Play-Games' in *Thoughts Concerning Education* (1693), Locke austerely advises that 'A smooth pebble, a piece of paper, the mother's bunch of keys, or any thing they cannot hurt themselves with, serves as much to divert little children, as those more chargeable and curious toys from the shops, which are presently out of order and broken.' He recommends that children be encouraged to make or invent their own amusements, and continues:

> Play-things which are above their skill to make, as tops, gigs, battledores, and the like, which are to be used with labour, should indeed be procured them. These 'tis convenient they should have, not for variety, but exercise; but these too should be given them as bare as might be. If they had a top, the scourge-stick and leather-strap should be left to their own making and fitting. If they sit gaping to have such things dropped in their mouths, they should go without them.

No mention yet of the kind of educational game that was to evolve in England half a century later, to the benefit of the publishing industry and the putative delight of children, but clearly the ideological grounds for such inventions were being prepared. 'Good contrivances' would soon be devised and would pour into the market place.

XV

R oyal children have always presented a special case, and their playthings have been well documented. In 1644, Cardinal Mazarin commissioned sets of playing cards to instruct the infant King Louis XIV of France who had ascended the throne at the age of four years and five months. These are works of art and wit, and one may hope that the little king enjoyed them, despite their instructive purpose, as we at Bryn ignorantly enjoyed Belisha and Millionaire.

Playing cards were not in themselves new; they probably date back to the twelfth century in China and Korea, and to the fourteenth century in Europe. We know that cards were played, perhaps too often and for excessively high stakes, at the court of Edward IV in England. But the idea of cards as an educational tool for the young was a seventeenth-century novelty. The four series commissioned by Mazarin were devised by Jean Desmarests (1596–1676) of the Académie Française, and designed by the Florentine artist and engraver Stefano Della Bella. They portrayed mythological stories, the kings and the queens of France, and images representing different parts of the world. The monarchs, as evocatively described by historian Catherine Perry Hargrave, were 'separated into groups, with dreadful but amusing finality, by a single adjective in the upper right-hand corner – pious, clever, cruel, unfortunate, celebrated, saintly, good, wise, brave, happy and capricious'. That is how history is crystallized. Thus, Blanche of Castille is 'saincte', and Eleanor of Acquitaine is 'capricieuse'. Le Jeu de Géographie is a set of cards that shows figures emblematic of their region or nation, in national dress, accompanied by a brief description. America, the Queen of Clubs, is represented by a bare-bosomed woman in a small chariot drawn by two unlikely creatures that look like a cross between an armadillo and a tiger.

Desmarests, in an explanatory booklet addressed to the queen regent, specifically stated his educational purpose:

> *Ce sont des Jeux en apparence que je présente à votre Majesté*
> *mais en effet c'est un livre, et une estude pour les Jeunes Princes,*
> *aussi sérieuse pour le moins que divertissante.*
> [These may look like toys that I present to your Majesty,
> but in fact they are a book for the young princes to study,
> and they are as serious as they are amusing.]

These French cards were not, I have discovered, the first history and geography cards. Henry Peacham, in his celebrated book on courtesy, *The Complete Gentleman*, written in 1622 for the ten-year-old William Howard, launches into a poetic hymn of praise to geography in his chapter 'Of Cosmography', which he describes as 'an imitation of the face, by draught and picture, of the whole earth and all the principal and known parts thereof…a science at once feeding the eye and mind with such incredible variety and profitable pleasure that even the greatest kings and philosophers…have bestowed the best part of their time in the contemplation hereof.'

This chapter concludes with an exhortation to the young

scholar to exercise his pen in drawing and imitating cards and maps:

> I have seen French cards to play withal, the suits changed into
> maps of several countries in the four parts of the world, and
> exactly coloured for their numbers, the figures 1, 2, 3, 9, 10 and
> so forth set over their heads; for the kings, queens, and knaves,
> the portraits of their kings and queens in several country
> habits; for the knave, their peasants and slaves; which ingenious
> device cannot but be a great furtherance to a young capacity
> and some comfort to the unfortunate gamester when that he
> hath lost in money he shall have dealt him in land or wit.

Thus are the minds of gamblers ingeniously tricked into improvement.

(In *The Beautiful and Damned*, F. Scott Fitzgerald's Anthony Patch prefaces his desperate, alcohol-soaked career with a lonely, fourteen-year-old passion for stamp collecting, which his despised grandfather 'fatuously' considered was teaching him geography. Despite his grandfather's endorsement, Anthony loved his 'new stamp-books or packages of glittering approval sheets' and would lie awake 'musing untiringly on their variety and many-coloured splendour'. He never forgot his stamps; they returned to haunt him.)

Peacham's recommendations show that French playing cards were being imported in the 1620s, and England soon began to make her own. As it happened, there were fifty-two English and Welsh counties, a number that divided conveniently into four suits of thirteen cards, each card furnished with useful information about the county it represented – its principal towns, rivers and products. In one of these sets, Lincolnshire (the Eight of Clubs) clearly shows Grantham and Newark and the straight stretch of the Roman road of Ermine Street, where Bryn now stands.

One early set of geography cards cast its net far wider than the counties of England. The eccentric engineer and engraver Henry Winstanley (1644–1703) designed and published in 1665 a pack that shows continents and their inhabitants, with colourful descriptions on each card. The British Museum has a full set, only recently completed, buried in its depths. I have discovered that ancient playing cards and early jigsaws have a tendency to sink to the dusty depths of institutions, or to make their way uncatalogued to distant warehouses.

In Winstanley's set, spades represent Africa, diamonds Asia, clubs America, and hearts Europe. Each card shows a male and female character in ethnic dress or undress, accompanied by weaponry or other indicators of nationality or culture; the text, with very inconsistent spelling, describes the products, habits and religion of each place. Plantations in Mexico are credited to Madrid and plantations in New England to London. The country of Morocco (the Queen of Spades) is 'often ruined by the wild Arabians and their Civil Wars'; the natives of 'Guinys' (the Seven of Spades) are 'Rude and Barbarous thieves and most idolators'; the Romans (the Knave of Hearts) are 'all Romanists', whereas in Amsterdam (the Four of Hearts) 'Here is toleration of all sects in Religion'. The Swedes, we are told, are 'clothed in Furr' and, moreover, Lutheran. One of the finest cards is the Two of Diamonds, which represents Samarchand and the Zagathans:

Zagathay, or Uzbeck, is one of the great parts of Tartary, and its people are warlike but cruel. Most rich in droves of Cattel and have little more knowledge than their Beasts. Pagan or Mahomitan. In Tartary desert are people living in houses built on wheels which they remove in great numbers to the terror of their neighbours.

Colin Thubron, a writer who knows these regions well, tells me that Zagathay must be what we know as Jagathai, a name given to Central Asia between the death of Genghis Khan and the rise of Tamerlane. It is unlikely that Henry Winstanley, a Suffolk man, had much first-hand knowledge of the kingdoms he so colourfully describes, but Thubron says his information is surprisingly accurate. And Winstanley was not a parlour traveller. He took his love of topography to extremes. He is best remembered for having designed the first lighthouse on the Eddystone Rock off Plymouth, erected in 1700, which he saw through various designs and revisions, and which has been credited with saving much shipping. But this invention cost him his life; he was on the lighthouse, seeing to repairs, when it was destroyed in a storm on 26 November 1703, and he perished with it.

XVI

The invention of geography cards for the young King Louis in 1644 connects the goose game of the Medici court with the invention of the jigsaw and the game of Belisha. The earliest ancestor of Belisha was a French game, derived from the goose game. Le Jeu du Monde of 1645, based on a mutation of Le Jeu de l'Oie, was designed by the infant king's geographer, Pierre du Val. This was a game in which chance still ruled, but as you played you could learn the names (though not the relative locations) of the countries as you moved your counter round the track of the world; each numbered space was occupied by a small map. Du Val followed this ingenious invention with Le Jeu de France pour les Dames (1652), based on a traditional draughts board, in which the white squares were white, but the black squares were replaced by maps of the regions of France.

The concept of learning geography through play can thus claim to have originated in France, and some historians have wondered why it took so long to reach England, which was already full of cartography. Beautifully coloured maps were treasured in cabinets and hung as furnishings and tapestries in halls, galleries, studies and libraries. Artists portrayed landowners and explorers standing before backgrounds of maps, or surveying maps importantly spread upon tables. It would seem a short step to the kind of geographical table game that had been devised in France in the 1640s, but in fact the earliest known English version dates from a century later, from 1759. This, however, when it at last arrived, was very different from its predecessors.

The new game was called A Journey Through Europe, or the Play of Geography. It was designed by John Jefferys, teacher of geography, writing and arithmetic, and marketed by Carington Bowles, a well-known publisher of maps and prints based in St Paul's Churchyard. It was a track game, but in the form of a map, not a spiral. It was mounted on canvas, and could be folded and stored in a case like a real travelling map. The player twirled a flat-sided top called a 'teetotum' to obtain a number, and then advanced or retreated his counter accordingly, as in the goose game. The spaces here were embellished not with rustic images but with useful nuggets of topical patriotic information, such as: 'He who rests at 28 at Hanover shall by order of Ye King of Great Britain who is Elector, be conducted to No 54 at Gibraltar to visit his countrymen who keep garrison there,' or 'He who rests at No 48 at Rome for kissing ye Pope's toe shall be banished for his folly to No 4 in the cold island of Iceland and there miss three turns.' The winner was the first to reach London, 'the first city in Europe'.

The immense success of this new game was imitated over the next few decades in innumerable designs and variations, some combining the principles of the goose game with the format of the new tour of Europe, and introducing a variety of edifying elements to assuage the consciences of players.

F. R. B. Whitehouse, for many years chairman and managing director of the Chad Valley company, published in 1951 an illustrated book titled *The Table Games of Georgian and Victorian Days*, which gives an excellent account of the development of board games, while somewhat arbitrarily subdividing them into 'Instructional' games, games of 'Moral Improvement', and 'Games of Amusement'. Under the second heading, Whitehouse describes such items as The New Game of Human Life (1790), The Mirror of Truth (1811), and Virtue Rewarded and Vice Punished (1818), all of which provide a strong element of exhortation, ranging from lessons in civic duty to warnings about what happens to naughty children.

The pious moral content is in many cases offset, however, by the beauty of the design of the board, which must have added much to the pleasure of play. The New Game of Human Life, for example, published by John Wallis and Elizabeth Newbery in 1790, takes the player spirally through various imaginatively illustrated stages of life from infancy through manhood and the prime of life to sedate middle age, old age, decrepitude and dotage. The instructions for this game specifically advocated the use of a teetotum rather than dice. The New Game of Human Life was, of course, a game of chance, but the less this aspect was emphasized to its players the better. By this stage in history, we needed excuses for enjoying ourselves.

Many examples of these games survive in county museums and toy museums, each mirroring the ethics, dress and sometimes the historical events of the period in which it was designed. A tale like Bunyan's *Pilgrim's Progress* lent itself readily to pictorial representation, and the staging posts of the Slough of Despond, Vanity Fair and Doubting Castle became as familiar to players as the counties and castles of England. Many children firmly believed that these were real places. Such family board games are re-created to this day by publishers and toy manufacturers, and new and topical variants are on the market every Christmas.

The Chad Valley catalogue for 1954 advertises a board game called Dan Dare's Race in Space, as well as Muffin the Mule jigsaws and drawing slates, and any catalogue for any year offers a similar snapshot of the new, the traditional and the adapted. The impressive display in Robert Opie's Museum of Advertising and Packaging, now in Notting Hill, tracks the way in which trends in advertising and historical events are reflected through board games and jigsaws based on the days of Empire and two world wars, on movies and TV shows, on the launch of the sputnik and the space race. There is even a Twiggy Dress-the-doll Model Dress Book. Dress-the-doll books have a surprisingly long history.

(Opie saves these ephemera with a purpose: 'Whilst families tend to save mementoes from special occasions, it struck me that little was being done to keep the everyday material. When the thousands of pieces of this social history are assembled into some giant jig-saw, the result illustrates the remarkable journey we have all come through.')

The early board games designed for pure amusement betray their frivolity in their titles: Funnyshire Fox Chase, Royal Race Course, Comic Steeplechase, Waddling Frog. It was an old edition of the Funnyshire Fox Chase that first attracted Major Whitehouse to his pet subject. He advertised for information about similar games, and realized from the nature of the sparse replies he received that he had found a wider but less well-trodden field than he had thought. 'Not knowing what may turn up next adds tremendously to the interest of collecting these old games,' he sweetly and innocently wrote. I picture him as a pleasant, silver-haired, country gentleman, a kind father and an indulgent grandfather, who loved to show his grandchildren his valuable collection. I wrote to Chad Valley to find out what had happened to him, but no answer came, perhaps because Chad Valley, once toymaker to the queen, has been swallowed up by Woolworths, which itself is about to disappear. I did not pursue him further, for I did not wish to be disappointed. He might have been cast in the Alison Uttley mould.

In his history, Major Whitehouse confined himself primarily to canvas or linen-mounted games published between 1750 and 1850, but in his tenth chapter he briefly mentioned jigsaw puzzles, which he said were 'not games in the strict sense of the word'. In a foreword to the 1971 reprint we are told (by the then Vice-Chairman of Chad Valley, R. Swinburne-Johnson) that a book on the history of jigsaw puzzles by Linda Hannas would shortly appear as a companion volume to Whitehouse's own work.

And with the jigsaw puzzle, an entirely new form was born.

XVII

The first jigsaw puzzles took the form of 'dissected maps' and the earliest of these were credited to John Spilsbury (1739–1769). Spilsbury was an engraver, printmaker and cartographer, and as a young man he was apprenticed to cartographer Thomas Jefferys (*c*.1719–1771) of St Martin's Lane, who, like his namesake John Jefferys, became involved in manufacturing a geographical race game. (The two Jefferys may or may not have been related, but they must have known one another; this was a small world.) Thomas Jefferys, despite an appointment as cartographer royal to George III in 1760 and a successful career as a publisher of maps of the Americas, was declared bankrupt in 1766, the very year that his pupil Spilsbury is said to have hit upon the concept of the jigsaw.

Spilsbury's idea was dazzlingly simple. He mounted maps on thin mahogany board and cut them along country or county boundaries with a fine marquetry saw, then boxed them up for children to reassemble. In retrospect, it seems astonishing that nobody had hit on this concept before. (And perhaps somebody had.)

These puzzles seem to have been specifically designed and sold as an amusing educational aid for children, and it is no coincidence that they arrived on the market during the extraordinary boom in child-oriented products that marked the second half of the eighteenth century. For those trying to follow the prescriptions of Locke and Rousseau, they fitted the bill exactly. They pleased parents and publishers alike, and children may well have enjoyed them as much as I did when young.

I first read of John Spilsbury in the pioneering work of jigsaw-puzzle scholarship by Linda Hannas, *The English Jigsaw-Puzzle 1760–1890*, which, as we have seen, Major Whitehouse had announced as forthcoming in his book on board games. This book, published in 1972, was the starting point of my historical quest. Linda Hannas was the first writer to devote a whole book to the art and history of the jigsaw, and she dedicated many years to her subject, gathering together a fine private collection of puzzles, which was sold through Sotheby's on 27 July 1984. She died in October 2004, not long before I read her book, though it took me a long time to discover this, and I kept hoping I might be able to meet her and talk to her about her obsession. I would have liked to have asked her more about what attracted her to the subject, how she became a collector, what collecting meant to her, what first attracted her to jigsaws, whether she continued to enjoy assembling them. But I came just too late, my letters went unanswered and, anyway, even had I written in time she might well not have wanted to see me. Experts may be possessive about their material and do not always welcome the interest of others, as I have found to my cost. They do not want newcomers peering at their treasures.

Linda Hannas (née Morris) was the London-born English wife of Torgrim Hannas, a Norwegian resistance fighter, intelligence officer, bibliophile, scholar and antiquarian book dealer who presented his library of Scandinavian linguistic literature to the British Library in 1984, the same year that his wife sold her jigsaws. (He died in 1998.) Antiquarian book dealers are collectors by trade and inclination. I was for years involved with a dealer who specialized in literary periodicals, and I learned from him the value of completing the set, the excitement of finding the missing number. I never knew whether I was deeply bored by this activity, or whether I found it, as he did, of compelling interest. On the whole, I think boredom prevailed, and to this day I don't really like reading periodicals, but his company shed a certain glamour on them. He was a glamorous figure, despite his dusty trade.

Ah, the brief, illicit hours I spent with this too-much-married man, faithfully and faithlessly, amidst the book stacks, in dark basements and leaking warehouses! (This sounds like a scenario from a story by Edith Wharton or Anita Brookner, but it wasn't quite like that, for we were both in our thirties, and between us we had too many children. This is one of the reasons why our stolen basement hours were brief. We were conscientious parents and we had to get back to pick up the children from school.) For his sake, I still keep my eyes open for odd copies of *The Dial*, or *Horizon*, or *Encounter*, or *The Nineteenth Century and After*, or *Granta*, or *delta*, where one might hope to find the first publications of D. H. Lawrence or Angus Wilson or Sylvia Plath or Ted Hughes or Peter Redgrove. It is too late, as my friend died years ago, and I don't know what to do with these items when I spot them. But I keep looking. It is a habit. I was pleased to be able to recognize the first appearance of Hardy's famous *Titanic* poem, 'Convergence of the Twain', in a periodical in my husband's archive. I feel it ought to be worth a few bob.

Mrs Hannas's decision to part with her slowly acquired collection, a good twenty years before her death, must have been hard to make, and probably indicated a greater family dispersal. Even less dedicated scholars than she find it hard to part with their jigsaws. Attics and storerooms are full of old puzzles, often deplored by spouses and derided by children, taking up space, gathering dust, waiting for a query from someone like me, who wants to know why they are still there and what they represent. After dinner parties, late at night, out they come, for my admiration. I am sorry I did not meet Mrs Hannas.

Linda Hannas's study, which provides a checklist of more than five hundred items, is a landmark in the story of children's games. Her commentary is excellent, her illustrations alluring, her detailed descriptions vivid, and her detective work impressive. Her account of how she managed to establish the identity of an elusive family business of early puzzle manufacturers, the Barfoots, deserves a wider readership; she tracked them down through their distinctive trademark of a swag of roses. I pursued, not very methodically, some of the museum items she lists, and often found the originals, preserved in old cardboard boxes and entwined with old string, to be dismayingly duller than their photographic reproductions, which often lend a gloss to objects that are in reality stained and defective. This made me admire her perseverance the more.

An exhibition at the Museum of London in 1968 (then in its former home in Kensington) called *Two Hundred Years of Jigsaw Puzzles* displayed many of her discoveries and attracted some interest. A boom in 'pastimes' objects, Victoriana and heritage decor was on its way; Laura Ashley's first shop opened in the same year in South Kensington, and shortly afterwards, in the winter of 1971–2, an exhibition of biscuit tins from 1868 to 1939 at the Victoria and Albert Museum proved popular, drawing on a similar mixture of nostalgia and curiosity. Michael J. Franklin, the biscuit tin expert, typically gives tips about prices as well as information about manufacturers and artists in his 1979 book, *The Art of Decorative Packaging*. The boom continued, and the first of what was to be a successful chain of shops called Past Times, providing replica heritage objects of some sophistication, opened in Oxford in 1986. These shops also, of course, sell jigsaws.

Linda Hannas's 1972 study was not, however, merely an essay in nostalgia and a stimulus to the collecting habit. It was of interest to professionals as well as amateurs, and soon after its publication her observations were beginning to make their way into the mainstream of essays and bibliographies. The historian J. H. Plumb in his article on 'Children in Eighteenth-Century England' (*Past and Present*, May 1975) was one of the first to cite her work at some length, and two years later Lawrence Stone in *The Family, Sex and Marriage in England 1500–1800* (1977) mentioned dissected maps in the context of Enlightenment educational theory and practice (although he does not credit Hannas by name). Raphael Samuel, in *Theatres of Memory* (1994), a work that provides an excellent and surprisingly sympathetic analysis of the Laura-Ashley, old-postcard, Teas-with-Hovis, retrochic phenomenon, draws on and praises her discoveries in his discussion of playing cards featuring monarchs, and jigsaw puzzles featuring chronological tables of English history.

Many scholars have now followed in the footsteps of Hannas, exploring the history of jigsaw puzzles and the allied terrain of children's books, movable books, flap books, flick books, dress-the-doll books, harlequinades, peep-shows, pin-prick pictures and other ephemera. (Canadian writer Jill Shefrin, for some twenty years associated with the Osborne Collection of Early Children's Books in Toronto, made herself an expert in this field and contributed much new scholarship.) John Spilsbury's name is now familiar to anybody interested in this esoteric area of knowledge. A prize awarded by the American Association of Game and Puzzle Collectors (AGPC) is named after him, and he was the answer to a question on *University Challenge* on 27 November 2006, when he scored a point for the team who guessed him correctly. He has a short entry in the new *Oxford Dictionary of National Biography*, where his life appears under the same heading as that of his older brother Jonathan, also an engraver.

Both had appeared (in a group entry, along with Jonathan's daughter Maria, a successful artist) in the original DNB, but no mention is made there of dissected maps. The new entry, in contrast, gives John full credit for his invention and cites Linda Hannas as a source. Maria Spilsbury, not surprisingly, now has a long entry of her own: she is credited with a gift for large crowd scenes, painting cottages and cottage children, pastoral and nursery scenes in crowded canvases, many of which favoured the kind of images that later became (and have remained) popular with jigsaw-puzzle manufacturers, though she has not yet, as far as I know, been awarded the accolade of jigsaw reproduction.

Spilsbury's novel device has been so lastingly popular, and has given rise to so many variants, that it is hard to imagine a world without it. We can only wonder whether he suspected, when he died in 1769 at the early age of thirty, that he had launched a winner. Probably not, I fear.

The map format of the earliest puzzles reflected the fashions of the day, when maps were appearing everywhere, in prints and on fans, handkerchiefs and embroidered samplers. John Spilsbury not only invented the puzzle: according to the *ODNB* he also took advantage of the more frivolous fashion for printed silk kerchiefs, offering one that boasted a 'New and most accurate map of the roads of England and Wales; with distances by the milestones'. This growing love of cartography was no doubt connected with the increasing ease of travel and the spread of Empire; maps and puzzles in map form were considered patriotic as well as instructional. Despite the vastly extended range of jigsaw subject matter, a sense of the original geographical connection survives, and classic map jigsaws are still in production. (Educational kerchiefs did not confine themselves to maps; John Clare was given one with a poem by Chatterton imprinted on it.)

When they were little, my children had a Galt jigsaw of the

counties of England, and I was recently given an old plywood Victory puzzle of the same subject, called Industrial Life in England and Wales, which shows Leicestershire to be full of sheep and suitcases, Nottinghamshire of lace and oak trees, Lincolnshire of vegetables and chickens, whereas little Rutland is too small to feature any industries or products at all. It is coloured bright blue, like a lake, but as the jigsaw was made long before Rutland Water ('one of the largest man-made reservoirs in Europe') was created in the 1970s, this must have been a prophetic coincidence.

I have a friend who claims that the only jigsaw she ever does is a map of the departments of France, the names of which she is determined eventually to commit to memory. I persuaded her to bring some pieces of it to the Pizza Express, opposite the British Library, where I inspected them over our invariable lunch of *melanzana parmigiana*. The pieces were non-interlocking, like those of the earliest puzzles, and although I assembled three large chunks of the smiling blue Atlantic without much difficulty, I ran into trouble with Saône and Bourgogne. Learning the names of the French departments is complicated by the fact that, like the boundaries of English counties, they keep changing; Seine and the Charente have become *maritime*, according to Georges Perec in *Penser/Classer* (1982), in order to avoid the shame of being *inférieure*, and 'in the same way, the "*basses*" or "low" Pyrénées have become "*atlantiques*", the "*basses*" Alpes have become "*de Haute-Provence*", and the Loire "*inférieure*" has become "*atlantique*".' Departments are sensitive.

Map jigsaws are not always as easy to assemble as you think they will be. One Christmas, Gus Skidelsky commissioned for me a jigsaw based on an old Ordnance Survey map that centres on a house-shaped piece representing the site of our Somerset home. The bit with the sea was very difficult, as were the winding footpaths through the ancient woodlands. But I learned place names I had not known; I learned the lie of the land before our house was built. Maps and jigsaws continue to fit together well and profitably. They interlock.

Not everybody is as enthusiastic about jigsaw maps. Jill Shefrin tells me, 'Ironically, the only jigsaw puzzles I had as a child were maps of Canada and the United States, and it is only in the last few years that I have begun to assemble jigsaw puzzles myself. I only really enjoy those which are made from interesting paintings.'

Nicholas Tucker, however, remembers with pleasure a jigsaw map with little Rutland. I knew Nick when I was a teenage schoolgirl living in Granville Road in Sevenoaks. Nick (now honorary Senior Lecturer in Cultural Studies at the University of Sussex) is a scholar of children's literature, and although I haven't seen him in many years, I've followed his career through articles in the newspapers. While I was thinking about writing this book, I read a particularly interesting piece by him about childhood in the *Independent on Sunday* (9 July 2006). It appeared at a time when the press was in one of its periodic fits of moral panic about the miseries of modern childhood. Not so, wrote Nick; the old image of a past Golden Age, of a *Cider-with-Rosie* idyll in the Cotswolds, is largely illusory, and most children are on the whole healthier, happier, more comfortably dressed, less terrified by hellfire, better educated and closer to their parents now than they used to be.

Prompted by this, I wrote to him about the Teas-with-Hovis activity of jigsaws, and asked whether he knew any jigsaw historians. He responded immediately and helpfully with many suggestions, and also volunteered some personal memories:

Jigsaws played a huge part in our Granville Road childhood. They always had bits missing, so that one got almost as used to a particular space as one did to a piece. And the pictures that gradually emerged; once they came together, it was almost as if a chord of music suddenly played. There was a Red Indian in a canoe, given to me by Father Christmas at a London store, which was always particularly atmospheric. We also had old, pre-war jigsaws of Victorian-looking battleships, scenes from silent films – I can see them all now. A woman standing on a round table, all long legs, while a man swatted at a mouse. No one questioned what was going on – we simply accepted it as part of the quite often occasionally crazed world of the adult.

My aunt and mother – both still alive – carried on doing jigsaws when almost anything else, including dominoes, had become too much for them. I suppose the obvious symbolism is making order from chaos, but with the nice fall-back position that order is always attainable in the end so long as one works hard for it.

I find it interesting, and comforting, to discover after all these years that the Tucker family was so little worried by the missing pieces. The Tuckers were a comforting presence, down the road. They weren't anxious, or neurotic, or depressed, like us. Or so it seemed to me when I was fifteen. My mother used to mutter that the Tuckers had no stair carpets. I have no idea whether this was true or not, or how she made this discovery. It wasn't the sort of thing I would notice. But I did think that it was none of her business.

Nick's grandfather used to make wooden jigsaws and favoured the tradition that went right back to John Spilsbury. 'One particularly useful one was the counties of Britain. I still have a vague idea of what Montgomeryshire and Flintshire looked like, and how easy it was to lose Rutland!'

Rutland, the smallest county. The Ram Jam Inn on the Great North Road is in Rutland, or it is at the moment. Over the years, Rutland has been lost to the map of England, and restored to it.

ɔundaries of this part of Middle England shift from
Sometimes the poet John Clare was born in one
mes in another – his natal village, Helpton, used to
ɪptonshire, but is now in Cambridgeshire. We were
letters to Long Bennington to 'Nr Newark, Notts',
although I think it was really in Lincs. (This was before the days of
postcodes, before the days when Bryn had to have a street number,
before the days when it was demoted to '80 Main Street', a number that I could never memorize.) Auntie Phyl liked Rutland and
was pleased when it came back on the map. The symbol of
Rutland is a horseshoe, because it is a county through which so
many travellers pass. I have been happy in Rutland.

XVIII

My first physical encounter with a Spilsbury map was a significant moment, a jigsaw epiphany. I discovered that examples of Spilsbury's earliest works were held in the Map Room of my familiar haunt, the British Library, and I thought I would go to visit them. I do not often venture into the Map Room. I spend most of my time in Humanities Two, a pleasant place that I find conducive to study and within which I am conservative about my choice of seat, as I used to be in the old BM Reading Room. But off I boldly went, up one floor into the alarmingly unknown, to see whether I could set eyes on the famous Spilsbury maps.

After some negotiation with various helpful members of staff, I was presented with Spilsbury's Map of Europe Divided into Kingdoms, in an edition dated 1767 (or was it 1766?), some two years before Spilsbury's early death. There had been some question as to whether it was available to view, or hidden away for conservation, but eventually it appeared, in its mahogany box, and to my surprised delight I was allowed to sit there at a large desk and assemble it. I didn't even have to wear gloves. (I have always hated wearing gloves, even outdoors in bitter weather. And yes, just as I was warned, my fingers have grown stiff, possibly as a result of this phobia.) I was politely asked to check whether any pieces were missing, and I was able to confirm that the pieces representing Scotland, the English Channel, the Low Countries, Sardinia, Corsica and the Gulf of Finland were indeed absent, as a note in the box that housed them confessed. I wondered how many decades ago, how many centuries ago, those pieces had vanished.

I also had time to assemble a map of Africa in forty pieces, which arrived in a box with the handwritten inscription 'A gift of Lady Cecilia Johnston, May 27, 1792'.

There was something exhilarating, touching and anarchic about being allowed to handle and assemble the pieces of these dissected maps, with their delicate colouring of pink and green and acqua and yellow. I was not sure that I should have been given permission to touch; it seemed too much of a freedom. The sense of escape from books and words was physically and mentally liberating. Those who spend much of their lives writing and reading often yearn for a different form of activity. Some go fishing, some garden, some go on long walks, some take up watercolours or bookbinding or cabinetmaking, some work at jigsaw puzzles.

I think one of the reasons I am drawn to these puzzles is precisely because they have no verbal content; they exercise a different area of the brain, bring different neurons and dendrites into play. Like many people, I use the word-based, verbal, left side of my brain too much, and have begun to think, in the light of recent neurological research, that one of the causes of my stammer is a defective link between the left and right hemispheres – nothing to do with childhood trauma or parental expectation. I have a bad spatial sense and suffer from embarrassingly poor powers of facial recognition (this is a recognized condition, called prosopagnosis), and I like jigsaws partly because they give me a quiet chance to look at wordless patterns. I feel this must be good for me, and it surely can't be harmful. Stroke patients are sometimes advised to do jigsaws as an aid to recovering a loss of spatial sense. (Neuropsychologists Roger Sperry and Robert Ornstein did a lot of work on the cerebral cortex in this context, and it was Ornstein who advised Doris Lessing to encourage her son to do jigsaws after he suffered a stroke.) Chess might be even better for me, as it is clearly a spatial game, but it is too competitive, too demanding, too intellectual.

Many writers (including W. H. Auden, Georges Perec, Julian Mitchell, Julian Barnes, Ronald Harwood and Jonathan Raban) have been addicted to crossword puzzles, but I have never taken to them either. The hours of freedom from words are a relief to me, though of course I acknowledge that, paradoxically, I then seem to feel the need of words to try to analyse the nature of this freedom.

That's because writing is an illness. A chronic, incurable illness. I caught it by default when I was twenty-one, and I often wish I hadn't. It seemed to start off as therapy, but it became the illness that it set out to cure.

Some writers admit that they find writing therapeutic, others (like Julian Barnes) strongly deny it. Angus Wilson said that he began writing fiction on the advice of his analyst in Oxford while he was recovering from a breakdown, although he was not always happy in later years to be reminded of this. The protagonist of Doris Lessing's *The Golden Notebook* suffers from writer's block and starts to write again at the suggestion of her analyst. Sylvia Plath in *The Bell Jar* wrote out of revenge, and Wordsworth wrote some of his greatest and most enigmatic lyrics (the Lucy poems) out of what he calls 'self-defence'. Writing is a protection, a cure, an affliction. It makes you ill, and it offers to cure you. Writers need a rest from writing and from words, words, words.

Before I return to the historic jigsaw, I offer a description of a modern, 750-piece jigsaw, purchased in 2007 from the RSC shop in Stratford-upon-Avon, that is a true challenge to the prosopagnosis sufferer. The image says it is 'based on the Flower Portrait of William Shakespeare', and it is composed of hundreds of tiny, head-and shoulder photographs of real people, forming a mosaic that represents the playwright's well-known bust. Pale and under-exposed people make up his noble forehead and his collar; darker and more red-faced people his hair and his jacket. At first sight I thought this puzzle, because brightly coloured, would be easy to assemble, but it is not, because the juxtapositions are completely arbitrary, and there is no overlap from one little square to the next.

I had assumed that the photographs would be of famous actors and actresses in Shakespearean roles, illustrating the verse on the side of the box that tells us that all the world's a stage, yet they are of 'ordinary people', of diverse ethnic origins but probably all British, in contemporary dress. It took me a while to work out that a few faces are cunningly repeated, sometimes identically, sometimes reversed – the chap in the jaunty, seafaring cap, the yellow-haired clown, the boy with his baseball hat at a funny angle, the royal-looking lady in a dark-blue hat. As I laboured away at this task, I found myself giving identifying labels to the faces, much as I have to do in real life, memorizing them as 'big white face with glasses', 'Mother Teresa', 'bearded cleric', 'evil baby', 'disco type', or 'nice lady in grey V-neck with pearls'. Of particular appeal was the 'generic Oxford academic', a style that I identified with my son Adam – all variations on a wry, cheerful, bespectacled, smiling face, which one may see any day attached to young men walking or cycling along the street in Oxford, but never ever in Ladbroke Grove. You could walk for a year without seeing that face in Ladbroke Grove.

My father also suffered from prosopagnosis and frequently offended friends and neighbours by failing to recognize them. As I was walking along the beach with him one summer at Filey, a woman in a flowered bathing suit greeted him warmly and tried to engage him in conversation. It was obvious that he had no idea who she was. In the end she told him her name, and he appeared to recognize it, and chatted politely for a few moments. As he walked away he kept muttering to himself, 'The penny didn't drop, the penny didn't drop', an interesting phrase that I had never heard before, and that I connected with the penny-operated, cement-block pebble-dashed lavatories on the seafront, and the more thrilling slot machines in the amusements arcade.

The woman had lived next door to us during the war in Pontefract, but of course I hadn't recognized her either. She didn't wear a flowered bathing suit in Pontefract.

XIX

There is no information or educational content in that brightly coloured, demotic, multicultural, RSC jigsaw, and its connection with the Spilsbury maps in the Map Room is almost as remote as its connection with Shakespeare. One could gain little virtue or knowledge from its assembling: it is 'just a game', a pastime. The jigsaw has come a long way from its schoolroom origins, both in appearance and in function. Its instantly recognizable, interlocking pieces, with their familiar, standardized, die-cut shapes, bear little resemblance to the pale, thin, smooth, sliding, aristocratic, wooden slices in Lady Cecilia's mahogany box, with its swelling pink imperial theme. Yet these devices have a common ancestor, a common descent.

The innovative concept of dissection caught on rapidly, spreading throughout England and beyond, as the British Empire spread. Imitations of the early Spilsbury geography puzzles soon became familiar objects in upper-middle- and upper-class schoolrooms. John Wallis, the Darton family, James Izzard, Robert Sayer, Elizabeth Newbery and other members of the growing army of publishers of children's books began to produce a wide variety of tempting designs, and as they became more widely disseminated, they became cheaper. Scholars have recently been searching assiduously for references to these puzzles in eighteenth- and early nineteenth-century correspondence, educational literature, fiction, and art, and I have trawled, less assiduously, in their wake, following their markers. I enjoyed the quest, and have made some discoveries of my own.

The most widely known mention, and one that I must have read many times, is to be found near the beginning of Jane Austen's *Mansfield Park* (1814), where we discover Maria and Julia Bertram looking down on their poor little cousin Fanny Price because she is not acquainted with the dissected map of Europe. In the first weeks of Fanny's residence at Mansfield Park, evidence of her prodigious ignorance is brought regularly in fresh reports to Lady Bertram in the drawing room: 'Dear mamma, only think, my cousin cannot put the map of Europe together – or my cousin cannot tell the principal rivers in Russia – or she never heard of Asia Minor – or she does not know the difference between water-colours and crayons! – How strange! – Did you ever hear of any thing so stupid?'

It is not surprising that there were no dissected maps in Fanny's simple Portsmouth home; they were not cheap, though models could be bought more cheaply without the sea. Spilsbury's prices ranged from 9s to £1 1s, making these objects more expensive than the vast numbers of children's books that were now pouring into a rapidly expanding market. Like du Val's Le Jeu de France pour les Dames and the playing cards designed for Louis XIV a century earlier, they were playthings for the privileged, educational aids for the advantaged. The poet William Cowper, writing to his friend William Unwin in September 1780 with advice about Unwin's son's education, invokes an aristocratic precedent, in the form of Lord Spencer (the first Earl Spencer) and his son's geography lessons:

I should recommend it to you therefore…to allot the next two
years of little John's Scholarship, to Writing and Arithmetic,
together with which for Variety's sake and because it is capable
of being formed into Amusement, I would mingle Geography.
A Science which if not attended to betimes, is seldom made
an Object of much Consideration…Lord Spencer's Son when
he was 4 years of Age, knew the situation of every Kingdom,
Country, City, River & remarkable Mountain in the World.
For this Attainment, which I suppose his Father had never
made, he was indebted to a Plaything; having been accustomed
to amuse himself with those Maps which are cut into several
Compartments, so as to be thrown into a Heap of confusion,
that they may be put together again with an exact Coincidence
of all their Angles and Bearings so as to form a perfect Whole.

'A Heap of confusion' is a good phrase.

The second Earl Spencer, incidentally, remained a credit to his
enlightened education; although born into a fast-living family
where card games and gambling were far more popular than
books, he became a dedicated bibliophile and collected one of the
greatest private libraries in Europe.

Geography, as Cowper here notes, was often an overlooked or
despised element in the school curriculum and not taken very
seriously. My father thought geography 'a soft option' and teased
my son Joe for pursuing it at school, but I enjoyed trying to answer
Joe's O-level questions with him. (Joe Swift's solution to global
population control was appropriately Swiftian: shoot the babies.)
But many have equally plausibly maintained that maps are more
fun for little children than algebra, Greek and Latin. Thomas Fuller
dedicated the first book of his popular *A Pisgah-Sight of Palestine*
(1650) to 'The Right Honourable Esme Stuart, Earl of March and
Darnley, Lord Leighton, etc' whose 'tender months' at that point

had not yet completed a year, but who, Fuller trusts, might in due course grow into the book, as he would grow into his clothes. And meanwhile, Fuller hoped, he might 'take pleasure in the maps which are here presented'.

The fifth book of *A Pisgah-Sight* is dedicated to another titled infant, the Right Honourable John Lord Burghley, and Fuller again fondly mentions his maps, explaining that he is hoping to plant a ripening nursery of patrons. And his maps of the Holy Land are indeed quaint and wonderful, full of whales, ships, mountains, camels, ravens, angels, cities and soldiers, with a splendid depiction of the dark Dead Sea (MARE MORTUUM, MARE SALSUM, MARE ASPHALTITIS) and the blazing towers of Sodom, Gomorrah, Zeboim and Admah. Mount Pisgah itself is proudly shown, with Moses, aged 120 years, standing aloft upon it and surveying the whole land of Canaan. (Fuller slyly remarks that Moses could see Palestine so well because he had a clear view from the top and enjoyed miraculous eyesight for his age.)

These maps are far more friendly and entertaining than the notorious illustrations in that other staple of children's pre-Enlightenment Sabbath reading, Foxe's *Book of Martyrs*. John Day's woodcuts for the *Book of Martyrs*, which were recut and recopied and reprinted for three hundred years, terrified generations with their graphic portrayals of tortures, whereas seventeenth-century pictorial maps of the counties of England, decorated with heraldry and scenery, offered harmless, peaceable and instructive visual pleasure. Fuller's Palestine was a playful and entertaining land, full of miniature wonders and, although Biblical, happily free from religious gloom and exhortation.

Children used to enjoy inventing imaginary countries, before they had virtual worlds to play with. Fanny Burney's nephew created a land called Protocol, and she entertained the daughters of George III with stories of this place. Thomas Malkin, a child prodigy who died in 1802 at the age of six, also invented an imaginary kingdom, of which we have a fuller record: he created a detailed map of the island of Allestone, together with an account of its history, treaties, kings, customs and folklore. We know about Thomas through a memoir written by his father, Benjamin Heath Malkin, schoolmaster, antiquarian and topographer, which records the brief life and death of this remarkable infant. *A Father's Memoirs of his Child* is distinguished by a frontispiece designed by Malkin's friend William Blake, and includes a memoir of Blake as well as a generous selection of his poems, made available to a wider public for the first time – another signpost in the dawning recognition of the singular state of infancy. Malkin describes his son's precocious achievements and quotes at length from his letters. The child, he writes, has a 'most happy art in copying maps' and 'a remarkable habit of inventing little landscapes…cutting up waste paper into squares and drawings.'

Like the young Brontës and, many years later, the adult J. R. R. Tolkien, Tom created a well-charted realm. He also played with ready-made, dissected maps in the Spilsbury fashion. In one of his letters, dated 18 January 1799, little Thomas writes: 'I have a new map. Thomas can put it together and when Mama takes some counties out Tom can tell what they are.' His father assures the reader that 'His dissected maps, from which he had very early acquired his knowledge of geography, afforded him pleasure and interest to the last. He had some Counties of England in his hands, reading the names of the towns in them, within half an hour of his dissolution.' However, he also, interestingly, tells us that 'he ceased to talk of the imaginary country' during his illness. The father was relieved that the child's brain, dissected after his death, showed no sign of abnormality. He had feared that his son had died of some form of brain fever, and clearly worried that he had been subjected to excessive mental stimulation.

This is a very sad story. The death of children was commonplace at this period, but it is still a sad story. And, sadly, we don't have a picture of little Thomas Malkin playing with a dissected map, although we can witness him being borne up to heaven by one of Blake's angels. But we can more happily see Masters Thomas and John Quicke at work on a map of Europe in a pastel portrait by William Hoare, dated *c.*1770, which may be the earliest image of a jigsaw in art. In this newly post-Locke, family-oriented age, portraits of children engaged in natural activities were popular. Hoare, a Bath-based artist, specialized in portraits of young people, and drew his own daughter in many informal poses. In this portrait of the Quicke children, he portrays the younger boy holding the stubby shape of Italy in his hand and looking up to his brother for approval or affirmation. Family groups of this period often show educational scenes, with parents reading to children, or children holding books or sketching, with books strewn casually (but not carelessly) upon the nursery or drawing room floor. Little dogs remained the most favoured accessory (Hoare painted a fluffy little girl in a fluffy white dress holding a fluffy little white dog, where the substance of animal and child merge in a worrying manner) but the portrayal of pursuits that illustrated parental concern and interaction also became popular. Some of these ostentatiously affectionate groupings may protest a little too much, but the Quicke children playing quietly with their map, without visible adult interference, seem to me to be happy with their task.

(Can it be possible that little Miss Hoare was the artist who later drew the obscene cartoon of 'A modern Venus', which survives in Horace Walpole's collection? This is reproduced in Diana Donald's *The Age of Caricature* (New Haven, 1996) where she describes it as 'a playful visualisation of the physique suggested by the "pouter pigeon" fashion of the 1780s, with its puffed out bosom and rump.' I disagree. I find it more repulsive than playful.)

Maria Edgeworth, one of the most influential of educational theorists after Locke, endorses the use of the jigsaw, manifesting as she does so her characteristic attention to closely observed details of child behaviour, worthy of a Tavistock-trained child psycho-therapist. In *Practical Education* (1798), written with her father Richard Lovell Edgeworth, she observes:

> Whoever has watched children putting together a dissected map, must have been amused by the trial between Wit and Judgement. The child who quickly perceives resemblances catches instantly at the first bit of the wooden map, that has a single hook or hollow that seems likely to answer his purpose; he makes perhaps twenty different trials before he hits upon the right; whilst the wary youth, who has been accustomed to observe differences, cautiously examines with his eye the whole outline before his hand begins to move; and, having exactly compared the two indentures, he joins them with sober confidence, more proud of never disgracing his judgement by a fruitless attempt, than ambitious of rapid success. He is slow, but sure, and wins the day.

Auntie Phyl and I were much given to fruitless attempts, and not inclined to sober confidence; it was more fun that way. We were keener on resemblances than differences.

Maria Edgeworth also introduces puzzle maps into her *Early Lessons* (1801), where she provides a lively description of young Frank's struggle to reassemble his older brother Henry's dissected maps, and his loss of the 'little crooked country of Middlesex', for which he searches everywhere: 'under the tables – under the chairs – upon the sofa – under the cushions of the sofa – under the carpet – everywhere he could think of'. He is happy when at last he finds it, on a table where it had been concealed by a large book of prints, and the next morning he succeeds in hooking every county into its right place: 'He was much pleased to see the whole map fitted together — "Look at it, dear mama," said he, "you cannot see the joining, it fits so nicely."

Not to see the joining — that is satisfying.

The 'lost county' is a recurrent motif in jigsaw lore. It is the little land of lost content.

XX

In an age when theories of education were so widely discussed, the provision of dissected maps is a sure marker of progressive teaching methods. And they were found in the highest of social circles. Lady Charlotte Finch (1725–1813), an aristocrat with connections as grand as those of the Spencers, used maps to instruct her charges, who included two future kings, George IV and William IV. She was governess to the fifteen children of George III, and is credited with supervising what has been described a progressive nursery, which encouraged child-centred learning. Queen Charlotte herself took an exceptionally close interest in her children's education, read Rousseau and Fénelon, and is said to have kept a volume by Locke on her bedside table.

Zoffany's sumptuous family portrait of *Queen Charlotte with her Two Eldest Sons* (*c.*1764–5) is a speaking tableau of childhood, with multiple messages: it shows the elegantly robed and jewelled young queen in her dressing room, with the two-year-old Prince of Wales and his one-year-old brother Frederick grouped around her in colourful fancy dress, both somewhat dwarfed by an enormous but docile boar-hound. The Prince of Wales is dressed, warrior-like, as Telemachus, son of Ulysses and Penelope, and Frederick as a tiny

Turk with a pretty, silvery turban and a diminutive gown of blue and gold. The mood is playful but imperious, for the room is full of the rich spoils of trade and Empire: a richly patterned Turkish carpet, a French clock, a lavish display of Flanders lace, and life-size lacquered Chinese mandarin figures standing on either side of a tall gilt-framed mirror. On the far left of the painting, we may see on the palace lawn, through the gorgeously draped window, a solitary flamingo, representing far-flung lands and voyages, and on the far right, reflected in a mirror, discreetly attentive, the profile of a woman who is taken by some to be Lady Charlotte Finch, representing the world of learning.

It was Lady Charlotte who ordered the fancy-dress outfits for the little princes, as she recorded on 6 September 1764. Dressing children in historical costume was popular at this period, as Reynolds' child portraits bear witness; little boys were immortalized in the garb of Jupiter, Hannibal, Bacchus and Henry VIII, images that curiously combine playfulness with pathos and an ominous sense of destiny. Zoffany's little princes and Reynolds' heroic children provide a striking contrast with Hoare's painting of the Quicke brothers, who are shown fair and square, without parody, as themselves, engaged in a proper children's activity, not aping the aspirations of adults or providing a sly moral for the superior viewer. The Quicke portrait, like Chardin's portraits of children playing the goose game or solemnly absorbed with knucklebones, or shuttlecocks, or toy drums, or windmills, shows respect.

The geographical allusions of Zoffany's work remind us that geography and dissected maps were of more than academic interest to kings and princes. George III was to see the maps of the Americas redrawn, and his lavish embassy to China under Lord Macartney in 1792–4 was rebuffed. It was important for heirs to the throne to be able to locate their plantations, their colonies and the empires of their rivals.

Lady Charlotte's equipment for teaching geography included, as well as the more usual globes, two elegant mahogany cabinets, one with thirteen shallow drawers, the other with three deeper drawers, furnished with brass locks and handles, perhaps designed for travelling between the royal residences in and around London. They contained several maps, two by Spilsbury, and one of North America from a printed plate from the *Atlas méthodique* of Jean Palairet. Across a vast tract of the north-west of the map of America are inscribed the words 'Partie Inconnue'. Jill Shefrin has written a monograph on these cabinets, their contents and Lady Charlotte's teaching methods, engagingly titled *Such Constant Affectionate Care*, which gives due prominence to Spilsbury's invention. These cabinets are the first though not the last example of royal patronage of the puzzle, but it is not known (or not yet known) whether they were commissioned directly from Spilsbury by Lady Charlotte. In 2000 they were offered for sale by a private owner and spent some years in limbo with a dealer awaiting an export licence before a successful appeal was made through the Department of Culture, Media and Sport to save them for the nation. This appeal, as reported by the press, slightly overstated Lady Charlotte's accomplishments, for it claimed that she herself was the inventor of dissected maps, an attribution that has long been dismissed as false. But the value of the cabinets (they sold for £120,000) certainly bears witness to a growing interest in Spilsbury and other early jigsaws both from scholars and from collectors. In 2007 they were put on display at Kew Palace, and I am told they will travel between Kew and the Museum of Childhood at Bethnal Green.

Kew Palace is an appropriate home for the puzzles, for the royal family used Kew as a retreat for many years, and here in various houses, palaces, lodgings and gardens the princes and princesses enjoyed fresh air, picnics, games and botanizing. Flora Fraser, in her tragicomic royal saga *Princesses* (2004), described Kew as 'a full-blown royal campus, which the royal children rarely left during the summer months, where servants intrigued against each other, and where tradesmen in the village that had grown up around the church on the Green vied for preferment'. Queen Charlotte's *cottage ornée* survives today as a tourist attraction, and Kew Palace (originally built as a merchant's residence in 1631) has been renovated to give a sense of the family life of George III, the queen and their many children. Other items on display include a 'baby house' complete with furnishings embroidered by the princesses, cut-paper silhouettes, a silver rattle and a silver ink-stand, globes, musical and scientific instruments, and examples of George III's accomplished architectural drawings. The message of Kew Palace is mixed; it was a place of domesticity and safety, but it was also a place of suffering and frustration, eventually contaminated for the king by memories of bouts of illness, confusion and constraint.

The baby house has an unusual wallpaper. Its colour is what I call turquoise, and what the experts call verditer green, and it shows a pattern of irregular amoeba-like blobs outlined in white floating against a turquoise background dotted with tiny spots in a darker shade of green. (I was complimented by the Deputy House Manager on my visit to Kew for wearing a colour-coded turquoise T-shirt, which we took to be a happy omen.) The baby house colour scheme has been picked up in the house itself. In the queen's boudoir, on the first floor, the walls are a strong clear verditer, with a Greek-key border of black and green, re-created from an early nineteenth-century fragment uncovered during restoration. The curtains are black and yellow chintz, and there are two little tables, one a green-baize card table, the other a sewing table with a work-basket, at which the queen and the princesses would spend hours on their knotting and netting. It is not a room of excessive grandeur.

Today, the ghosts of frustration and illness have been banished to the unrestored attics, and a more positive spirit of years of domesticity, artistic endeavour and earnest education prevails. Flora Fraser's account of the childhood of the princesses gives a vivid portrait of the texture of their lives – the music, dancing and drawing lessons with a succession of governesses, the elaborately dressed theatrical tableaux, the promenades, picnics and birthdays, the conscientious acquiring of foreign languages. In the evenings they sewed, while listening to renderings of the works of Walter Scott; sewing was euphemistically known as 'working', although the objects made were mainly ornamental gifts. (Auntie Phyl and I used to say that we 'worked' at a jigsaw, and women of her generation kept their sewing things, as did the queen, in a 'work-basket'.) The poor Princess Royal, unlike the rest of her family, was not at all musical, hated the endless evenings of Handel ('I think that my dislike for music rather increases') and was keenly conscious of her poor ear, which restricted her skill in dancing. (My sister Helen said to me the other day that we would not have done well as princesses, as none of us had a good ear. She is right.)

The claim that Lady Charlotte invented dissected maps and puzzles rests largely on a misleading note to this effect, of a later date, which was found with the cabinets. Nor, as it now appears, was John Spilsbury himself necessarily the inventor. He was probably the first commercial bookseller to market them, but Jill Shefrin has put forward the name of an earlier originator, Madame Jeanne-Marie Le Prince de Beaumont (1711–1780), a writer, teacher and well-known reteller of fairy stories, who entered 'cartes de géographie en bois' in the prospectus for her exclusive and expensive school in Henrietta Street, Cavendish Square, London, in an advertisement of *c.*1755–60. (This, alas for patriotism, would make the jigsaw in part a French invention.)

There are several references of the period to Madame de

Beaumont's 'wooden maps', including one by the well-connected court favourite Mary Delany (1700–1788), who refers to them specifically, and as early as December 1759, in a letter to her sister Anne Dewes. Mary Delany spent many evenings with the royal family and children, and was well acquainted with Lady Charlotte; the paths of Lady Charlotte and Madame de Beaumont also, according to Shefrin, 'crossed over a period of years', the former putting into practice the educational theories of the latter. Caroline Lennox, Lady Holland, also referred to these maps; writing in 1762 to her sister Emily about her son Harry, who was being educated *à la Rousseau*, she notes that 'he works very hard all day out of doors, which is very wholesome…He eats quantities of fish and is so happy and pleased all day. At night we depart a little from Monsr. Rousseau's plan, for he reads fairy-tales, and learns geography on the Beaumont wooden maps; he is vastly quick at learning that or anything else.' This sounds a very pleasant regime.

So who is to know who first thought up the notion of the dissected puzzle? Maybe Spilsbury was no more than the clever exploiter of another's idea. Maybe a private commission from Lady Charlotte for the royal nursery set him on his path to brief prosperity and a small, posthumous fame. Maybe Mary Delany was the go-between.

XXI

Mary Delany, born Mary Granville, was an inventive woman. Through ingenuity and resourcefulness she made the best of a poor start in life and a dismal, semi-forced first marriage to an elderly husband, Alexander Pendarves, who died leaving her less well off than her relatives had expected. She and her friend Lady Charlotte Finch were both acquainted with marital distress. Finch's marriage to the Honourable William Finch produced four children and had at first been companionable, but shortly after her appointment as royal governess in 1762 he became mentally unstable (he died in 1766) and is said to have been violent towards her. So she left him for a life shared between Kew and an apartment at St James's, and a career caring for two families of growing children, her own and the queen's. A historian might hesitate before connecting her husband's illness with her demanding employment at court, but a novelist need not be so circumspect.

Mary Delany, who remained childless, remarried happily some twenty years after her first husband's death, but by this time she had developed her own skills and interests, as well as a distinctively independent attitude to the social whirl. She had a keen (and often satiric) eye for fashion and display, which she loved to describe in vivid detail; fabrics, trimmings, patterns and colours ('scarlet damask, gold tabby, pale lemon lutestring, silver frosted tissue, mouse-colour velvet') glow and sparkle and flutter under her pen, and she was full of advice to country cousins about ribbons and gloves. (She would certainly have advised Alison Uttley and Auntie Phyl that ribbons for the elderly were not a good idea. She had strong opinions about ribbons.)

Mary Delany first came to the notice of the royal eye at Queen Caroline's birthday celebrations in 1728, where she made (in her own words) a 'tearing show', like a jay in borrowed feathers, in jewels borrowed from Lady Sunderland and a gown she had designed herself. 'The Queen thanked [Lady Carteret] for bringing me forward, and she told me she was *obliged to me* for my pretty clothes, and admired my Lady Carteret's extremely; she told the Queen they were my fancy, and that I drew the pattern.' But Delany, much as she loved clothes, was also a true mistress of the half-arts. She took up the crafts of japanning, shell-work and cut-paper-work, creating from simple and largely inexpensive materials objects of great and sometimes lasting beauty.

These pursuits were popular with many aristocratic women, some of whose skills went well beyond the conventional needle-work, bag-making and knotting that helped to kill time. Charlotte Boyle, credited with 'real genius' by Horace Walpole, ambitiously covered the wall panels of a room at Boyle Farm, Thames Ditton, with black Japan-work (*verre eglomisé*) using lampblack and gold-leaf applied to glass with isinglass. Elizabeth Vesey at Lucan House in Ireland decorated her dressing room with 'Indian figures and flowers cut out and oiled, to be transparent, and pasted on her dressing-room window in imitation of painting on glass'. Delany, who helped her friend Mrs Vesey with this task, thought it had 'a very good effect'.

Delany herself was, however, the most innovative of all.

Germaine Greer in *The Obstacle Race* (1979) generously described her as 'the most civilised person in the most civilised era of English culture', and listed with admiration her prodigious activities, which included 'the making and sticking of pincushions, Japan-works, pastel portraits, copies of great masters, designs in shell-work, lustres, candelabra, cornices and friezes in cut-paper on wood, chenille work, cornices made of shells painted over like fine carving, upholstery, quilt-making, embroidery, cross-stitched carpets, miniature playing-card painting'. Delany worried that her mind was 'too much filled with amusements of no real estimation', a characteristically self-deprecating view that women tended to take (and still take) of crafts that cannot be dignified with the name of art. Late in life, she wrote to her niece Mary:

> Now I know you smile and say what can take up so much of A.D.'s [Aunt Delany's] time? No children to teach or play with; no house matters to torment her; no books to publish; no politicks to work her brains? All this is true but idleness never grew in my soil, tho' I can't boast of any useful employments, only such as keep me from being a burthen to my friends, and banish the spleen.

(Greer, in a not uncharacteristic volte-face, seems somewhat capriciously to have turned against Delany since she wrote *The Obstacle Race*, complaining in the *Guardian* in 2007 that she ought to have learned how to paint instead of wasting her time in cutting up paper. This article provoked predictable indignation in twenty-first-century women artists who work in patchwork, needlework and the soft arts, a spat that reminded me of that large, American, feminist, mixed-media artwork, Judy Chicago's *The Dinner Party*, collaboratively created in 1974–9. I saw it in a warehouse in Islington. It was interesting but ugly. The delicacy of its needlework was not its distinguishing feature, whereas the delicacy of Delany's work is undisputed.)

Delany was modest about her achievements but, while it is true that her name is not registered in the ranks of the great masters that she copied, her creativity and originality were fully recognized in her lifetime. It is agreed that her finest works were the paper collages of her old age, made after the death of her second husband Dr Delany in 1768. She began this extraordinary composite work in 1773 or 1774, when she was in her seventies, producing over nearly ten years a 'Flora Delanica', consisting of a series of nearly a thousand exquisite, delicate and botanically accurate, closely observed series of cut-paper mosaic flowers. These remarkable artefacts, which are as beautiful, fresh and natural as they are ingenious, were made by a process of her own devising, which portrays each flower as though it were alive upon its stem. They are, it must be admitted, in a different league from Auntie Phyl's gummed elves.

Her flowers were admired for their artistry by Reynolds, and for their accuracy by Joseph Banks and Erasmus Darwin. Queen Charlotte (who loved Delany and signed herself in letters to her as 'your very affectionate queen') plied her with rare specimens and praise, and presented her with a beautiful, gold-spangled, satin pocket case containing, as Delany's waiting-woman put it, 'a knife, sizsars, pencle, rule, compass, bodkin'. Her mosaics were miracles of craftsmanship. Her 'Burnet Rose' (*Rosa spinosissima*), with its delicate white and cream flowers, has a stem showing sixty-five thorns, cut in one piece with the stem, and her 'White Flowering Acacia' has literally hundreds of leaves cut in different shades of green. The simpler flowers – the Chinese lantern, the marsh vetch, the corn poppy – are also very beautiful. She wielded her scissors with genius. Occasionally she would incorporate a part of a real plant – a leaf, a floret, a seed pod – in a collage. All this creative activity can hardly be dismissed as time-wasting, although it was certainly time-consuming.

It seems far from impossible that Mary Delany might have hit spontaneously upon the puzzle principle, so adept was she at the arts of dissection and reassembly, of combining and re-creating, of making something from almost nothing. Maybe she and Lady Charlotte Finch discussed these matters as they watched the royal children play at Kew. Maybe, as Shefrin suggests, 'future research will reveal yet another, earlier inventor'. Dates are set to be challenged. Historians love to bowl them over, one by one: 1760, 1759, 1758... How far back in time may the dissected puzzle be traced? And how far, and how quickly, did it travel?

XXII

It's a pity that we don't have any paintings or drawings of George III's children playing with their Finch/Spilsbury cabinet. But we have recently been introduced to a puzzle-playing child from another royal family, portrayed by Goya with a piece of a dissected map in his hand. This portrait, of the six-year-old Spanish prince Don Luis María de Borbón y Vallabriga (1777–1823), was painted in 1783, when Goya was beginning to make himself known as a supremely successful (yet supremely uncompromising) portraitist of Spanish royalty and aristocracy. It shows the little boy formally dressed in blue breeches and tailcoat standing in front of a large map, holding a piece of a puzzle in one hand and a pair of compasses in the other. This child was the nephew of King Carlos III of Spain, and son of the king's semi-exiled younger brother, also Don Luis, and it was painted at his father's palace not far from Madrid.

During the same visit and in the same year, 1783, Goya painted one of his most famous and expressive groups, *The Family of the Infante Don Luis de Borbón*, which shows the Infante Don Luis, his wife, their three children, and a beautifully differentiated retinue of attendants, in an informal and intimate late-night setting. To me, this scene seems intended to demonstrate domestic happiness and solidarity, although art historian Xavier Bray points out that the darkness and the composition also suggest isolation and exile, and perhaps foreshadow the imminent death of the ageing Infante. The Infante plays a game of solitaire (with cards identified as the powerful Ace of Coins, the Horse of Clubs and the Two of Clubs) on a candle-lit, green-baize card table, watched by his much younger wife Teresa, who is dressed in a loose white gown. Her long hair is being braided by a hairdresser, and other members of the household gather round, one or two staring inquisitively out of the frame at the viewer, others watching the play of the cards. Little Don Luis, in profile, follows the game; his younger sister Maria Teresa gazes at the figure of Goya (who has included himself and his easel in the corner of the foreground of the composition) while a round-eyed infant is held aloft in a governess's arms. It is an Enlightenment scene with a curiously free egalitarian spirit, giving interest and dignity to all its subjects, young and old, master and servant, and perhaps defiantly illustrating the family's triumph over the disapproval of the king and the difficulties encountered by progressive thought in a Catholic country still dominated by the Inquisition.

(The devout and despotic king disapproved of his brother because he had refused to follow the career ordained for him, and had instead pursued a worldly and amorous life. Having been appointed cardinal-archbishop of Toledo at the age of seven and archbishop of Seville at the age of fourteen, Don Luis had rebelled against his ecclesiastical destiny, and had gone his own way. The little boy holding the piece of dissected map was to become President of the Regency of Cadiz during Ferdinand's captivity and has been credited with reining in the activities of the Inquisition. Jigsaws, as I maintain, are good for the character.)

Paintings celebrating the ideal of the 'new' companionate

marriage are a good hunting ground for images of children's playthings. The Duke of Orsuna was the head of another enlightened and progressive Spanish family much loved and much painted by Goya, and his 1788 portrait of the duke with his elegant intellectual wife and four children includes the obligatory small dog and a miniature, beautifully made, black toy carriage on a string. Surely this family must also have had dissected maps in its nursery? Lady Holland (born Elizabeth Vassall, and wife of the third Lord Holland) met the family on her travels in Spain with her husband in 1804, and wrote warmly in her journal of the duchess's liveliness, her handsome children, her 'national magnificence and hospitality', describing her as 'the most distinguished woman in Madrid from her talents, worth and taste'. She also praised the duke's exceptional library, 'chiefly of classics, history, voyages and books of science, which he intended for the use of the public, but this intention he was not permitted by the Governt. to carry into effect'.

Lady Holland's Hispanophile husband was, one might note, the nephew of Charles James Fox and of his younger brother Harry, who was reared on fish, fairy stories and Rousseau. Charles James, the apple of his father's eye, was more spectacularly indulged as a small child by his doting father Henry Fox, the first Lord Holland. This devoted parent, having recovered from the shock of producing a baby with skin 'all shrivelled' and staring eyes who looked incredibly 'like a monkey', soon fell in love with the company and conversation of his precocious second son, whom he found 'infinitely engaging & clever & pretty'. He could deny him nothing; he is said to have allowed him to smash his father's watch, to tear up his state papers, and to ride on a saddle of mutton while paddling his feet in the gravy. (Stella Tillyard, in *Aristocrats* (1994), has him riding on a patriotic joint of roast beef, and she is no doubt right, but I prefer my saddle-of-mutton version.) In *Family, Sex and*

Marriage in England 1500–1800 (1977), Lawrence Stone quotes this anecdote from Lady Louisa Stuart:

> A great dinner was given at Holland House to all the foreign ministers. The children came in at dessert. Charles, then in petticoats, spying a large bowl of cream in the middle of the table, had a desire to get into it. Lord Holland insisted he should be gratified, and, in spite of Lady Holland's remonstrations, had it placed on the floor for the child to jump in and splash about at his pleasure.

Permissiveness, some thought, could be taken too far, and stories like this (some but not all of them apocryphal) contributed to the Victorian backlash against the early 'indiscipline' that had turned Fox into a gambler and a debauchee.

Fox, as a little boy, was painted by William Hoare, who also painted the Quicke brothers with their dissected puzzle. Fox is shown in a silk dress, wearing a splendid headdress and clutching a King Charles spaniel. Already, as an infant, he looks like a contender who would not be content to play the game of patience.

XXIII

Since Mrs Hannas sold her collection in 1984, more early jig-saws have come onto the market. They are not as rare as once thought, and interest in them has increased. The Sotheby's sale catalogue of the Hannas collection stated that there were 'only six known Spilsbury jigsaws, four of which are in this collection'. Her map of Europe 'Divided into its Kingdoms' had an estimate of £200–£300 and was described as 'lacking three pieces'. Spilsbury's 'England and Wales', lacking many pieces, plus another better copy, together with 'two engraved maps coloured by hand, mounted on wood, and cut to form puzzle', formed a lot also estimated at £200–£300, the same price as that of a further lot consisting of Spilsbury's 'The World' together with 'a smaller engraved two hemispherical map dated 1762 which is Spilsbury's earliest known imprint, torn'. A map of 'Asia, divided into its Empires, Kingdoms and States', described as possibly the first jigsaw puzzle to have an interlocking border, was included in a lot estimated at £150–200.

Interestingly, all these items went for far more than their estimates: the map of Europe fetched £1,650; 'England and Wales' went for £880; 'The World' for £984; and Asia for £352. Prices were rising, and jigsaws were becoming increasingly collectible.

The dates shift, and the dissemination of puzzles throughout Europe and the rest of the world has not been fully charted. Nevertheless, it was the traditional founding date of 1766, true or false, that introduced me to Kevin. He sent me off on a new wild-goose chase, which was to take me far from the story of the jigsaw, and far from my Somerset evenings with Auntie Phyl. This is how it happened.

The thrill of my first physical contact with the Spilsbury maps in the British Library was so great that I was fired with eagerness to see as many old jigsaws as possible, as soon as possible. And by soon I meant immediately, that very day. (I am not patient by temperament, which is one of the reasons why I believe jigsaws are good for me.) I returned the wooden maps in their boxes to the appropriate counter in the Map Room and decided to set off at once in search of their Victorian successors. It is not often now that I try to do two things in one day. I knew that the Museum of London had holdings of puzzles, and indeed at that stage believed that Linda Hannas had bequeathed it her collection, so I thought I would go there and see whether I could find them. At that point, I innocently trusted that they would be spread out in glass cabinets, awaiting my eager inspection. I longed to see them. I don't know how I have preserved this optimism of easy access for so long.

It is, in theory, easy to get from the British Library to the Museum of London via King's Cross on the underground, and had I been in less of a hurry I would have gone on the tube, courtesy of my old person's Freedom Pass. But I knew from past experience that the Barbican is itself a giant puzzle. Its exits and entrances, like those of the reconstructed King's Cross, are bewildering, its layers labyrinthine. So I resolved to take a cab, which would take me straight to the right hole in the fortress wall. I usually resist travelling by taxi, for reasons that do not involve expense, but I decided to save time and make an exception to my rule. I would ask to be dropped off at the correct entrance, and thus gain at least half an hour of working time.

This was a lucky lapse of rigour. When I stated my destination, the taxi driver said to me, reasonably enough, 'Doing London in the day, are you?' I was mildly offended; I was a scholar, not an ageing tourist from out of town, going from museum to museum with nothing better to do. Did I look like an idler? So I said pompously, 'No, I'm doing some research.' He changed gear at once and politely asked about my subject. When I told him, he enquired, 'So when was the first jigsaw made?' I was able to reply, with unusual precision if not necessarily with historical accuracy, 'In 1766.'

He thought about this for a moment, as we headed east. Then he said, 'No, that can't be right. There must be earlier jigsaws. Think about it. What about mosaics?'

I thought about this challenge, and have continued to think about it. As he spoke, little brightly coloured particles of memory began to scatter and glitter and connect in the back of my brain. Tesserae, tesserae. Click, click, click. Mosaics, patterns, kaleidoscopes, tapestries, pictures. Dispersion, cohesion, mastic, gum, glue. Mimesis, mimicry. Children in antiquity, playing with pebbles and bones and teeth on a cave floor. Tragic children, dying early in their droves, before they had had much chance of any fun. Greek knucklebones, Greek fivestones. Roman pavements, Roman masonry, Roman *spolia*, architectural salvage. Hadrian's Villa and the Doves of Pliny, Florentine table tops, *pietre dure*, *opus sectile*, inlay, marquetry, intarsia. Monte Oliveto, Urbino, Gubbio. Disconnected moments of epiphany, moments of recognition. Reconstructions, reassemblings, replications. Collections, cabinets of curiosities. Simulacra, copies, reproductions. Calendar art, conversion art, paper flowers, elves made of gummed paper. The half-arts, *die Halbkünste*, the *compositae*.

The jigsaw model of experience and of the universe.

The model in which the scattered pieces from the first dispersal are reunited at the end of time.

XXIV

I first went to London with Auntie Phyl. She took me and my sister Susan to see the sights. I had never been further south than Bryn. I was about eleven, I think, with a centre parting and little brown plaited pigtails, and a hopeful smile and Clark's shoes and wrinkled knee socks and a nice cloth coat with a nipped waist and buttons and lapels. We stayed for a few days in Bloomsbury, in the Kenilworth Hotel (or was it the Ivanhoe?), and I found every moment of our sojourn extraordinarily stimulating and exciting. London was wonderful to me. There were moments of terror, like the moment at breakfast when the waiter asked me, 'Black or white?' and had to repeat his question several times. I had no idea what he was talking about, as he hovered threateningly over my cup of coffee with a heavy silver-plated jug of hot milk. And Auntie Phyl had to tell me that in a hotel I didn't need to make my own bed. I had never stayed in a hotel before. I found it hard to believe that somebody else would make my bed for me. At home, we always made our own.

London, the greatest city in the world, was known to me through books, and through the Monopoly board, and as the destination of the parlour travellers in Belisha. I knew of Mayfair and of

Marble Arch. Auntie Phyl had been whetting our imagination for years, with tales of the zoo, and Kew in lilac time, and St Paul's cathedral, and Trafalgar Square, and the British Museum, and Madame Tussaud's, and the lights of Piccadilly Circus, and the underground, and the Lyons Corner Houses. All these things we now saw and sampled. We fed the pigeons and went to the zoo. Auntie Phyl was tireless in those days, and thought nothing of climbing the Monument, or the stairs up to the Whispering Gallery. We had our supper in the Corner House on the junction of Oxford Street and Tottenham Court Road, where, if I remember rightly, there was a live orchestra playing for us. She and I usually ordered the same dish, which was called *omelette aux fines herbes*. I thought this the height of sophistication. The speckling of green on the neatly folded yellow flap, all reposing like a quiet oval fish on an oval silver salver – this was a luxury, yet a luxury that did not make us feel uncomfortable or outclassed.

I do not think that Auntie Phyl referred to the Corner House waitresses as 'nippies', as others knowingly did, for I do not recall hearing the word at that age, and I remember being slightly surprised by it when I first came across it. I suspect she might have disliked its familiarity and its condescension. Like me, she was a little nervous with waiters, waitresses and other figures of authority, whom she considered to be more than her equals. Like me, she much preferred public transport to taxis. Like me, she was not a good employer and did not enjoy bossing people about or giving instructions. In her later years she came to rely heavily on Joyce, as cleaner, carer, confidante, neighbour and friend, and on Joyce's husband Eddie as handyman, mechanic, gardener, neighbour and friend, but she relied on their good nature rather than on any contractual relationship. I used to worry that neither of them ever got paid.

Joyce had looked after my grandmother at Bryn in her last

illness, and after Grandma's death she inherited the care of Auntie Phyl. I remember Auntie Phyl saying to me once, after some slight tiff, 'I'd better keep on the right side of Joyce. I'd be sunk without Joyce.' I often think of that phrase, and see Auntie Phyl sinking, heavily, helplessly, beneath the waters.

But when she was in her thirties, she was tireless. She was over-awed by upmarket restaurants and fancy department stores, but she relished the adventure of staying in a hotel, or taking a journey across Europe, or catching a liner to Scandinavia, or a tourist coach to East Germany. In her own way, she was enterprising. One year, astonishingly, she drove to Istanbul. (She shared the driving with my father, and, unlike my mother, she did drive.)

Our week in London was a treat. I wish I could remember more of it. We liked the little zoo-born polar bear, Brumas. That year at Christmas we bought each other little white Brumas replicas, made of soap. Auntie Phyl allowed us to indulge these childish longings without making us feel silly. Both my parents often made me feel silly. They wanted us to grow up. They didn't really like children. They didn't dislike them, but they found them tiring and tiresome. My mother said she liked babies, but she was impatient with noisy, dirty, independent, uncontrollable youngsters. Their company bored her. Neither of my parents had been very happy as children, and, unlike Auntie Phyl, both had longed to escape from South Yorkshire. My mother saw childhood as a state to be endured, a time of hard work and study, of pleasure deferred. We were praised for high marks and passing exams, but nothing else we did seemed to be of value. A disappointing university grade (an Upper Second instead of the expected First) was mourned like a death in the family.

When I tried to have some fun as an adolescent, I would be told, 'Wait until you get to Cambridge, you can do that when you get to Cambridge...' It never seemed to occur to them that any of their children might not get into Cambridge. I distrusted this attitude. I had the sense to know that the competition for places was fierce, but they seemed to expect I would be offered one as of right. The pressure to follow in their footsteps was unquestioned and intense, so intense that none of us actively rebelled against it. It seemed to be the only way to get away. Cambridge had liberated them, and in turn it was expected to liberate us.

Auntie Phyl never imposed such expectations on us, because nobody had expected much of her. She let us enjoy ourselves.

I can't remember whether Auntie Phyl took us into the National Gallery, but I have a photograph of us amongst the pigeons in Trafalgar Square.

I loved the underground, and the famous map of it, from which we could work out how to get to anywhere from anywhere. (The maze-loving Georges Perec, of course, saluted this map.) It all seemed too good to be true. The names of the stations enraptured me – Regent Street, Chalk Farm, Swiss Cottage, Russell Square, Earl's Court. The map was so clearly marked, its routes so logical, so reassuringly easy to follow. We always knew where we were when we were underground on the underground. We could not get lost. It made visitors feel at home, in control of a vast strange city, which was our own and not our own. It was an immense romance.

I don't think we can have done Hampton Court on this visit, for how could there have been time? But I do remember taking Auntie Phyl there, many years later, when she was staying with me in London while recuperating from her cataract operation in Moorfields Eye Hospital. We had a lovely day out, wandering in the gardens, sitting in the sun in an outdoor café taking tea and cake, and talking to another couple of elderly idlers at the next table. She did appreciate an outing.

Hampton Court, like East Hardwick, is a bright and sunny place in my memory. It is festive and light-hearted, a palace built for pleasure. Sometimes, when I am in very low spirits and beset by troubles, I think that I might cheer up if I were to take a trip to Hampton Court. And in the blazing hot summer of 2006, in so many ways a bad year for Michael and me, I did just that. I went for a day out to the Hampton Court Flower Show, where my son Joe was presenting show gardens for the BBC programme *Gardeners' World*. He sent a car to collect me from the Lion Gate. I watched him, proudly, as he spoke to camera, and I wished that my father could have seen him. A keen gardener himself, my father would have been so surprised and pleased to find he had a gardening grandson. Auntie Phyl and Joyce often saw Joe on telly, and Joyce and her friends in Long Bennington continue to follow his career with interest. But my father died too early to know of Joe's metamorphosis.

Joe refused to have much truck with higher education or university. He probably thought there'd been too much of that kind of thing in the family. He did his A-levels, in his own relaxed and laid-back fashion, and then he found his own way. He seemed to know what he was doing. His father and I didn't interfere. We were and remain full of admiration for his independence.

XXV

I like being a tourist and seeing the sights. So I shouldn't have reacted in that defensively hoity-toity manner when Kevin asked me whether I was up in London for the day. But I'm glad I did, for otherwise I might not have started to think about mosaics, and the mystery of patterns and composites. I might not have seen that they, too, are part of the plan.

I made a date with Kevin, who agreed to take me on a tour of London in his cab, starting from the City of London, to look for mosaics and other jigsaw analogies. We met at Farringdon Station, and he chose our route. He showed me the new buildings and the old, the complex infill and patterning of Roman London, and the succeeding waves of two thousand years of overbuild and underpass. We gazed at Minster Court in Mincing Lane, and at the sparkling isometric diamonds of the windows of the Gherkin, and at the rugged brick remains of the Temple of Mithras, and at Tivoli Corner at the Bank of England. We drove over Holborn Viaduct, beneath which the shops of the printmakers, mapmakers and puzzle producers of Holborn Hill have long been buried. He described to me the legendary Knowledge that London taxi drivers are obliged to acquire. London is a jigsaw, and he knows better than to most of us how the pieces fit together.

Unlike many taxi drivers, he approved of the bold new architecture of the last twenty years and pointed out the high-rise buildings of the City that he liked best. But he also took me to St Ethelburga's in Bishopsgate, a medieval church that was blown up by a massive IRA terrorist bomb blast in 1993. The tower and the west front of the building had collapsed, and the church was so badly damaged that it was thought it would have to be demolished, but much of the original material has been salvaged and reused. The church may now be impressively photographed, if you are clever enough, with a view of the diamonds of the Gherkin soaring up like a spacecraft behind its modest façade.

The restoration of St Ethelburga's, Kevin suggested to me, had been a kind of giant stone jigsaw. (Kevin should have written a chapter of this book.) At his prompting I discovered how frequently the word 'jigsaw puzzle' is used about restoration projects. Angkor Wat, the Dead Sea scrolls, the stained-glass windows of Lincoln cathedral, the shredded Stasi files of East Germany, the three seventeenth-century Chinese vases that were broken by a careless member of the public in the Fitzwilliam Museum in Cambridge when he tripped over a shoelace – all these and many more similar undertakings have been described as 'jigsaws'. The Fitzwilliam snatched advantage from adversity by creating a 'Reconstruct your own Fitzwilliam vases' twenty-piece jigsaw-puzzle postcard, retailing at a modest £1 from its seductive online shop.

XXVI

Fashions in restoration change. I was shocked to read that all the heads of the figures of that vast, struggling mountain of antique marble known as the Farnese bull are fake, and a lot of the limbs, too, and that all the animals except the dog and the bull are late additions. There it stands in the National Museum in Naples, this monument to successive waves of antique, Renaissance and eighteenth-century taste, surrounded by pious admirers, but much of it is guesswork. It is now widely considered by art historians to be remarkable only for its size, and for the miraculous preservation of the sculpted rope tied to the bull's horns. The giant legs of the neighbouring figure of Herakles, also salvaged, like the bull, from the Baths of Caracalla, are very controversial. They have been lost and found and restored and re-restored. We don't do so much of that now, or not with such classic masterpieces. It's a long time since anyone tried to stick a head on the *Winged Victory of Samothrace*, or arms on the *Venus of Milo*. Only pranksters and surrealists and post-modernists and Oulipeans play around like that these days.

It's said that it was Louis XVIII of France, whose brother lost his head, who put an end to the idea of providing the *Venus of Milo* with new arms. I don't know whether that's true or not.

With lesser works, and with more recently or chance-destroyed churches like St Ethelburga's, we still strive for the authentic. We try to put the pieces back in place. A craftsman working on a panel of the 1894–5 Tiffany Ascension window of the Calvary Methodist Church in Pittsburgh complained that it 'was like doing several jigsaw puzzles piled on top of each other and mixed up at that'. The restorers had to undo the work of previous restorers, who had incorrectly put back some of the 8,268 pieces of glass, like a delinquent mother-in-law driven mad at Christmas.

In the past, fidelity to a historical template was less highly prized than it is now. The large round Bishop's Eye window in the south transept at Lincoln, with its flowing stone tracery, is filled with a composite of fragments of medieval painted glass that makes no attempt to reproduce the original design, thought to have been of the Last Judgement. The cathedral was seriously damaged by Parliamentary troops at the time of the Civil War, and much of the coloured glass was destroyed or dispersed. In the late eighteenth century the surviving fragments were reassembled and rearranged in the frame of the stone rose with no regard to subject or content, achieving what scholars critically describe as a 'haphazard array' that is 'pleasing to the eye but devoid of content'. The north transept rose window retains most of its medieval glass *in situ*, but the south rose is an eighteenth-century folly in a Gothic frame. Meaningless, but nevertheless glorious.

Auntie Phyl took us from Bryn to see Lincoln cathedral. We liked the Lincoln imp in the angel choir. She had a gift for capturing a child's attention by pointing out such things. The rose windows were too big for me, too bright, too high, too far away, and I had no interest in their iconography, authentic or jumbled, but I could see the imp and the angels. We liked to talk about such memories. 'Do you remember when we went to see the Lincoln imp?' 'Do you remember the horseshoes at Scarrington?' So we built up our picture of the past.

In Somerset, I took Auntie Phyl and Daisy to Cleeve Abbey, a beautiful group of Cistercian monastic buildings standing not far from Nettlecombe, and an easy outing from Porlock. I have come to know it well. I went round it on one occasion with a friend who had once been a Cistercian nun, and she explained its architectural and religious significance to me, stone by stone, in great detail, all of which I have now forgotten. (This friend was going to write a memoir called *Stark Mad in White Linen*, but she never got beyond this inspired title, and she is dead now.) Auntie Phyl and I just liked the look of Cleeve and its happy situation. I like the gatehouse and the ruins and the stonework and the well-kept greensward and the little river and the moat full of green tresses and yellow flowers – primroses, irises, monkey flowers, marsh marigolds, as the seasons changed. In the Middle Ages the abbey was rightly known as Vallis Florida, the Valley of Flowers.

Cleeve has a famous decorated tiled pavement, dating from the thirteenth century, now protected from the elements by English Heritage and a new tent-like structure. The pattern of the pavement is simple. Yellow, ochre, terracotta and brown tiles, bearing heraldic devices of chevrons, lions, fleur-de-lis and double-headed eagles, are arranged diagonally, divided by darker bands of plain tiles. Part of the arrangement is complete and lies *in situ*, but at one end of the exposed rectangle bits and pieces of broken tile, as in the Lincoln windows, have been jumbled up and laid together randomly. For Cleeve Abbey, like Lincoln, has been through many changes, and after the Dissolution it became a gentleman's residence, and then a farm, with the cloister serving as a farmyard, the dormitory as a barn, and cattle lodged in the monastic buildings. Thomas Hardy would have read its history well.

One of the most precious objects I salvaged from Bryn is a square tile. I think it may once have been used as a teapot stand. It is decorated with a symmetrical, six-petalled, white flower, the sort of boldly simple daisy one used to draw at school when learning how to use a pair of compasses. The white petals, separated by light-green-grey bells, are set into a dark-blue background, a blue of an intense and luminous richness, and the flower is surrounded by a dark-brown border with a simple, light-brown, fronded, curving motif. The tile itself is thick, and heavy, and always cool to the touch, as though it remembers a cloister or a church or a grotto, although it was never set in any floor or wall. On its underside (which is perforated with small holes) it tells me that it was made by the Campbell Tile Company in Stoke-upon-Trent, so perhaps it represents a link with the Bloor potters. I think there were several of these spare tiles at Bryn. The weight of it is a comfort to the hand, and its simple symmetry is a pleasure to the eye.

At school in York, I received no education in the visual arts at all, or none that I can remember. We learned nothing of paintings, and next to nothing of architecture, although we were so well placed to study it. We went to York Minster for special occasions, but it remained to me a vast and impressive but incomprehensible mass of stones. The school was a Quaker school, which may explain why this branch of our education was so conspicuously neglected. There was a principle involved here, of plain living and high thinking. We attended Quaker Meeting twice weekly, on Wednesdays and Sundays, in a plain Meeting House. We dressed plainly. Visual ornament was not encouraged. There were some books on art in the school library, and I remember browsing through the paintings of Delacroix with an intense and presumably erotic emotion, but when I was discovered at this private occupation it was suggested to me that these works were 'morbid'. I suppose 'morbid' is a fair word for *The Massacre at Chios* and the *Head of the Girl in a Cemetery*, but it was discouraging.

I liked the girl's low blouse, her crazed bare shoulder, her china-white eye, her wild coiled hair, her tragic intensity. I tried to find a place for my feeling for her in *The Sea Lady*, but I couldn't fit her in. I managed to work in Chios and the massacre, but I couldn't find a home for the girl in the cemetery. I don't think she will ever be made into a jigsaw.

We knew that York was a historic city, because we regularly walked under Micklegate Bar and along its Roman and medieval walls, two by two in a crocodile. We even had a Roman soldier's tombstone propped up in a basement corridor under the school, and in the sixth form those of us doing A-level Latin were allowed to avoid the shivering, bare-kneed misery of hockey by digging for dull shards of Roman pottery in a trench in one of the school gardens. But the aesthetic impact of the monumentality, the historicity of York eluded me almost totally. When we went on outings to Rievaulx or Fountains Abbey (and I suppose these out-ings must have been intended to be educational rather than devout, as they were for the history boys in the movie of Alan Bennett's play), I could induce myself to thrill at the sight of the bare ruined choirs, but I think that was because they appeared to me in a pantheist poetic guise, filtered through the works of Walter Scott and Charlotte Brontë. In my reading preferences, I was already graduating from Walter Scott to George Eliot, but my artistic responses remained those of an unschooled child.

Kevin knew a great deal about the architecture and history of London, which I imagine he had taught himself. The palimpsest of the city fascinated him, and he kept an eye on its changes. He likened the labyrinth of arches and tunnels that burrowed under St Pancras and King's Cross to great cocoons. Their mouths, as they opened onto the street that flanks the stations, used to house car mechanics, wine stores, junk shops, machine tools, but who knows what was hidden in the further reaches of their long, subterranean bellies? Lost treasures from the National Gallery, or the bones of mastodons? Kevin liked the idea of this hidden hinterland. Most of the tunnels are now sealed up and redeveloped, spruced up in pale-pink and ochre brick, and St Pancras Station, next door to the British Library, now boasts, according to the press, 'the longest champagne bar in Europe'.

(The St Pancras hotel has been closed, undergoing restoration, for most of my adult life. A friend tells me that his father used to sell asbestos samples to the railway men when they had offices in this building. His sister died of mesothelioma, as, more inexplicably, did my father.)

What creatures of the future had once lain in these cocoon burrows behind the stations, awaiting metamorphosis? I wonder whether Kevin saw the BBC TV series *Quatermass and the Pit*, which was first shown in 1958, before he was born and before I had a TV set. I recall a plot about an unexploded bomb, which turned out to be a spacecraft containing fossilized creatures from millions of years ago. The bones and skulls of the ape-like bodies were embedded in the wall of the underground, behind the Victorian brickwork.

An urban myth claims that some of the tunnels of the underground can never be restored because if you start to mess about with bits of the crumbling brickwork the whole of London will collapse into a giant crater. We just have to live with them as they are, held up and stuck together by the glue of time.

Kevin and I didn't get to see the restored Butterfly Mosaic in Camberwell, on the wall of the old Public Baths building on Wells Way, but he told me about it. We did the Borough and Waterloo and the wine bars, but we hadn't time to go to the Camberwell Beauty. Michèle Roberts, in her kaleidoscopic and evocative memoir, *Paper Houses*, celebrates this mosaic. It is part of her patchwork of London memories. Kevin would be impressed by her knowledge of the Knowledge.

XXVII

I did not open my eyes to art and architecture until I went to Italy, at the age of seventeen, when I studied Italian for three months at the Università per Stranieri in Perugia. Nobody had warned me about these marvels. My father had been in Italy with the RAF, but he did not speak much of his memories. The Roman forum, the Capitoline Museum, the Appian Way, the Villa d'Este, the paintings of Giotto, the hill towns of Umbria, the Piazza della Signoria, the *Primavera* of Botticelli: how could such things be, in a world that also gave birth to Nether Edge? I fell in love with antiquity and with the Italian Renaissance, with light and marble and stone, with carvings and capitals and gemstones and mosaics, with fountains and avenues and obelisks. A sense of history rushed over me like a torrent. A walk in the Campagna made me feel faint with joy, and ruins and cypresses and broken columns filled my dreams. The tomb of Cecilia Metella enraptured me. I had not read any Goethe then (and probably still thought his name was pronounced Go-eth) but when years later I came to read his *Italian Journey* and first heard the phrase 'Sehnsucht nach Süd', I recognized the sense of yearning that had swept through me when I was seventeen. It was a longing for the South.

London and Rome are both ancient composite cities, full of spoils, and the discovery of Rome illuminated my love of London. I began to see new layers of the past.

I recently came across a book titled *The Eloquence of Appropriation: A Prolegomena to an Understanding of Spolia in Early Christian Rome*, which describes in some detail the process of recycling that is so poignantly visible in Rome. Its author, Maria Fabricius Hansen, a Danish academic, deals with a specific timespan, but her book prompts thoughts about the universal processes of recycling and adaptation. In England, stained glass from churches has reappeared in follies and in private libraries; church masonry has been used to build town houses, priories and abbeys have become hotels; antique marble pillars have become garden ornaments; and an Egyptian obelisk has been erected on the London Embankment.

Thomas Hardy, with his keen apprehension of entropy, was affected by the reuse of identifiable relics. In *The Woodlanders* he describes the ruins of Sherton Castle, where two or three of the arched vaults 'had been utilized by the adjoining farmer as shelter for his calves, the floor being spread with straw, amid which the young creatures rustled, cooling their thirsty tongues by licking the quaint Norman carving, which glistened with the moisture'. His not very attractive, new, red-brick house at Max Gate was built over the remains of a Neolithic stone circle and a Roman-British cemetery, and a sarsen stone still stands in its garden. Hardy was proud of his 'skellingtons'.

Stones may be reborn. There's a phrase for this, as the book on antique *spolia* told me. *Rediviva saxa*. And if stones, why not we?

I find even the title of this book about *spolia* oddly moving. It describes a process of melding, joining and reassembling that affirms not entropy but continuity and survival and the grand aesthetic of time. This may not have been what was intended by the architects of early Christian Rome, but this is what they have achieved in posterity. Maria Fabricius Hansen (of the Department of Art History of the University of Aarhus, and herself perhaps in the grip of the Northern longing for the South) is at pains to point out that appropriation, before the Romantic movement and our own authenticity-conscious age, was ethically and visually much more acceptable than it is now. Plagiarism was no crime, and originality and authenticity were not necessarily virtues.

Jacob Burckhardt and Bernard Berenson may have judged the recyclings of Late Antiquity as a falling off from the creativity of Classical Antiquity, but that is not how Hansen sees them. She writes in praise of heterogeneity, plurality and diversity. Her photographic plates show some striking examples of recycling – of classical capitals transformed into baptismal fonts, of pagan columns erected upside down in Christian churches, and, most famously, of the miscellaneous panels, figures and reliefs of the Arch of Constantine rearranged in a new configuration with a radically different purpose, the sum having a different meaning from the parts. Constantine's Arch, with its reused materials from the reigns of Hadrian, Trajan and Marcus Aurelius, was described as a 'scrap-book' by art historian Martin Robertson, but she allows it more dignity.

It may be, as Hansen suggests, that Constantine and the early Christian emperors saw these transformations as a purging of paganism, as a deliberate profanation of the sacred stones of the old gods. Walking on a pavement of antique marble fragments furnished with outworn pagan inscriptions was literally an act of 'trampling on the enemy'. The enemy is now long dead, and most of the creeds have faded, but the stones remain, reassembled, like the painted glass of Lincoln cathedral, to please the eye; they acquire, in the process of survival, other meanings and send us other messages. They cry out to us, with their own eloquence, through interpretation after interpretation.

The pieces of the jigsaw scatter and are recombined in a new pattern that does not always strive to work from a lost template. (Is that because there is no fixed state, no frame, no archetype? The model may be evolution, not rediscovery.) Stone jigsaws, city jigsaws are around us everywhere, and not all the heroes of salvage are purists and conservationists. There are few emperors in this story. Some have been building contractors and demolitionists and scrap-metal merchants. John Mowlem of Swanage, stonemason and son of a quarryman, made a fortune as a young man in London, Dick Whittington style. With his nephew, the contractor George Burt, he spent much money refurbishing his home town with miscellaneous objects and reused materials, including 'the lamps from London Bridge, an illuminated clock made for the Great Exhibition of 1851, and the Cheapside entrance to the Mercers' Company, re-erected as the town hall for Swanage in 1881'. Hardly Constantine's Arch, but quite a memorial. This elaborate façade, described in Pevsner (Dorset, 1972) as 'an overwhelmingly undisciplined example of the City of London style' of the mid seventeenth century, became redundant when Cheapside was being widened; the original proposal had been to incorporate this fantastic erection, with all its swags and fruits and putti, into a new building on the old site, but it was decided that it was so thickly covered with 'London black' that cleaning and restoration would be too expensive. So it was moved to Swanage where, it was later noted, 'at this remote spot Nature's cleansers have perfectly done their work'.

Saxa rediviva.

I don't know how these speculations connect with my sense of the safety of the frame, the safety that Auntie Phyl provided at Bryn, but I know they do. One of the pleasures of the jigsaw-puzzle world lies in that safety, of knowing that all the pieces will fit together in the end. But where is the frame of an evolving city? Or of an expanding universe? Where are the boundaries? As a child, like many children, I was intrigued, aroused and tormented by the question: 'Where does space end?' I used to lie on my back and gaze at the sky and try to imagine the boundaries of infinity. I could make myself feel quite faint with my own stupidity and desire. I am still waiting to find an answer that I can begin to understand.

Very large round numbers make me feel giddy. How do we know that we are made up of a hundred trillion cells and a hundred billion neurons, as neuroscientist Steven Pinker so casually remarks? Did he count them all, one by one? How do we know that 'between one and three million' Cambodians died in Year Zero? That Cambodian number upset me so much that I wrote a novel about it, not because I wanted to justify Pol Pot, but because I didn't like the large yet vague roundness of the large number. Who were all these in-between people? Didn't they count at all? Could they be counted? The larger estimate has been revised downwards, and a sociologist in Chicago called Patrick Heuveline has tried to answer my query by devising a system of accounting, using electoral registers that attempted a more precise figure. I was pleased to think I had prompted him to that effort. It spared some of the unnumbered dead.

Led by Kevin, I have strayed out of my frame and along a branching spiral track of free associations. But no associations come for free. They cost the neurons dear.

XXVIII

I used to think until quite recently that one would grow out of mental pain. One would simply become, towards the end, too old and too numb to feel it. I didn't like the prospect but, looking around me, at old people I knew and old people I didn't know, such insensibility seemed, like death, inevitable. As Hopkins warned us: 'creep,/Wretch, under a comfort serves in a whirlwind: all/Life death does end, and each day dies with sleep...' Bodily pains would replace the pains of the spirit. The intensity of despair would be overtaken by arthritis or cancer.

That's what I used to think, or fear, or hope. When I was a child, my father had encouraged me to believe that the depression from which I suffered would pass with adolescence and, to a degree, he was right. Bringing up three children, working and writing to support the family and pay the mortgage, cleaning, shopping and cooking, left me too busy to sink too low for too long. I began to think that brisk activity, followed by a stiff whisky, could cure anything. My mother's angry depression seemed to me to be clearly related to her inertia and frustration, which afflicted so many educated and half-educated women of her generation; if she'd had more to do, if she hadn't had so much domestic help, if she'd been able to pursue a career, if she'd been more active, if she'd gone out for walks, things might have been different. I did notice that my father's depression had not vanished with age and, indeed, began to gain on him towards the end, but I never thought this could happen to me. My father was too well mannered to indulge in complaints and laments, and I think he found some solace in a sense of religious and social hope, but he did, in his seventies, reveal dark moments of the kind of lonely melancholy that besieged Dr Johnson. He suffered as a boy and as a young man, and he began to suffer again when he retired from the bench and lived in too close a seclusion with my mother. Or that's how I read what I observed. I should have taken warning from that.

I keep the telephone number of the Samaritans to hand. I have a very high regard for them. They have saved me on a couple of occasions. I worry now about the 1471 facility, because the anonymity of the phone calls was so reassuring. I don't understand the new technology of witholding numbers, and I suspect no phone calls are really secure. The Samaritans assure me that they never try to contact a caller without consent, except in the most extreme circumstances, and I trust what they say. But the very possibility is disquieting.

At times I feel some pride in my continuing capacity for feeling really, really bad. I think of the envious comment of a friend of mine, at a party, observing a well-known, hard-drinking novelist who is even older than we are: 'How can she still manage to get so drunk, at her age?' The friend who made this comment is not herself abstemious or censorious; her remark was made in a spirit of admiration. Drinking and suffering require stamina.

My father published two novels while he was a county court judge. The first, which appeared in 1971, was a workmanlike detective story; the second, *Scawsby*, which appeared in 1977, was a more ambitious book about multicultural adoption, set partly in a north-eastern fishing village not unlike Filey. It is far-sighted, humane and moving. Adoption was a subject in which he had a keen professional and personal interest, and he was well acquainted with multi-ethnic issues. In his unsensational plot he includes the question of underage sex, of which he took a lenient and rational view that would horrify most of today's journalists, and there is an 'honour killing' (a phrase not then current). He manages to evoke sympathy for the perpetrators of this crime as well as the victims, which not many writers would have attempted to do or have succeeded in doing. He was not inhibited by anxieties about political correctness. He was correct from his heart, not from fear of misunderstanding.

He was working on a third novel, set in a northern solicitor's office, after he retired. He asked me to read this work in progress, about which he said he was not confident, and I made some comments which he may have found discouraging, though I hadn't meant them to be so. I wish now that I had been more positive. My mother was angry with me about this. 'You should have told him it was going well, whatever you thought of it,' she said. 'It kept him busy. It gave him something to do.'

She should have followed her own advice. Once she said to me, 'I'd have written novels too, if only I'd had the time.' And maybe she believed that.

When I was young I used to repeat to myself, as one of my early mantras, some lines of Joachim du Bellay on the ruins of Rome. I found them more congenial, less terrible than the Terrible Sonnets of Hopkins, which I had learned at school. I bought my copy of du Bellay, an ancient, yellowing, 1918 Librairie Garnier paperback, in Cambridge in February 1959, in my last year at university, two or three years after I first went to Rome. It is still with me, its stitched and aged spine brown and peeling like bark, scattering Sibylline fragments whenever I handle it, and looking as old as the ruins it laments. These are the lines from *Antiquitez de Rome* that I know by heart:

> Tristes desirs, vivez donques contents:
> Car si le temps finist chose si dure
> Il finira la peine que j'endure.

Edmund Spenser translated these lines, but I've never been able to commit his version to memory. It runs:

> My sad desires, rest therefore moderate:
> For if that time make ende of things so sure,
> It als will end the paine, which I endure.

But time doesn't finish either, ever.

I had some grand and solemn moments in Rome aged seventeen, but I also had some trivial ones. Early one morning, after a night spent for some reason on the Stazione Termini, my friend (my friend of the *melanzana parmigiana*) and I tried to buy a ham sandwich at dawn in an espresso bar. The chap kept barking at us 'Crudo o cotto?' rather as the waiter in the Kenilworth had reiterated 'Black or white?' We weren't stupid, we knew what both these Italian words meant, but we couldn't imagine why he was using them. It seemed a very Lévi-Strauss kind of question. Who on earth would want raw ham, at six o'clock in the morning? Raw ham, in a *sandwich*?

I know better now.

Rome is an education.

XXIX

W e didn't do art history at school, nor did we study the history of England very seriously. We did some ancient history, of which vestiges remain in my memory, and they may eventually have added to my appreciation of Rome. The eighteenth century, the age of the dissected map, was a huge bald space in my education, containing one or two random, disconnected, free-floating pieces – Fielding's *Tom Jones*, which we were surprisingly allowed to read as an A-level set text; the building I knew as Bryn; Dr Johnson; Fanny Burney's *Evelina*; Tar McAdam; the Prince Regent; the Bath Assembly Rooms; the rotation of crops and Turnip Townsend; *She Stoops to Conquer*; my father's silver candlesticks and the invention of Sheffield plate. These did not add up to any kind of a whole. I had no chronological sense of the social background of the period, and I have pieced it together laboriously, inade-quately, over the years. I am still very hazy about the connections.

But I do now know that the jigsaw puzzle was not always known by this name. Its name is a recent coinage, dating from the late nineteenth century, and derives from the tool known as a jigsaw. These tools, which have a very narrow blade used for fretwork, began to appear in the late eighteenth century, but the name by which we know them was not widely used for another hundred years. I have been using the term 'jigsaw puzzle' anachronistically, as did the Sotheby's catalogue of the Hannas Collection in 1984. It is mere chance that what we now call jigsaw puzzles are not called fretsaw puzzles, as the terms 'jigsaw' and 'fretsaw' are, I am assured, more or less interchangeable. We could now have been saying, 'I'm doing a fretsaw of the *Garden of Earthly Delights*,' or 'I've just finished a fretsaw of Tutankhamen, and the gold bits were very difficult.' That sounds very odd. Or jigsaws might have been called Zig Zaws, or Zag Saws, as some early models were. Those trade names might easily, perhaps more easily, have caught on. But they didn't.

The treadle jigsaw dates back to the 1870s, and puzzles were named after it within a decade or so. We had a need for the concept and the word entered the vocabulary. Maybe the idea of 'jiggling' bits together had something to do with its permanent adoption (and the words do have a very distant etymological affiliation). The sound of the word fitted the meaning.

The word 'fret' has less happy, less playful connotations: more Drabble than Tucker.

A detailed history of the development of jigsaw-puzzle making in the nineteenth and twentieth centuries is beyond my scope and my ambition, and probably the patience of all but the most committed reader, so I shall not tackle it in any depth. If I tried, I would largely be paraphrasing the research of others, and that seems pointless. Also, I would make a very bad job of it. I am not good at describing technology or mechanical processes. I can hardly tell a hawk from a handsaw, or a fretsaw from a jigsaw. The only treadle with which I was ever acquainted was my Auntie Phyl's venerable, black-and-gold, smooth-bodied Singer sewing machine, which stood in the guests' dining room at Bryn, and I could never get that to work properly. The thread snarled, the needle juddered and stabbed, the fabric snagged and puckered. I liked the silver bobbins, which looked like little science-fiction chrysalides incubating another life form, but I never understood how to load them. For Auntie Phyl, the machine sang smoothly along the seams. She had the knack.

I have, I think, almost grasped the basics of the technical processes by which the hand-cut, non-interlocking, wooden puzzles of the eighteenth century were developed into the mass-produced cardboard puzzles of today. The jigsaw and later the die cutter (which was like a kind of giant pastry cutter) were the tools that made these changes possible, and made jigsaws as we know them cheaply available to a large public, thus changing the social class of the jigsaw, and turning an aristocratic schoolroom aid into what I would argue is one of the cheapest, most democratic and most accessible of all entertainments.

A hospital in Connecticut has recently introduced a jigsaw-puzzle table into the waiting room of its department of oncology and radiation, and the puzzles have proved popular with those whose 'loved ones' are undergoing treatment; they provide 'moments of interaction' that cut across 'the lines of gender, age, and status'. I am told that in England they are occasionally provided in the jury room to entertain jurors during interminable court delays. Several people have reported to me on the use of the jigsaw in bonding with new in-laws at family gatherings. This is all a far cry from the days of Lady Charlotte, and the princes at Kew, and Lord Spencer, and the little Spanish Infante painted by Goya.

I am not particularly interested in the technical processes of manufacture, but the social ends of jigsaws interest me very much.

We did not do wooden jigsaws with Auntie Phyl. We did cardboard ones. Was this because of the war? I don't know. Recently, on advice, I have indulged myself by purchasing one or two expensive modern wooden models, and I can see that there is something satisfactory about handling the pieces and clunking them together. One could learn to despise cardboard. I am sure the Queen orders wooden jigsaws from her jigsaw club. But why acquire expensive tastes, if you are happy, as I am, with the mass-produced?

In the 2006 film about the aftermath of the death of Princess Diana, we can see Helen Mirren as the Queen in an authentically old-fashioned-looking drawing room in Balmoral, where an unfinished jigsaw is displayed upon a table. I couldn't see whether it was made of wood or cardboard, or what the image was.

The only concession I made to research on the fretsaw front was to pay a visit to a friend who is a skilled amateur cabinetmaker, and who possesses a fine collection of wood-working tools, including a replica of an eighteenth-century tool chest that he made himself, based on the 1796 Seaton chest now in Rochester Museum. I felt I had to try to get some kind of grasp of the processes in question, but what I chiefly acquired from listening to David and handling the items in his collection was a sense of the hand-crafted beauty of the tools themselves, with their ivory or wooden handles, their fine blades, their distinctive personal histories. These objects, like their products, are now collectors' items, growing rarer and more expensive year by year. And, in their presence, it became easier to see why the early dissected maps would have been beyond the reach of Fanny Price's family in Portsmouth. Each mahogany map was hand-made, by craftsmen. They were not throwaway toys, destined to join the junk of the nursery.

David is a carpenter's son, and for him cabinetmaking is a pleasure and a skill that has offset a professional career spent at desks and in meetings. Like me, he enjoys an escape from words. I can see that creating an intricate and beautiful three-dimensional object gives a great and lasting satisfaction. The art of marquetry moves and excites him. His partner's tastes are minimalist, but he loves the rich complexity and intricacy of wood and veneer, of inlay and *trompe l'oeil*, and maybe he hopes one day to introduce some Florentine fantasy into her austere domain.

I have another witness to the lure of the manufacturing process, whose account illustrates very clearly why a ham-fisted person like me is wise to stay well away from saws and blades. My correspondent Anthony Brown writes:

I had wanted to make my own puzzles for ages, even as a child. I had a fret-saw in my tool kit, but the broad blade and the inability to fix the wood securely resulted in most unsatisfactory pieces, far too loose for any pleasure in puzzle doing. After my apprenticeship as an engineer, I used to collect old calendars from the firm's offices after the New Year holiday. I still have the drawer-full which I accumulated.

Then I acquired an old treadle jig saw, which was subsequently stolen, but easily recovered with the help of the police when I saw it in an antique shop. (In fact, I only realised that it and a few other possessions had been stolen from our outhouse when I saw the jig saw in the shop window; I couldn't believe that there could be another one.)

Unfortunately, I have always been too busy with other priorities, although I did buy a scroll saw last year, in a moment of wishful thinking. My efforts on the treadle saw were fun and interesting, but frustrating, both in the making and in the subsequent doing. I have listed the plywood which I'll need on the long list of timber which I must order from the saw mill. But even when it arrives, there are other wood-working priorities.

One can see, from this kind informant's dilemmas, that there is a whole other world of puzzle expertise into which Auntie Phyl and I would have been most unwise to enter. She was critical enough of my attempts at sewing; it would have been unwise to let me loose with a saw. She was not all that good with her fingers, either. Her rock cakes were a bit rough and ready, and her pastry was never as light as my mother's.

People who make their own jigsaws are in a different league and have very different interests from those who merely assemble them. They are craftsmen.

One of the reasons why the jigsaw appeals to me, as I have already suggested, is that it is *pre-made*, its limits finite, its frame fixed. No ordinary degree of manual clumsiness (and mine is advanced, and inevitably advancing) can yet prevent me from finishing a jigsaw. It can't be done badly. Slowly, but not badly. All one needs is patience. (The French used to call puzzles *les jeux de patience*, and the Germans called them *Geduldspielen*. Now they both call them *puzzles*.) In this aspect, the jigsaw is the very opposite of the novel. The novel is formless and frameless. It has no blueprint, no pattern, no edges. At the end of a day's work on a novel, you may feel that you have achieved something worse than a lack of progress. You may have ruined what went before. You may have sunk into banality or incoherence. You may have betrayed or maligned others. You may have to scrap not only the day's work, but the work of the preceding week, month, year, lifetime. You may have lost ground, and for ever. You may have lost your nerve, and indicted all that you have achieved. Writing fiction is frightening. Some novelists find the safety of a reliable formula, but I never did, nor did I really wish to.

Editing *The Oxford Companion to English Literature* for five years, and then revising it for other, shorter stretches, was a comfort to me, for at the end of each day I could say, 'I have made progress. I have added entries on Samuel Bamford and Sylvia Plath and Philip Larkin and Angus Wilson, revised entries on Samuel Johnson and Oliver Goldsmith, received and checked entries on Hopkins and

Horovitz and Horror.' The pieces fitted together, they interlocked. Asterisk led to asterisk in a finely articulated and complex pattern, in a vast jigsaw. This was satisfying. The end was sure to come. There would be spare pieces that never found a home and would have to be discarded, and missing pieces where dates or titles were lost and unavailable, but the book as a whole, as a self-referring entity, would be completed. Assembling and fitting the pieces together was a form of carpentry.

Writing novels is not like that.

Coleridge, in Chapter 22 of his *Biographia Literaria*, draws a famous distinction between FANCY (the drapery of poetry) and IMAGINATION (its soul), and at one point invokes the image of dissected maps, suggesting that Wordsworth sometimes woodenly (my word) combined instructions and described construction programmes of a pre-existing plan, rather than drawing on the deeper resources of the imagination. Referring to a landscape passage in *The Excursion* (Book III, 23–73), which describes in sequence yew tree, stream, crag, rock, stones and 'a tall and shining holly', Coleridge comments that the draughtsman or painter could have presented these images to the eye far more economically and satisfactorily. He continues:

Such descriptions too often occasion in the mind of a reader, who is determined to understand his author, a feeling of labour, not very dissimilar to that, with which he could construct a diagram, line by line, for a long geometrical proposition. It seems to be like taking the pieces of a dissected map out of its box. We first look at one part, and then at another, then join and dove-tail them; and when the successive acts of attention have been completed, there is a retrogressive effort of the mind to behold it as a whole. The Poet should paint to the imagination, not to the fancy.

Here, while dismissing or deprecating the satisfaction of this 'retrogressive effort of the mind', Coleridge in fact accurately describes the particular pleasure to be gained by the completion of a large jigsaw puzzle, the moment when the small local struggles of murky corners or blank blue skies or confusing geometric repetitions or (in Perec's classic example) of 'the belt buckle of a uniform which turns out *in extremis* to be a metal clasp holding the chandelier' are resolved, and the whole emerges from the parts. The Jackson Pollock ceases to be an intense and frustrating battle with arbitrary splashes and streaks and blobs and blisters of paint, and becomes an intentional and recognizable work of art, caught within the frame of its canvas. Venus of Urbino emerges smiling from a sea of complacent apricot pink. Brueghel's 246 children join the everlasting game.

This is not to suggest that those who do jigsaws delude themselves that they are creating a new work of art. They are not so stupid. It isn't an art. It isn't a hobby. It isn't even a craft. Making a jigsaw puzzle from plywood is a craft, and as we have seen a tricky one, but doing a ready-made cardboard or wooden jigsaw doesn't qualify. It isn't quite a game, either. It is a different kind of act. But what kind of an act is it?

It could be argued that Georges Perec, in the immensely complex, enjoyable and intricate *La Vie: Mode d'Emploi*, uses the jigsaw as a central metaphor for the tragic futility of human endeavour and the tedium of existence, a *vanitas* motif constructed in the French metaphysical mode. And that is one way of looking at his novel and at this pursuit. The jigsaw has been used with satirical overtones in this manner by playwrights and film-makers who portray characters with nothing better to do and no thoughts to think, pointlessly wasting time as they work away at broken images, at puzzles without solutions. Crazy old Mrs Winemiller in Tennessee Williams' *Summer and Smoke* (first performed in 1948, but set in 1916) is told by her daughter to be quiet and work on her 'picture puzzle', but she complains, 'The pieces don't fit! The pieces don't fit!' She is in her disruptive second childhood, demanding to be bribed into good behaviour by promises of ice cream and cigarettes. Orson Welles makes brilliant play with the jigsaw motif in *Citizen Kane*, where the missing piece of plot is Kane's childhood sleigh, Rosebud. The film is full of rich imagery of grandiose Roman rubble, towering crates, crazy collections of antique statuary and junk, newspaper cuttings and fragments, and amidst the fragments, stranded in a dark echoing chamber by a cold baronial fire, sits Kane's wretched second wife, endlessly assembling and reassembling large jigsaws of conventionally pretty landscapes. Her activity is pointless, her loneliness intense. Her problems, like her husband's, are insoluble.

Kane's second wife, Susan Alexander, is said to have been modelled on Randolph Hearst's wife Marion Davies. In a photograph by Cecil Beaton, Davies appears with some other society ladies assembling the pieces of a jigsaw. The photograph was taken in St Donat's Castle in Wales, which Randolph Hearst had purchased in 1925. These pieces fit neatly together.

Perec's jigsaw motif may be seen as the apotheosis of this conceit (though there are other ways of seeing it). The inspiration for *Life: A User's Manual*, translated by David Bellos, came to Perec, he claimed, while he was working on a huge jigsaw puzzle portraying the port of La Rochelle. His protagonist, Percival Bartlebooth (and the name has a deliberate echo of Melville's nay-saying Bartleby the Scrivener), is obsessed both by ports and by jigsaws. As the heir to a considerable fortune, he constructs a way of spending time that he trusts will occupy him fully until his death. Laboriously, over a period of some years, he undertakes to learn the art of painting watercolours, for which he has no natural aptitude whatsoever (just as Kane's wife had no natural aptitude as an opera singer).

Then he sets off with his servant and valet Smautf to travel the world, painting the harbours of the many ports where his ship puts in. These paintings Smautf dispatches back to Paris, where they are hand-mounted on wood and hand-dissected into puzzles. Bartlebooth will then return to Paris to spend the second half of his life reconstructing these harbour scenes, which, when reconstructed, will be deliberately destroyed. It doesn't quite work out according to plan, but that is the plan.

The massive and elaborate pointlessness of this project is like a parody of the wagers, voyages and contests to be found in the pages of Jules Verne, and indeed an epigraph from Verne's *Michael Strogoff* fronts the work: 'Look with all your eyes, look!' But the effect of this extraordinary work is in no way nihilistic; it shares the vigour and sense of adventure of Verne himself, and a richness of detail that recalls the work of Balzac and Zola.

Those who believe that they are spending their lives usefully and progressively on humanitarian projects, or on bringing up their children, or on achieving wisdom, or on running a country, may well be appalled by the reflection of nothingness that Perec's long novel plays back, and which certainly constitutes part of its impact. Bartlebooth, crouched over his self-imposed and self-destroying task, is making nothing. Is he an image of the artist? Is he a Beckett-inspired version of Everyman, trapped in a possibly heroic but ultimately ridiculous effort to delude himself that life is not void?

Sitting over a jigsaw as an adult, one may well feel foolish. When I described my new subject to a fellow author from a grander background than mine, her initial distaste was patent. Jigsaws? Yes, she remembered them. As a child, when she had stayed in country houses with her parents, there had always been a jigsaw on the table in the morning room, and guests would toy with a piece or two in passing, as though they were on a luxury liner. Clearly this pursuit for her represented the fatuity of the underemployed, upper-class life.

She herself is one of the most influential writers and journalists of her time, a modern superwoman, and to her the notion of time-wasting seemed alarming, perhaps even threatening. (For do we not all, towards the end of our lives, become redundant, however busy we may have been in our prime?) Our conversation moved on to other time fillers and killers, like knitting and needlework and crochet, which again she appeared to regard with anxiety and contempt. I am sure that, like Huizinga, she would have disapproved of bridge, with its connotations of middle- and upper-middle-class female idleness, although chess, being a more masculine and intellectual game, might perhaps have been more acceptable to her.

I have always felt a little judgemental about bridge myself, but that is largely because I never learned to play, and I suspect I could never get to grips with it even if I had tried. In one of my late novels, *The Seven Sisters*, I describe a group of friends who meet through reading Virgil in Latin in a reading group; they go on a trip in the footsteps of Aeneas, which is quite a highbrow form of tourism (a Jules Verne or a Martin Randall art-tour outing, not a Thomson's Holiday) and, as they travel, their Virgil tutor offers to instruct them in the art of bridge. They take to this, very happily, for after all, they say to themselves, they are on holiday, and their tutor's presence sanctions the diversion. I was quite pleased with this unexpected little moment in the plot, which came to me out of the blue as I was contemplating the ways that we find to amuse ourselves as we grow older. It seemed liberating. And I was pleased when a friend at dinner told me that she had enjoyed my novel, and had been relieved to find that I and my characters hadn't been superior or condescending about bridge. She revealed herself as a keen bridge player and described the pleasure she gained, when travelling abroad, in coming across people with the same interest. She could find a new small temporary world of friends anywhere in the world, she said. I was impressed by this testimony and resolved never to think or speak ill of bridge or bridge players again.

Maybe, when I have finished this book (which, like Penelope's tapestry, could go on for ever), I shall set myself the task of driving the Belisha route, from Oban to London, stopping off at every one of the beauty spots and towns and villages illustrated in the pack of cards. It would be a pointless and glorious undertaking, somewhat in the Bartlebooth mode, but much more fun.

XXX

Our capacity for disapproving of and moralizing about one another's amusements, as of one another's artistic tastes, is almost limitless. Class prejudice and religious intolerance lie behind most of these attitudes, and most of us are guilty. Huizinga disapproved of bridge, and Plutarch of fishing, which he considered 'a filthy, base illiberal employment'. John Northbrooke's 1579 treatise against dicing condemned it as 'the mother of lies, of perjuries, of theft, of debate, of injuries, of manslaughter, the verie invention of the Divels of hell'.

Some people disapprove of jigsaws, some of knitting, some of chess, and many more of dancing and lotteries. (Chess is forbidden in some states under Islamic law.) Willard Fiske's *Chess in Iceland* (1905) is a treasure house of commentary on social attitudes to games and gaming; he quotes as a classic example of the partisan spirit Mauritio Bardinelli's 1604 dismissal of cards (suitable only for stablehands and cobblers), chess and dice in favour of backgammon. Backgammon, he claims, is 'a perfect diversion, adapted to every lofty intellect…it is not a sport which strains the mental powers, but is cheerful, varied, diverting'. This resembles Boswell's view that Johnson should have played draughts for the sake of his spirits. Bardinelli also applauds the fact that backgammon is played sitting down.

David Hume, too, endorsed backgammon as a relief to the spirits and a cure for mental exhaustion. Worn out as a young man by venturing too far into the terrible wastes and forlorn solitude of abstract thought, and dreading the storms of controversy he had aroused amongst 'metaphysicians, logicians, mathematicians, and even theologians', he learned to take comfort in human society and the conversible world: 'I dine, I play a game of backgammon, I converse, and am merry with my friends.' He became well known as a man who enjoyed a good dinner (Gibbon described him, with friendly admiration, as one of the fattest of Epicurus' hogs) and, more remarkably, he appears to have learned how to cook himself, writing on 16 October 1769 in his fifty-ninth year to his friend Gilbert Elliot that his temporary lodgings in Edinburgh were

> very cheerful, and even elegant, but too small to display my great Talent for Cookery, the Science to which I intend to addict the remaining Years of my Life…I have just now lying on the Table before me a Receipt for making *Soupe à la Reine*, copy'd with my own hand. For Beef and Cabbage (a charming Dish), and old Mutton and old Claret, no body excels me. I also make Sheep head Broth in a manner that Mr Keith speaks of it eight days after, and the Duc de Nivernois would bind himself Apprentice to my Lass to learn it…All my Friends encourage me in this Ambition; as thinking it would redound very much to my Honour.

Hume, one of the greatest philosophers of history, did not over-rate the life of the mind. He believed that other pleasures, if pursued with equal passion, were of equal value. He played billiards, and enjoyed a game of whist of an evening with the old lady who lived on the floor below him. This is from his one of *Essays*, 'The Sceptic':

> The inference upon the whole is, that it is not from the value
> or worth of the object, which any person pursues, that we can
> determine his enjoyment; but merely from the passion with
> which he pursues it, and the success which he meets with in
> his pursuit. Objects have absolutely no worth or value in
> themselves. They derive their worth merely from the passion.
> If that be strong, and steady, and successful, the person is happy.
> It cannot reasonably be doubted, but a little miss, dressed in a
> new gown for a dancing-school ball, receives as compleat
> enjoyment as the greatest orator, who triumphs in the
> splendour of his eloquence.

Dr Johnson disagreed with this position, arguing, according to Boswell, that 'A peasant and a philosopher may be equally satisfied, but not equally happy. Happiness consists in the multiplicity of agreeable consciousness. A peasant has not capacity for having equal consciousness with a philosopher.' But Hume knew how unhappy philosophy could make a man, and he spoke and wrote of what he knew.

Herbert Spencer is famous for claiming that 'A propensity to play billiards well is a sure sign of a misspent youth,' whereas Jeremy Bentham more provocatively argued that

> Prejudice apart, the game of push-pin is of equal value with
> the arts and sciences of music and poetry. If the game of push-
> pin furnish more pleasure, it is more valuable than either.
> Everybody can play at push-pin: poetry and music are relished
> only by a few. The game of push-pin is always innocent: it were
> well could the same be always asserted of poetry.

Whatever added to the sum and aggregate of human happiness, considered Bentham, was in itself justifiable, as quantity was more worthy of consideration than quality. This remains a challenging proposition.

Despite studying Utilitarianism with some interest at Cambridge, under the heading of 'The English Moralists' (a miscellaneous grouping that included Plato, Aristotle, Kant and Marx), I've never been quite sure what kind of a game push-pin is, and am relieved to see frustrated dissension on this point expressed on the internet, some of it under the eloquent heading, 'What the fuck is pushpin?' It's amazing how much the student mind can glide over without stopping to query – the Royal Game of the Goose, the twelve good rules, nine men's morris, push-pin, jigsaws in *Mansfield Park*. I never bothered to get to grips with any of them. But it's never too late to learn. The *OED* defines push-pin as 'A child's game, in which each player pushes or fillips his pin with the object of crossing that of another player' and gives examples from Shakespeare, Herrick, Marvell and Cowper, which leave me none the wiser. What *kind* of pins? Pins as in ten-pin bowling? Pins as in the pins stuck into Alison Uttley's sacred pincushion? Or pins as in spillikins?

My husband has always thought it was a game somewhat like shove ha'penny. But I don't know what shove ha'penny is either. Is it a kind of pitch-and-toss? And what, please, is pitch-and-toss?

The antiquarian and engraver Joseph Strutt, in his classic compendium titled *The Sports and Pastimes of the People of England* (1801), is as dismissive as he is unhelpful. All that he has to say is that 'Push-pin is a very silly sport, being nothing more than simply pushing one pin across another.'

My grandchildren liked that game in the Minehead arcades when you tried to make pennies fall over a shelf, in a cascading copper waterfall. They could teeter on the brink impossibly, banking up, and then suddenly, orgasmically, they would let themselves go. I liked that game too. We used to play it in Filey when we were children. It's very silly, but it's fun.

Jane Austen, we are told in *A Memoir of Jane Austen* (1870) by her nephew James-Edward Austen-Leigh, was good at spillikins. Nobody could throw them with as steady a hand as she, and her performances with cup and ball were marvellous. 'The one used at Chawton was an easy one, and she has been known to catch it on the point above an hundred times in succession, until her hand was weary. Sometimes she found a resource in that simple game when unable, from weakness in her eyes, to read or write long together.'

That's what novelists do when they need a break. They play solitaire, or free cell, or do a bit of a jigsaw, or play cup and ball.

Jane Austen was an affectionate and patient aunt. She wrote to her sister on 24 October 1808 from Southampton, as she tried to divert her nephews Edward and George from grieving for the death of their mother: 'We do not want amusement; bilbocatch ['biloboquet', i.e. cup and ball], at which George is indefatigable, spillikins, paper ships, riddles, conundrums, and cards, with watching the ebb and the flow of the river, and now and then a stroll out, keep us well employed.' This is a sad testimony to her brave efforts to amuse the little motherless boys.

Those who read books tend to despise those who don't. My mother disapproved very strongly of homes without books, and those for whom the word 'book' meant 'magazine'. (Though it has to be said that she herself had subscriptions to *Woman* and *Good Housekeeping*, and for me one of the first indulgences of returning from boarding school for the holidays was the pleasure of going through a thick pile of carefully saved back numbers. I particularly loved the agony column of Evelyn Home, and to my surprise have discovered that in real life she was a Quaker called Peggy Makins.) Francis Spufford, in *The Child that Books Built* (2002), an account of his childhood reading, states: 'I have a cultural sanction for my addiction. Books get cited over and over as the virtuous term whose wicked other half is Nintendo, or MTV, or the Web.' But those who read his story to the end will discover that he agrees with Bentham that reading is not necessarily innocent, for his addiction led him into pornography, a journey he appears to regret.

Disapproval of card games is traditional and comes in various degrees of intensity. Mary Delany's objections were measured; she wrote: 'I am not so great an enemy to cards as to be uneasy at them, but I would not make it my business to secure company *for that purpose.*' Caroline Lennox, who cultivated the life of the mind, couldn't resist cards and gambling, but felt uncomfortable about it: 'I can't help when I play deep having an unpleasant feel about it, as if I did something wrong; perhaps a little vanity at not acting consistent with the rest of one's character. In short, I don't quite know, but tho' I love it I don't feel pleasant at it.' Lady Mary Coke, in contrast, had no such scruples. She played regularly, often at court, tediously and painstakingly recording in her journal each evening's losses and gains; these were usually in the region of seven or eight guineas, though sometimes they were very much higher. Jane Austen (in a letter to her sister Cassandra, dated 7 October 1808) records being 'tricked' into playing commerce with friends in Southampton for a three-shilling stake, but at that rate she could not play more than one pool, as she 'could not afford to lose that, twice in an evening'. (Lady Mary balanced her persistent gambling with some healthy hands-on gardening, which has not yet been considered a debauched activity.)

Card games were endemic in aristocratic circles in the eighteenth century. How else could leisure time be passed? Innumerable group and family portraits record their subjects playing cards, and often without any hint of satire, though sometimes criticism may be intended, and art historians are always searching for it. A few rakes played for high stakes, losing thousands of pounds in an evening. Others played to alleviate boredom. The diarist John Hervey gives a chilling glimpse of life under George II, on the night of the birth in 1737 of the 'poor little ugly she-mouse' of a daughter of the Princess of Wales. Unaware of the turn of events, at Hampton Court

> the King played at commerce below stairs, the queen above at
> quadrille, the Princess Emily at her commerce-table, and the
> Princess Caroline and Lord Hervey at cribbage, just as usual,
> and separated all at ten of the clock; and, what is incredible
> to relate, went to bed all at eleven, without hearing one
> syllable of the Princess's being ill, or even of her not being
> in the house.

That phrase, 'just as usual', is deadly.

Decades later, nothing much had changed. George III's daughter Princess Elizabeth, born in 1770, and pining for a husband as she felt her beauty fade, wrote in despair in 1802 from the regular family holiday in Weymouth to her confidante Lady Harcourt:

> Read to the Queen the whole evening till cards, when I play at
> whist till my eyes know not hearts from diamonds and spades
> from clubs. And when that is over, turn over cards to amuse the
> King, till I literally get the rheumatism in every joint of my
> hand... News there is none, but who bathes and who can't, and
> who won't and who will, whether warm bathing is better than
> cold, who likes wind and who don't, and all these very silly
> questions and answers which bore one to death and provoke
> one's understanding.

The bad example set by some of the royals, and notably by the Prince Regent himself, was in part responsible for the evangelical revolt against loose living and high stakes. Jane Austen's disapproval of the amateur theatricals in *Mansfield Park* is taken as a significant marker in this shift towards propriety, for, in her high-spirited girlhood, there had been little sign of such censoriousness. But her reservations about the tone of the amusements at Mansfield Park were mild compared with the condemnations of Mrs Sherwood, the autocrat of the nursery and the author of the best-selling and much reprinted *History of the Fairchild Family* (3 volumes, 1818, 1842, 1847). Mrs Sherwood (born Mary Butt) denounced card games with evangelical intensity, and in her memoirs she luridly describes the small-town life of her grandparents' generation in Coventry and Lichfield as bedevilled by raucous card parties. The ladies, she said,

> always played for money, and often quarrelled so violently over
> their cards as actually to proceed to pulling of caps... It was
> astonishing how fifty or sixty years ago this mode of spending
> the evenings prevailed among the ladies in towns. As the
> market and the church filled up in the morning, so did cards
> occupy almost every evening of females in a certain class.

This doesn't sound quite like the dull royal evenings, or like the peaceful games of cribbage, piquet, speculation, quadrille and vingt-et-un enjoyed by the county families in Jane Austen's novels, though it is true that the vulgar Mrs Philips in *Pride and Prejudice* enjoyed 'a noisy game of lottery tickets' with her nieces, and 'a little bit of hot supper afterwards', and we see the more refined characters in *Sense and Sensibility* recoil from the noisiness of a game of consequences.

Playing for money was, as Mrs Sherwood says, considered

normal. Harriet Martineau, who was born into a religious Huguenot family in Norwich, and who was herself as a child of a neurotically religious persuasion, records the pleasure of winning at cards without a hint of self-reproach, although she was by nature of a disapproving temperament: she disapproved of women writers who sustained themselves with alcohol when working late, and she disapproved of Mary Wollstonecraft because she succumbed to sexual passion. But playing cards did not carry an odour of sin.

The Wordsworths played cards at Dove Cottage, when they weren't reading Chaucer or Shakespeare to one another. But I don't think they played for money. The Coleridge children did jigsaws, but I don't know whether the Wordsworths did.

Elizabeth Gaskell's *Cranford*, set in the 1840s and early 1850s, also records without any note of censure the continuing prevalence of cards, although Gaskell was the wife of a minister (albeit a tolerant Unitarian one). The ladies of Cranford play 'the decorous, highly respectable game of Preference' regularly, nearly every evening, with passion and commitment, gulping down their tea in order to get at the game more quickly. 'Cards were a business in those days, not a recreation.' They played for threepenny points (these would have been little silver threepenny coins), and it was customary for each player to contribute a shilling towards the expense of each new pack of cards, placing the coin discreetly under one of the candlesticks as the green-baize tables were laid out for the game. Gaskell does not hint at any rowdiness or impropriety at these gatherings, and the gentle ladies of Cranford certainly did not indulge in the pulling of caps, though occasionally 'a few squibs and crackers' were let off at the end of the evening at careless or unlucky partners. All the ladies, we are assured, were in bed and asleep by ten.

Elizabeth Gaskell smiled on the quiet amusements of her townswomen, who learned to fill their empty and impoverished days with harmless and mutually supportive activities – paying morning calls, knitting garters, talking about the London fashions, making candle-lighters (known to Miss Matty in Cranford and to us at Bryn as 'spills') from coloured paper, and embroidering Queen Adelaide's face in loyal wool-work.

Auntie Phyl taught us how to make spills by making little twists from old newspapers. We used them to light the little paraffin Kelly lamps that saw us to bed before electricity reached Long Bennington. I enjoyed this thrifty and simple activity of recycling. We kept the spills in a pot on the mantelpiece.

Elizabeth Gaskell had an affectionate temperament and an easy tolerance of eccentricities. She was fond of her old ladies, and writes about their small world with confident indulgence, while eschewing the sentimentality that often afflicted the prose of Mary Russell Mitford, her contemporary and a fellow chronicler of country ways. Mitford's *Our Village*, which provides a close parallel and an interesting comparison with *Cranford*, is a little overloaded with apple cheeks and dimpled faces and sparkling eyes and primroses and cowslips and hollyhocks and carnations and mossy dells and elves and fairies. The words 'delicious' and 'beautiful' are sprinkled too lavishly on the page, and even her admirers admitted that she enamelled too brightly. Her violets are too violet, her bluebells too blue. She was an ardent rambler and gardener, and her garden at Three Mile Cross, near Reading, was her solace for the hardships of a life that had, in fact, been thrown off course and nearly ruined by her father's gambling. Dr George Mitford (the professional title was largely honorary) was all too fond of cards. He had managed to get through a large fortune of some £70,000, which he lost on whist, piquet, speculation and greyhounds, playing for much higher stakes than the Cranford ladies, and his daughter had to write hard and fast to save him from his creditors and the King's Bench Prison. She might well have taken to speculation herself, for in 1797 at the age of ten, with a beginner's luck, she had personally selected a winning number in the Irish Lottery; she chose 2224, because the digits added up to ten, and the ticket won her £20,000. Her father got through that, as well as his own and his wife's inheritance, thus consigning his daughter to a life of scribbling. She gave up betting, and took up writing and gardening. He went on betting.

Most of Mary Russell Mitford's nineteenth-century prose sketches would translate easily into twentieth-century Heritage jigsaws. When South Africa-born novelist Barbara Trapido in *Brother of the More Famous Jack* (1982) describes a house in Sussex as being 'like a house one might see on a jigsaw puzzle box, seasonally infested with tall hollyhocks. The kind one put together on a tea tray while recovering from measles', she could be describing many of the dwellings described by Mitford or painted by Helen Paterson Allingham – images of archetypal, timeless, modest, rural tranquillity, still faithfully reproduced and sold in village shops in the third millennium, despite the advent of more upmarket art jigsaws.

When Mitford was writing about her universal village for the *Lady's Magazine*, she seems conscious, like Gaskell in *Cranford*, of describing a vanishing Golden Age (and one that would vanish all the more rapidly if others were to continue to uproot and replant wild flowers as vigorously and profligately as she). Does the brightly coloured jigsaw box cast a shadow and a question over what was or was not the Real Thing? Elizabeth Gaskell solved this problem with exceptional tact and grace in *Cranford* and *Cousin Phillis*, where the lament for a passing way of life is securely placed in a context of inevitable progress and change, but Mitford, writing to stay afloat (and writing village sketches because they paid better than the poetry, tragedies and historical dramas that she had considered her true *métier*), was pushed (like Alison Uttley, though for different reasons) into some kind of falsity of sweetness that strikes us uneasily now. She wrote for the market. It was her father's fault.

Helen Allingham (a family connection of Mrs Gaskell) also painted for the market, to support her ailing husband and her three children; her watercolours of Surrey cottages were for some years very popular, although they went out of fashion during her lifetime. But they lived on as jigsaws in the 1920s and 30s, enjoyed in an age when urban sprawl was destroying some of her subjects and vastly inflating the prices of others.

Mrs Sherwood would have disapproved intensely of Dr Mitford and his gambling, if not of his daughter's filial loyalty. She was by nature evangelical, censorious and dogmatic, and maybe her descriptions of the card parties of her grandparents' era are exaggerated. Yet her popular *The History of the Fairchild Family* is not an austere work, and it strikes a more lurid note than the cool, enlightened and rational tales of her contemporary Maria Edgeworth. Mrs Sherwood's stories were popular with children not for their moral lessons and interpolated hymns and prayers, but for their sadism and gluttony. They are packed with racy descriptions of childish naughtiness, violent retribution and sudden death, accompanied by tempting descriptions of roast fowls, venison, currant-and-raspberry pies, buttered toast and damascene plums. It is a rich and unwholesome mixture.

Children like unpleasant stories, and I was very fond of (though rather frightened by) some punitive tales called *The Misfortunes of Sophy* (*Les Malheurs de Sophie*), translated from the French of the Comtesse de Ségur (1799–1894) by Honor and Edgar Skinner. These volumes had a little of the Fairchild family spirit; they are full of horrors, which is why I remember them so well. Sophy was a greedy, hot-tempered, disobedient, rash and bold four-year-old, who stole sweets and tormented animals and let her wax doll melt. She was a bad little girl and a bad mother to her doll. Sophy was naughtier than I could think of being. Her worst misfortunes are associated with the disgrace of cutting off the heads of her mother's goldfish, and drowning her tortoise while trying to give it a bath. I was appalled and frightened by these events, for I would never knowingly have been unkind to animals, and continue to be shocked by the fact that Maggie Tulliver in *The Mill on the Floss* let her brother's rabbits die. I am surprised these Sophy stories were given to me when I was so little. I was still at East Hardwick when I first read them; the book was presented to me at Christmas 1944, 'for good progress', by N. Royston, Head Teacher. I was five years old.

Is it significant that Miss Royston described herself as Head Teacher, not as headmistress?

De Ségur's morality tales were very popular in France. They are part of Georges Perec's enormous tapestry. Madame Marcia, antique dealer, has a varied collection of wares in her shop, including lubricious animated watches, 'trinkets, curios, scientific instruments, lamps, jugs, boxes, porcelain, bisque ware, fashion plates, accessory furniture, etc.', and a clockwork mechanical toy that 'could have come straight out of *Le Bon Petit Diable*, that Victorian children's story-book by the Comtesse de Ségur: a horrible old hag, spanking a little boy'. In de Ségur, in the French style, the sadistic/erotic and the pedagogic meet. In Sherwood, there is no such overt recognition.

I was never exposed to the Fairchilds as a child, for they had already been out of fashion for a century, though I discovered one of Sherwood's popular evangelical stories in a tiny bijou edition hidden away in a drawer in Grandma Bloor's bedroom at Bryn. It was titled *Little Henry and his Bearer*, and it was a missionary work set in India. I wonder whether my grandmother had ever read it. She was not a religious woman, and she was not much of a reader. I don't think I ever saw her reading a book. I don't know what she would have made of the literary interests of so many of her direct descendants.

My grandmother preferred a game of cards. We used to play a game called Nap (after Napoleon) at Christmas, when Grandma and Auntie Phyl came to stay in Sheffield, and later, in Wylam-on-Tyne, where we lived when my father became county court judge of Northumberland. This, I think, was the only card game we ever played under my parents' roof. Grandma loved her game of Nap. We played for halfpennies, which was unusually exciting and seemed slightly irregular and un-Quakerly, but we never came to blows over the spoils of the kitty.

My father used to encourage me, a moody adolescent, to stop sulking in my bedroom reading books and to join the family card game. 'You shouldn't look down on games,' he said. 'What's the point of admiring Jane Austen, and then despising the way her characters spend their time? Come and play.' He actually said that, in more or less those words. It was a reproof that left its mark. He also confided, that same Christmas, that he dreaded taking Grandma Bloor her early morning cup of tea. 'Every morning, I think I'm going to find her dead in her bed,' he said. And she did look, had always looked, remarkably unhealthy – overweight, and with a bad yellowish colour. But she didn't die under his watch. She went home to Bryn, after that last family Christmas, and died in the brass bedstead from Leeds in the care of Joyce and Auntie Phyl.

My father always brought me an early morning cup of tea when I was staying as an adult at my parents' home, first in Northumberland, and then in Suffolk. I don't like an early morning cup of tea, I much prefer coffee at that hour, but I was touched by his kindness, so I always drank it, in gratitude. I could never have said I didn't want it.

Mrs Sherwood disapproved of cards, and she would have disapproved of halfpenny Nap, but she approved of geography, Biblical maps and the jigsaw. These were all classified as educational. The Fairchild children, Henry, Emily and Lucy, are instructed by their father in the use of the globe and the locations of Europe, Africa, America and the Garden of Eden (which, we are firmly told, is to be found upon the borders of the river Euphrates), and they are also introduced to dissected maps. Visiting a richer friend with a very tidy and well-stocked nursery ('enough to furnish a toy-shop'), the children are asked to select a toy each. Henry seizes upon a Noah's ark; Lucy 'chose a dissected map of England and Wales, and another which formed a picture, and Emily, a box of bricks and doorways, and pillars and chimneys, and other things for building houses'.

The dissected puzzle is condoned, and its subject matter is no longer confined to maps. It did not take publishers long to realize that the rapidly expanding market for children's books and games could be profitably exploited by the Spilsbury concept of deconstruction and reconstruction. You didn't have to stick with geography. If you could cut up maps for entertainment, you could cut up anything. You could teach Bible stories or the history of the kings and queens of England. You could illustrate *Pilgrim's Progress* or *Robinson Crusoe* or the adventures of John Gilpin. You could teach the alphabet, or natural history, or mathematics. Or you could provide pictures that had patriotic rather than purely educational content; soon the first royal images in a long tradition of royal jigsaw subjects began to appear, featuring Queen Victoria's coronation, and Queen Victoria and her consort riding in Windsor Park. Pictures of great events, such as the conflagration at the Tower of London (1841) or the Great Exhibition (1851), or the exploits of General Gordon were not bought principally for their instructional aspects.

Queen Victoria, like her successor Queen Elizabeth, did jigsaws. Whether she ever attempted those portraying herself is not, as far as I know, recorded. (Jigsaws of royal figures now tactfully avoid dissecting the royal face, and it is no longer fashionable to stitch the royal face in loyal wool-work as it was in Gaskell's and Mitford's day, though I did once attempt a tapestry cushion of Anne of Cleves. It remains unfinished because I did not like it much and, anyway, the wool ran out.) We do know that one evening the young queen co-opted Lord Melbourne and her Lord Chamberlain Lord Conyngham to help her with a puzzle. 'The pleasantest gayest evening I have passed for some time', she notes in her journal. 'I sat up until half past 11.' She also played Fox and Geese, very happily, with her betrothed, Prince Albert. This once-popular board game is classified by Irving Finkel as a hunting game, and may or may not have some resemblance to the game of 'marelles', which Edward IV played some four hundred years earlier, featuring 'two foxes and forty-six hounds of silver overgilt'. Edward played for high stakes, forcing him to borrow from the Medici to finance his games and his wars, but Victoria and Albert were more prudent.

The tension between edifying and unedifying games reflects the tension between edifying and unedifying books, and is deeply rooted in the history of publishing for children. For many years I remained uninterested in children's literature as a genre (although, of course, like Francis Spufford I remembered my own early reading with pleasure and gratitude) and I have watched its rise to critical prominence over the past fifteen years with some surprise. Danny Hahn, who knows this field well, has helped me to cope with the growing mass of material, and was invaluable in the updates of *The Oxford Companion to English Literature* when it was still under my surveillance. But through my quest for jigsaws, and my memories of East Hardwick and of Auntie Phyl as village schoolteacher, I have been led into a subject that, like the life of Alison Uttley, has provided several surprises.

XXXI

I don't think it was Auntie Phyl who taught me to read. She taught me many other skills, but I don't think reading was one of them, although, of course, she did teach several generations of Long Bennington children. I can't remember how I learned. Possibly I learned with Miss Cooper at East Hardwick. One story has it that when my father came back from the war, he spent time getting to know me by sitting with me to spell out the words of *The Radiant Way*, a popular children's primer of the day. This may or may not be true. 'Pat can sing. Mother can sing. Sing to Pat, Mother. Sing to Mother, Pat.' Many people of my age were brought up on those simple syllables.

My mother was good at teaching grammar to older children (she loved grammar) but she was impatient with the younger ones. She was better with her grandchildren, and one of my happiest memories of her is her story about my son Adam, a hyperactive little lad who, when admitted to her bed very early one morning when she was staying with us in our first London house in Highbury, asked her to read to him. She groaned and said it was too early for her to open her eyes. Never mind, said Adam, I know my letters, I'll read you out the letters, and you can tell me what they say. My mother admired his spirit.

The name of the archetypal village schoolteacher, Goody Two-Shoes, is still well remembered, though not many people know who she really was. She has taken on another meaning. In February 2007, sitting at a pavement café in the Canaries, I overheard one Englishwoman say to another, of an absent third party, 'She's a bit of a Goody Two-Shoes, isn't she?' I was pleased to hear her name, even if it was being taken somewhat in vain, because I had recently tracked down the story of which she is the eponymous heroine.

She appears in a miniature sixpenny volume published in 1765 by John Newbery, the first publisher to realize the commercial potential of the juvenile market. It's a tiny book, small enough to fit in the palm of an adult hand, and a copy of it raises a smile even from the blasé staff at the issue desk of the Rare Books Room in the British Library. (It would be very easy to pop into your pocket.) It has been attributed to Oliver Goldsmith, and the opening chapter, lamenting Farmer Meanwell's eviction by Mr Graspwell, does indeed have an echo of the indignant, elegiac mood and simple world of *The Deserted Village*. It tells the tale of the poor orphan Margery Meanwell, who, after the death of her parents, sleeps rough in barns, lives on berries from the hedges, wears rags and has only one shoe; she earns the name of Goody Two-Shoes when a benefactor provides her with a whole pair, which she shows off to the village, crying 'Two shoes, see two shoes!' She learns her letters diligently and then teaches them to other little children, becoming 'a trotting tutoress', travelling from cottage to cottage, until eventually she is given a schoolroom of her own.

The booklet, which is in part a reading primer in disguise, is illustrated by charming rustic woodcuts of farms, cottages, children, birds and beasts, playfully attributed to 'Michael Angelo of the Vatican'. The child reader is addressed informally as each new picture appears. As Ralph the Raven is introduced the narrator prompts, 'and a fine bird he is. Do look at him.' We sense the comfortable presence of a kind aunt, pointing at the pictures as the pages turn. Alphabet games are introduced into the schoolroom plot, and it emerges that Ralph the Raven and Tom the Pigeon can learn to distinguish their letters too, thus anticipating the research of physiologists in Cambridge in the 1970s, who established that a pigeon could indeed learn the letters of the alphabet, even when they were disguised by different typefaces.

(The possibility of teaching animals to read and write has long fascinated humans. Pliny, in an affecting section on the sensibilities and talents of elephants in his *Natural History*, describes one that could write in Greek: 'Thus have I written, and made an offering of the Celticke spoils' is the sentence attributed to this clever beast in Philemon Holland's elegant translation. It must have taken some mastering. In 1785, a wonderful pig 'well versed in all languages' became the talk of London town, where his skill was portrayed in a fine print by Thomas Rowlandson. Robert Southey, in 1807, recalled that 'the learned pig was in his day a far greater object of admiration to the English nation than ever was Sir Isaac Newton'. Wordsworth also knew this pig.)

The tender-hearted story of Goody Two-Shoes is one of the best known but by no means the first of Newbery's productions for children. *A Little Pretty Pocket-Book*, which appeared some twenty years earlier in 1744, claims that place. It too had a brightly coloured jacket of Dutch flowered and gilt paper, and it consisted of a medley of rhymes and songs and alphabet games 'intended for the Instruction and Amusement of Little Master Tommy and Pretty Miss Polly, with Two Letters from Jack the Giant-Killer and also a Ball and a Pincushion'. (If you bought it without the ball and the pincushion, it cost twopence less.) Jack the Giant Killer was the monster-hero of earlier unedifying stories, loved by children but deplored by governesses, and here Jack is enlisted in the cause of virtue, instructing Tommy and Polly how to stick pins into either the red or the black side of their toy in order to gain merit. The book contains woodcuts showing children's games, each (somewhat randomly) attached to a letter of the alphabet, in a 'New Attempt to teach Children the Use of the English Alphabet, by Way of Diversion'. There are pictures of cricket, kites, maypoles, marbles, and shuttlecock, as well as many other sports and diversions, but there are, of course, at this early date no pictures showing children doing dissected puzzles. The nearest we get to this kind of activity is a picture of three characters sitting round a table playing a game of 'Squares', which looks like a card game but was probably a concealed advertisement for another of Newbery's educational games, the 'Sett of Fifty-Six Squares'.

The sticking of pins into balls and pincushions cunningly added to the pretty pocket book an element of interaction and physical activity for fidgety fingers. Alphabet lottery books also exploited this teaching method by encouraging children to learn their letters by sticking pins through the pages. A little alphabet book published by P. Norbury instructed that 'As soon as the Child can speak, let him stick a Pin through the side of the Leaf where the Pictures are, at the Letter on the other side, which you would teach him; thus let him do till he has by many trials run the Pin through the Letter.' In this manner, the child could learn C for Cock and Crocodile, or even X for Xerxes and Xantippe. I didn't find the instructions on where to stick the pins very clear, and it would have been unwise to experiment with a British Library copy, but no doubt a helpful schoolteacher or mother or governess or aunt would have showed you the technique. And as I was staring at Norbury's booklet, I suddenly remembered Auntie Phyl's sewing cards at Bryn. With a large needle and thread you could stitch the outline of a horse, or a dog, or a tulip. This was curiously satisfying, if not especially creative or intellectual. The products were not objects of beauty.

And Norbury's alphabet technique reminded me of something else. Sitting in Rare Books and Music, musing on children dead and gone, I began to see an explanation for a passage of a memoir that had been puzzling and distressing me for years.

Robert Southey, in his autobiography, which was written as a series of letters to a friend, describes his early childhood in the late eighteenth century. (He was born in 1774.) He was a lonely child, brought up in Bath between the ages of two and six largely by his eccentric aunt, Miss Tyler. He had no playmates, little exercise and was never allowed 'to do anything in which by possibility I might dirt [sic] myself'. He was obliged to share her bed, and as she always went to bed very late, he had to lie motionless for hours until she woke in the morning in order not to disturb her. 'These were, indeed, early and severe lessons of patience. My poor little wits were upon the alert at those tedious hours of compulsory idleness, fancying figures and combinations of form in the curtains, and watching the light from the crevices of the window-shutters.' His aunt was, luckily, acquainted with the Newbery family, and he was presented with a whole set of delectable Newbery books, 'a gilt regiment', 'splendidly bound in the flowered gilt and Dutch paper of former days'. Miss Tyler was also an impassioned theatregoer, 'an amateur and a patroness of the stage'; as he was considered too old to be put to bed before the performance began and could not be left alone with the servants, she took him to many incomprehensible yet delightful performances in Bath and Bristol: 'I had seen more plays before I was seven years old than I have ever since I was twenty.' He loved *Titus Andronicus* and *Cymbeline* and *As You Like It*, but *The Knight of the Burning Pestle* perplexed him terribly. Its sense of humour, he thought, was not accessible to a child.

His aunt, who hoarded everything except money, had a collection of playbills that Southey says Dr Burney might have envied, and they became one of the substitutes devised for my amusement instead of healthy and natural sports. I was encouraged to prick them with a pin, letter by letter: and for want of anything better, became as fond of this employment as women sometimes are of netting or any ornamental work. I learnt to do it with great precision, pricking the larger types by their outline, so that when they were held up to the window they were bordered with spots of light. The object was to illumine the whole bill in this manner. I have done it to hundreds; and yet I can well remember the sort of dissatisfied and damping feeling, which the sight of one of these bills would give me, a day or two after it had been finished and laid by. It was like an illumination when half the lamps are gone out. This amusement gave my writing-masters no little trouble; for, in spite of all their lessons, I held a pen as I had been used to hold the pin.

This passage, when I first came across it, struck me as little short of tragic: the thought of this poor solitary child, employed at this pointless indoor activity, has haunted me over the years, and I hope I have at last here found it a home. I need to draw it to wider attention.

And the reason why I had dipped into Southey's childhood memoir was in itself a little sad. I came across it when I was first revising *The Oxford Companion to English Literature* in the early 1980s. I had tried in vain to find a scholar eager to revise the entry on Southey, but nobody seemed to want him, nobody would adopt him, so I had to do him myself. (I got left with an odd crew, as I suppose I should have predicted: some so difficult that none dared take them on, some so obscure that none wished to take them on, and some plain dull.) Southey, unlike his friends Wordsworth and Coleridge, was and is deeply unfashionable. On *University Challenge* in October 2006 nobody recognized him as the author of the once-famous and long-lingering 'The Battle of Blenheim', with its bitter refrain: 'It was a famous victory.' The poem itself, his last claim to fame, was forgotten. In the revised entry in the *Oxford Companion,* I had to reduce Southey's sad revelation of his long loneliness to a few words, but at least I registered it, thus improving on the absence of any reference to his childhood in the volume of my predecessor, Paul Harvey.

I now see that perhaps Southey's pricking of the playbills was not quite as bizarre and deprived an activity as I had at first thought. Maybe it was merely an extension of the Norbery, learn-your-alphabet book-pricking, and not much more pointless than playing with a dissected map. So I need not have felt so sorry for Southey after all. And he lived on, despite Miss Tyler, because of Miss Tyler, to enjoy a long and successful life surrounded by friends and a large family. He married for love the daughter of a Bristol tradeswoman, whereupon Miss Tyler cast him off for ever, and eventually his home Greta Hall in the Lake District became something of a commune – not quite the pantisocracy of which he, Coleridge and his friend Robert Lovell had once dreamed, but a warm and crowded family home. De Quincey, in his essay on 'Southey, Wordsworth and Coleridge' in *Tait's Edinburgh Magazine* (1839), described it thus:

> The house itself – Greta Hall – stood upon a little eminence...
> overhanging the river Greta. There was nothing remarkable
> in its internal arrangements: in all respects, it was a very plain
> unadorned family dwelling; large enough, by a little
> contrivance, to accommodate two or, in some sense, three
> families, viz., Mr. Southey and *his* family; Mr. Coleridge
> and *his*; together with Mrs. Lovell, who, when her son was with
> her, might be said to compose a third.

Mrs Southey, Mrs Coleridge and Mrs Lovell were sisters, and Southey liked to describe the hill on which Greta Hall was built as 'the aunt-hill'. As well as aunts and nephews and nieces, Greta Hall also housed successive generations of cats, including Lord Nelson, Ovid, Virgil, Prester John and Hurlyburlybuss; it was Southey's belief that 'a house is never said to be perfectly furnished for enjoyment, unless there is a child in it rising three years old, and a kitten rising three weeks.'

(Southey and the three Fricker sisters spoke with a West Country accent; Wordsworth, however, presumably pronounced 'aunt-hill' as 'anthill', and when I was little I always called Auntie Phyl 'Antie'. I knew no other pronunciation.)

Southey has been credited with writing one of the best-known of all children's stories, *The Three Bears*, which survives in a prettified version. The character we know as Goldilocks was originally an old female vagrant, destined for committal to the House of Correction. Southey wrote this tale to be read aloud, preferably by several voices, by Mamma, or Papa, or, as he said, 'some fond Uncle, or kind Aunt'. The picture of a happy family gathered round a fireside reminds us of the long hours Southey spent as a boy lying painfully bored and lonely in bed, longing for the day to begin.

Not many writers describe boredom as well as Southey did. It is an ignoble and shaming state to which few are confident enough to admit. Graham Greene and Alberto Moravia admitted to it, and so, as I have noted, did my father. But most do not. (In 1960 Moravia published a novel, *La Noia*, which has recently reappeared in translation with the title *Boredom*; it originally appeared in English as *The Empty Canvas*, because his English-language publishers were, wrongly, afraid that boredom would not sell. I snapped it up on the strength of the title alone, and although it did not prefigure Perec's obsession with jigsaws, as I had hoped it might, it had some interesting material about an artist destroying his own canvases, which connects with the allied theme of the ephemeral sandcastle.)

The woodcuts in *Little Goody Two-Shoes* portray a vanishing world, and Newbery's productions mark a transition from an England still largely rural, to a country increasingly dominated by the purchasing power of the metropolis. The Newberys originally came from Berkshire and John Newbery's father, like the father of Little Goody Two-Shoes, was a farmer. The woodcuts remind me of the simple landscape I thought I could see in the deeply rural, flat, agricultural countryside round Bryn, where the cows and bullocks are to this day known as 'beasts', and where until recently the watermill by the river was used to grind flour. But these Newbery books were purchased for town children, who would enjoy the farmyard pictures of animals with which they were no longer necessarily familiar at first-hand. Children's toys and books have always harked back to the idyll of Home Farm. We learn our letters from building blocks that represent a way of life that has gone, and children who have never seen a live cow or a pig may discover them in illustrated alphabets and board games.

The Newberys moved to London in the 1740s and established themselves in the busy heart of eighteenth-century book production. *A Little Pretty Pocket-Book* was published at the sign of the Bible and Crown, but Newbery soon moved to the more famous Bible and Sun, near the Chapter House in St Paul's Churchyard. John Spilsbury, the mapmaker and the first puzzle maker, operated from Russell Court, off Drury Lane, a neighbourhood that is still home to cartographers, as well as to antiquarian and second-hand book dealers. The book and toy trade had its own well-defined territory, much of it within the City of London; it encompassed St Paul's Churchyard, Holborn, Covent Garden, Cheapside, the Strand, Fleet Street, Cornhill and Clerkenwell. Here many of the significant figures in the history of children's publishing were clustered, including the Newberys, their successor John Harris, John and Edward Wallis, and the Darton family. The geography of this neighbourhood was a board game of its own, with its interlocking lanes and alleys and rows and terraces and courtyards. J. H. Harvey Darton, the distinguished historian of children's literature, writing nearly two hundred years later in 1932 in the *Cornhill Magazine*, describes Ludgate Square as 'a small recondite Square... a kind of rectilinear maze, such as I liked to contrive on paper when I was a boy. It can be reached only by narrow one-way traffic lanes, and half-secret footpaths under archways.' He edited *The Chatterbox* story-book and annual from a building as 'elusive as Todgers's and as neat as a nest of Chinese boxes'.

And even today, after sixty years of blitz and demolition and grandiose post-modern reconstruction, some memories of the old region linger; there are still arches and byways and terraces and footpaths and courtyards and dank areas sprouting with stubborn buddleia. You can still get lost in the urban maze. But in the third millennium the only shop approaching a print shop or a bookshop in St Paul's Churchyard is a branch of Clinton Cards, witness, some would claim, to a new illiteracy. All the bookshops have gone. (Paternoster Row was wiped out in all but name on the night of 29 December 1940, along with six million books.) Two hundred years ago, this was the centre of the new world of juvenile literature. Everybody knew exactly where to go in London for children's books and games. Here is an extract from *Dame Partlet's Farm* (1804) published by John Harris, who succeeded John Newbery's widow Elizabeth Newbery as publisher:

At Harris's, St Paul's Churchyard,
Good children meet a sure reward;
In coming home the other day
I heard a little master say,

For every penny there he took
He had receiv'd a little book,
With covers neat, and cuts so pretty,
There's not its like in all the city;
And that for twopence he could buy
A story-book would make one cry;
For little more a book of riddles:
Then let us not buy drums or fiddles,
Nor yet be stops at pastry-cooks,
But spend our money all in books;
For when we've learnt each book by heart
Mamma will treat us with a tart.

A book rewarded by a tart: a pleasant bribery, the best of both worlds.

The publishers who followed in the Newberys' footsteps became more and more inventive. They made little boxed collections and cabinets of booklets that appealed to the eyes and to the fingers as well as to the mind. Movable books with 'turn up' or 'lift the flap' devices, peepshows, harlequinades and dress-the-doll books proliferated. Printers S. and J. Fuller, operating from a shop fancifully called the Temple of Fancy in Rathbone Place, London, created a dress-the-doll book in 1810 titled *The History of Little Fanny*, in which the head of Fanny could be inserted in seven different, hand-coloured, cut-out costumes, to the accompaniment of a moral verse telling us that Fanny will come to no good if she insists on playing with her doll instead of reading a good book – another device that has its cake and eats it. F. C. Westley's *The Paignion* (*c.*1830) is a slot-book with sixty-five cut-out, movable figures of adults, children, nurses and babies, and twelve delicately coloured, hand-painted scenes from everyday life such as the Pastry Cook's, the Chemist's, the Bazaar and the Drawing Room, with which a child could create many varied narratives and tableaux.

These were expensive items intended to be treasured, but the cut-out, like the jigsaw, may also provide one of the easiest and cheapest of home-made entertainments. You don't have to aspire to the artistry of Mrs Delany to gain satisfaction from this activity. In the opening section of Virginia Woolf's *To the Lighthouse*, six-year-old James Ramsay is amusing himself on his summer holidays by cutting out a picture of a refrigerator from the illustrated catalogue of the Army and Navy Stores, while Mrs Ramsay sits by him knitting a brown stocking. When he has finished the refrigerator, and it has been duly admired, she tries to find him a rake or a mowing machine, which would need 'great skill and care in cutting out', and thus distract him from his father's gloomy weather forecast. Children still like cutting out, as did little King Louis XIII. We can all remember those blunt-ended scissors.

I have a clear recollection of sitting under the privet hedge of Auntie Phyl's house in wartime Doncaster, playing with a paper doll that I could dress up in a Shirley Temple outfit, or in paper garments snipped out of fashion magazines or sewing patterns. The hedge towered above me, and I made myself a little house in its sour earthy roots. And when my children were much the same age as I was then, I made them two paper dolls, called Pierre and Cinabelle, which I persuaded them were so precious that they could only be taken out of their cabinet drawer as a reward for excellent behaviour. They were a special treat. The children entered into this bizarre collusion with surprising enthusiasm. We were in Paris at the time, living on a travel bursary, which is why the dolls had French names, and why we had no television. We had to make our own bedtime amusements in the rue Blomet.

XXXII

Booksellers, book dealers, printmakers and cabinetmakers have always encouraged the habit of collecting. Cabinets inspire a sense of order, which parents are keen to encourage, and a manufacturer who unites an appeal to the collecting impulse with an attractive container has hit on a winning combination. Children are notoriously bad at putting their toys away (see the controlling Mrs Sherwood for a vivid description of an untidy nursery, littered with 'English, French and Dutch toys, which generally lie pell-mell in any corner where the careless, listless, toy-saturated child may have thrown or kicked them') but some containers are so attractive that the act of restoring their contents may be presented as a pleasure in itself.

It is probable that Lady Charlotte Finch encouraged the little princes and princesses to take the responsibility for returning the pieces of their Spilsbury maps to the correct drawers of the mahogany cabinets with their own royal hands – though this in fact is not an easy task, as they have to be fitted in with great care, or the drawers won't shut. One of Lady Charlotte's successors, Miss Planta, bore witness to the fact that 'Princess Elizabeth is a lovely little fat sensible thing and so tidy that she never leaves her needles, or scrap of work without putting them all in a tiny bag, for the purpose', so one imagines that efforts towards discovering the fun of tidiness were considered part of a girl's education.

Jane Austen made a tiny bag for her sister-in-law, inside which was 'a little rolled up housewife', furnished with minikin needles and fine thread. In the housewife was a tiny pocket, and in the pocket was a slip of paper written as with a crow quill, with a little dedicatory poem. Austen's nephew wrote: 'It is the kind of object that some benevolent fairy might be supposed to give as a reward to a diligent little girl.'

Auntie Phyl, it has to be admitted, was not a tidy person. She let things lie. Her kitchen table was home to scores of objects, and must have been the despair of Joyce as she tried to introduce order and cleanliness to Bryn. My mother, who was a tidy person, found visits to Bryn in later years trying on this score, and occasionally remarked that the exemplary neatness of Joyce's cottage made her feel ashamed of her sister's squalor. In *The Peppered Moth* I described Auntie Dora's table:

> The kitchen table, once a plain wood, was covered with an
> unappealing pink-check stick-on badly fitted plastic coating,
> which began to peel round the edges, but stuck there, barely
> wiped, for decades. Biscuit tins gave way to – or rather, alas,
> were joined by – plastic boxes, Tupperware, melaware,
> polythene. Drawers burst and shelves buckled with hoardings.
> The new post-war rubbish was more durable than the old.
> It did not perish.

Auntie Phyl had many of the characteristics of the Good Aunt, but an old-maid neatness was not one of them. There was an anarchic streak in her. In later years one of our entertainments was to go up the rickety ladder to the apple-loft bedroom, where she stored apples from the orchard, and throw those that had gone rotten out of the window into the garden below. The loft smelled of cider and fermentation, and the soft, brown, decaying, apples smashed and splashed into the grass and weeds beneath.

The garden was too big for her. Without Joyce and Eddie she would never have kept it under any kind of control.

One of the most extraordinary of my childhood memories is of the day when we were allowed to set the field behind the house on fire. The grass had grown high and dry and yellow, and we were let loose in it with a box of matches. Even at the time I thought this was odd, and now it seems unbelievable, but it was so. We ran around, igniting clump after clump, and watching the flames spread and the grass flicker and then scorch and then blacken. It was thrilling. It was arson and anarchy. The flames flickered in my sleeping vision all night long.

Auntie Phyl was not as conventional as she looked. One day she told me about her walk to the village dump by the river. I remember that dump: it was, when I was a small child, full of archaeological treasures, like old marbles and patterned bits of broken crockery, but as the throwaway society flourished it began to receive larger and less attractive detritus. One day, walking the dog (at that time a bad-tempered Staffordshire bull terrier named Hanley), Auntie Phyl reported that she had discovered a large, brand-new brassiere, 'just my size', but that she had resisted taking it home with her. More worryingly, she also found a horse's head. 'I let Hanley have a bit of it,' she said, calmly. 'And when I took her back the next day she had a bit more.'

I can't remember now whether I ever put this dump incident in a novel. I don't think I did. I don't think I found a place for it. When you can't remember whether or not you've written about something before, it's time to stop.

XXXIII

A tiny bag, a tiny box, a baby house, a doll's thimble, Tom Thumb, Thumbelina. A cherry stone carved with scenes from the Old Testament, a minuscule, medieval, ivory sphere containing minuscule ivory figures playing chess, an antique intaglio the size of a thumbnail cut with nymphs by a fountain. Miniaturization is an industry of its own, beloved of connoisseurs, collectors, craftsmen, souvenir manufacturers and tourists, and it is also well represented in the book trade. At the turn of the eighteenth century John Marshall marketed a variety of boxed books and cards, for which he favoured titles like 'The Doll's Library' or 'The Doll's Casket'. His *Infant's Library*, manufactured around 1800, is a model bookcase containing sixteen little volumes. Adults today remember with affection their Nutshell and Thimble Libraries and their boxed sets of Beatrix Potter. Alison Uttley, who loved the diminutive, possessed miniature volumes of Shakespeare, the *Iliad* and the Greek New Testament as well as dolls' teasets.

Princes and popes and scholars of the Renaissance assembled *Kunstkammer* and cabinets and *studioli* housing paintings, miniatures, shells, sculptures, minerals, coins, jewels, games and scientific instruments, sometimes with the avowed ambition of bringing all the world's learning into a single space. The cabinet (like Auntie Phyl's kitchen table, but in a more orderly though sometimes in as random a manner) would contain everything. In 1782, a singular experiment in educational publishing on these principles was conducted by a German theologian named Johann Siegmund Stoy, who came from Nuremberg, the home of toys. He created a *Picture Academy for the Young*, which purported to offer a comprehensive view of the world's knowledge. It consisted of a compartmented box measuring seventeen by twelve inches, containing 468 copperplate engravings. It was an illustrated encyclopaedia in miniature, but an interactive one that you could rearrange using a complicated system of cross-references. This elaborate and unique object does not seem to have found any imitators in England, but the book dealers of St Paul's Churchyard appealed to some of the same instincts with their miniature pocket books and boxes, their curiosities and novelties. And Spilsbury, with his maps, put the world in a mahogany drawer.

The theme of pictures-within-pictures, of gallery paintings showing walls thickly plastered with densely hung pictures, and floors stacked with plaster casts and curiosities, has a lasting attraction for jigsaw-puzzle manufacturers. The puzzle solver gets many paintings for the price of one, and the satisfaction of being able to complete each small area separately, and then join the pieces into a pre-designed whole.

In 2006 the Courtauld Gallery mounted an exhibition based on a book titled *The Theatre of Painting* or *Theatrum Pictorium*, compiled by the Dutch painter and curator David Teniers the Younger. This handsome volume, published in 1660, is the first known illustrated catalogue of a collection of paintings, and it contains etchings and engravings of masterpieces by artists who include Titian, Raphael, Veronese and Giorgione. These works, which had been acquired by Archduke Leopold Wilhem of Habsburg, were copied from the originals in oil on wood (with one or two in oil on canvas) by Teniers, and Teniers' copies were in turn copied by engravers and etchers for the printed catalogue. This Borgesian replication provides food for speculation about the strange attractions of reproduction and miniaturization. Teniers was clearly captivated by the notion of pictures-within-pictures, and copies of copies, for he also painted large gallery paintings showing rooms crowded with wall-to-wall masterpieces being viewed by fashionable cognoscenti, idle spectators and the inevitable little dogs. His versions of the Old Masters are works of art in their own right, often adding a more sombre (and perhaps more secular) gloss to the Italian originals.

The Courtauld exhibition also contained a small portrait of an oil-on-canvas Doge, which scholar Margaret Klinge has suggested may have been cut out of a larger gallery painting of grouped figures, now lost. It is, perhaps, the surviving missing piece of a now dispersed and irrecoverable jigsaw. And the archduke's collection was in itself a collection of dispersed pieces, assembled from the spoils of earlier collectors forced to sell because of wars and disasters. Teniers captured and preserved all these works doubly and trebly, in a complex study in refraction.

Just as the Teas-with-Hovis plates or the kilted officer with his turbaned Sikh servant in the original Camp Coffee advertisement offer a vista of diminishing but perpetual self-reproduction, so paintings of cabinets and galleries offer an endless journey into an ever smaller and more toy-like world. This is more disquieting than reassuring.

Susan Stewart, in her essay on souvenirs and collections (*On Longing*), suggests that 'The miniature, linked to nostalgic versions of childhood and history, presents a diminutive, and thereby manipulatable, version of experience, a version which is domesticated and protected from contamination.' This is not very elegantly phrased, but it is true, and it clearly connects with the world of

Alison Uttley as well as with the cabinets of popes. Alison Uttley, as we know, was a supreme manipulator.

My father liked Camp Coffee, and we always had a bottle of this dark-brown syrup on the go in the kitchen cupboard. He maintained that if you didn't think of it as coffee, it was very pleasant. Sometimes we drank it at elevenses, but more often we used it to flavour cakes and custards. I like chicory in most of its forms, but it's a long time since I tried a cup of Camp.

Georges Perec was inspired by the Camp advertisement. In *La Vie: Mode d'Emploi* he describes a case of whisky by the name of Stanley's Delight, the label of which

> shows an explorer of white race, wearing a pith helmet but dressed in Scottish national dress: a predominantly yellow and red kilt, a broad tartan over his shoulder, a studded leather belt supporting a fringed sporran, and a small dirk slipped into his sock-top; he strides at the head of a column of 9 blacks each carrying on his head a case of *Stanley's Delight*, with a label depicting the same scene.

Camp has now changed its logo; it has been updated for modern times, with master and servant sitting side by side in egalitarian racial harmony. Robert Opie, scholar of advertising (whose museum contains a similar whisky advertisement for an imperial Edwardian brand of which I have never heard), claims that the new Camp logo is not much liked in India. Indians, he says, prefer the traditional.

Georges Perec was preoccupied by commercial art and advertising copy, by replicas, forgeries and transformations. He had worked in market research and he knew a great deal about the business of advertising. His first novel, *Things*, was intended, he said, to explore the way 'the language of advertising is reflected in us', and his two young protagonists, Sylvie and Jerome, drop-out students who 'had become market researchers by necessity and not by choice', are enthralled by the world of contemporary objects of desire. So is Perec himself, though in a slightly different mode.

La Vie: Mode d'Emploi is packed with detailed descriptions not only of promotional blotters and jigsaw puzzles, but also of elaborately faked works of art, mechanical toys and many kinds of kitsch. Engravings feature conspicuously, for engraving is the art of producing multiples, although Perec is equally interested (as was Baudrillard) in the concept of the unique object, the *unicum*, or uniquity – a concept inseparable from the twinned concept of the forgery and the fake. He would have been impressed by the achievements of the Greenhalgh family of forgers, based in Bolton, whose first effort was an implausible silver medieval reliquary containing a wooden fragment of the True Cross, which they claimed to have unearthed in 1989 in a park in Preston; they went on to hoodwink several distinguished institutions with their Assyrian and Egyptian antiquities. Their finest coup was a ceramic faun allegedly by Gauguin for which the Chicago Institute of Art paid good money. Shaun Greenhalgh made all these objects in his garden shed.

One of the many stories in Perec's maze of stories describes a more elaborate hoax. It concerns the duping of Bartlebooth's great-uncle James Sherwood, a Lancashire-born druggist who emigrated to America where he made a colossal fortune in Boston from ginger-based cough pastilles. He then attempted to alleviate the neurasthenia and lethargy of excessive wealth by collecting *unica*. 'In the jargon of the rare book, antique and curio trade,' Perec tells us, 'an *unicum*, as its name implies, is an object which is the only one of its kind.' This rather vague definition, he says, covers several classes of object, which include a monstrous double bass for two musicians, an animal species like the tendrac *Dasogale fontoynanti* from Madagascar, a postage stamp or engraving of which only one example survives, the pen that signed the Treaty of Versailles, the boxing gloves Dempsey wore to defeat Carpentier on 21 July 1921, or Rita Hayworth's glove from the film *Gilda*. 'Scepticism and passion,' he informs us, 'are the two traits of *unica*-lovers.'

The victim of an immensely lengthy and elaborate hoax, involving forged documents, hired actors, fake scenery, and a charade of vendors, Sherwood is brought to believe that he is on the track of the Holy Vase in which Joseph of Arimathaea captured the blood springing from the wounds of Christ. He purchases for $1 million a vase that turns out to be 'a slightly dissimulated gugglet of sorts, bought at a souk in Nabeul', but doubt is cast on the success of this deception when it appears that Sherwood is less downcast by the loss of a third of his fortune than might have been expected. Had he enjoyed the play-acting more than he would have enjoyed the acquisition of a real treasure, and regarded it as 'a powerful palliative for his melancholy', or had he paid the syndicate of forgers in faked twenty-dollar bills? Had he paid for a fake with fakes? The questions remain unanswered.

Perec's densely packed storehouse of a novel is stuffed with descriptions of pictures-within-pictures, with marquetry and mosaics, stained-glass windows, scrimshaw and globular glass snowstorms, patterned tiles and parquet floors, maps and plaster casts of Beethoven, inflatable dolls and patent ashtrays, paperweights and biscuit tins, souvenirs and old postcards and other items of bric-a-brac. Perec also lists a large monastery transported stone by stone from France to Connecticut and a simulacrum of Chartres cathedral constructed out of lard. The prose grows lyrical as it evokes, sublimely, 'a ceiling divided into octagonal sections, decorated in gold and silver, and more exquisitely worked than any jewel', and, bathetically, 'a linoleum mosaic of jade and azure and cinnabar rhomboids'. The novel is an unparalleled celebration of mimicry, artistry, craftsmanship, detritus and all the half-arts that have ever been invented, and it seems to me to contain some clues to the very heart of memory and of my personal past.

Which is odd, when I consider how different my life has been from Perec's, how long it took me to discover his work, and how hostile I was when young to most of the French avant-garde. I read Sartre and de Beauvoir eagerly, but I disliked the *nouveau roman* when I first encountered it at Cambridge (although I liked the cinema versions, such as *Last Year at Marienbad*) and the very thought of writing a book without the letter E irritated me. I thought this was frivolity itself. Games-playing! Games-playing! Life was too short for stuff like that, and books were too important.

I am a convert. I eat my words. Perec was a deeply serious man.

My interest in his work, however, although intense, remains selective. I greatly admire *Life: A User's Manual*, with its densely physical evocation of life in an apartment house in Paris, its cellular design, its cleverly overlapping stories, its obsessions, its closely observed descriptions of jigsaw practice and jigsaw mania, its sociological acuity, its multitude of 'things'. (Was he influenced, I wonder, by Zola's pullulating apartment-block novel, *Pot-Bouille*?) But I can't follow (or perhaps I mean I can't be bothered to follow) the structural use of the chess problem known as the Knight's Tour, which apparently involves moving a knight around the sixty-four squares of a chessboard without landing twice on the same square, and I can't grasp his employment of the Graeco-Latin bi-square. (I was unfortunately allowed to drop mathematics at the age of twelve, and that must be my excuse.)

I love Perec's lists, but I don't like some of his word games. I can't take the over-elaboration of the homophone experiments in which he phonetically distorts a name or an English proverb. Here are a couple of ludicrous examples: *Loup de wigwam: bêtes aux veines* (wigwam wolf: animal of the veins) becomes Ludwig van Beethoven, and *All's well that ends well* becomes *Alice vêle; Satan, soûl, hèle.* James Hadley Chase as *J'aime ça, les laides chaises* works a bit better, but even that's not a very convincing correspondence.

On the other hand, I very much like two homophones I came across recently in Gregory Benford's introduction to a translation of Jules Verne's *From the Earth to the Moon*, and I think Verne's admirer Perec would have liked them too. Benford, describing Verne's influence on other science-fiction writers, writes:

> Verne even influenced those who didn't quite know who he was. Isaac Asimov once told me that when he was still a young science fiction fan he found himself listening to a lecture about a great foreign writer, a master of fantastic literature. But Asimov couldn't recognise the name. Giving the French pronunciation, the lecturer said 'Surely you must know Zuell Pfern', and described *From the Earth to the Moon.* Asimov replied in his Brooklyn accent, 'Oh, you mean Jewels Voine!

That's a Perec kind of anecdote. 'Jewels Voine' is beautiful. Hyman Kaplan couldn't have put it better.

Wilful experiment used to annoy me. I was a *Mimesis* woman, brought up on the great Eric Auerbach and his magisterial version of what he calls 'The Representation of Reality in Western Literature', which he wrote in exile during the Second World War in Istanbul. (His concluding chapter, titled 'The Brown Stocking', discusses *To the Lighthouse* and James Ramsay cutting out his refrigerator.) I gained much and I missed much through this bias. I am catching up now.

I have even come to like the visual artists connected with Oulipo (they sometimes call themselves Oupeinpo) who have invented ingenious games with well-known images, fracturing them, swivelling them, slicing them, restructuring them and turning them inside out. I used to think this kind of experiment akin to a schoolboy's painting a moustache on the *Mona Lisa* or adding arms to the *Venus of Milo* and thinking it funny, but, again, I've changed my mind. Their efforts include reversing the image of Ingres's *Grande Odalisque* by turning her around on her couch in sixty-four slices so that she faces in the opposite direction, and creating new paintings from composite Old Master sources in elaborate collages. Some of the results are surprisingly attractive. (They claim to distance themselves from the collages of Surrealism by introducing technical constraints, but in my view this distancing is in itself something of a technicality.)

One of their proposals, the *Module Oupeinpien Universel* (*MOU*), devised at a meeting of Oulipo on 11 January 1997, is for a jigsaw described as a 'puzzlomorphic trammel-net, all of whose pieces have an identical shape', which can be permuted indefinitely. 'Every painting in the world (and all its reproductions), every printed page and poster, the entirety of existing images could thus be cut up using the *MOU*, and reassembled in a near-infinity of combinations.' Tristan Bastit (who is a real painter, not a fantasy figure) suggested creating 'a Potential History of Art (text and illustrations) on the *MOU* principle by cutting up the 4,008 pages of the *Universal History of Art* (in 10 volumes)'. This could be achieved, he said calmly, with the help of a jigsaw punch.

XXXIV

Johann Siegmund Stoy, inventor of the boxed picture academy, appears to have been an isolated and eccentric figure, whereas the Oulipeans thrived (and still thrive) on interchange. Perec, who has written so powerfully of the experience of half-crazed loneliness, was, paradoxically, for much of his life a gregarious and clubbable man, with many close friendships. Most of the early children's publishers were similarly interconnected, though by patterns of kinship rather than friendship; they came from closely knit family businesses, which intermarried and created long-lived dynasties. F. J. Harvey Darton, who chronicled the rise of these family groups, came from one of the most powerful; he was the great-great-grandson of William Darton, the founder of a durable publishing venture. The Dartons were Quakers, whereas the Spilsburys (John, the puzzle maker, and his older brother Jonathan) had leanings towards the Moravian Church, of which Jonathan became a member. An educational purpose informed both families, although John, with his dissected puzzles and printed kerchiefs, clearly had a commercial instinct as sound as John Newbery's.

The talented Spilsburys, unlike the Dartons, did not found a dynasty, although as we have seen John Spilsbury's name is now firmly recorded in history (or at least in the *ODNB* and the records of *University Challenge*) and the intricacies of the Spilsbury family tree have been disentangled. The name of Darton, however, is threaded through the long history of children's literature, and is still current. William Darton (1755–1819), writer, printer, bookseller, stationer and engraver, was the son of the landlord of the Coach and Six Horses in Tottenham, Middlesex, and was apprenticed to an engraver before setting up his own business. He became a Quaker, joining the Society of Friends in 1777, and ten years later began to trade in 1787 in White Lion Alley, Birchin Lane. It was from this address that he published *Engravings for teaching the elements of English history and chronology after the manner of dissected maps for teaching geography*, which has a claim to be the earliest historical jigsaw puzzle. He soon moved two streets to the east to 55 Gracechurch Street, where he formed a long-lasting partnership with printer Joseph Harvey (1764–1841). Darton's son, another William Darton (1781–1854), was to pursue the same line of business in the same neighbourhood, from an address in Holborn Hill.

Joseph Harvey, like the Dartons, was a Quaker, and the firm of Darton and Harvey, which flourished for well over a hundred years, had a strong ethical policy. It published anti-slavery literature for adults, and its many publications for children included works by two immensely successful sisters, Jane and Anne Taylor, who came from another prolific and thriving family business of writers and engravers. Anne wrote 'My Mother' (*Original Poems for Infant Minds*, 1804), and Jane wrote 'Twinkle, twinkle, little star' (*Rhymes for the Nursery*, 1806), which inspired many commercial spin-offs. Darton and Harvey also published the formidable Mrs Sherwood, whose memoirs were edited by F. J. Harvey Darton. It was William Darton Junior of Holborn Hill who invested heavily in table games and puzzles; his surviving products include an illustrated version of Anne Taylor's 'My Mother' in puzzle form, which was followed by 'My Bible', 'My Son', and 'My Grandmother'.

The firm of Darton and Harvey also published an author whose name was very well known to me as a schoolgirl in York, though I did not know much about him. In the school garden of the Mount there was a charming, eighteenth-century, octagonal summer house with an ogee roof, which was known to us as 'the Lindley Murray', after the Pennsylvanian-born Quaker grammarian (1745–1826) who eventually settled in York, and whose best-selling *English Grammar* was published by Darton and Harvey in 1795. Murray had been asked to write his famous *Grammar* in a 'humble petition' from three friends who were teachers at the Quaker school for girls in York, then located in Trinity Lane, and now known as the Mount School. His work was immensely successful in its day, and the school continues to prosper. It continues to be, as it was then, both Quaker and single sex, and the summer house named after him stands in its garden just as it always has. A history of the school written in 1931 tells us that it was then 'the haunt of schoolgirls, who would still talk of "the Lindley Murray", meaning a summer-house and not a book', and this was true when I was there in the 1950s.

My sisters and I were not sent to the Mount School because my parents were Quakers. They became Quakers as a result of sending us to the Mount. My mother had taught there, briefly, before her marriage, and had retained happy memories of its friendly and egalitarian spirit, so when my parents were looking for a suitable boarding school its name came up. My father thought we would have a less 'snobbish' education there than at some other well-known schools for girls, and he was right. I cannot remember precisely when he joined the Society of Friends, but it must have been at some point during the 1950s. (My mother, once a vocal,

Shavian, anti-chapel atheist, took some years to follow him.) My father, unlike my mother and my aunt, had a religious temperament, and intermittently attended the local Anglican church in Sheffield (now, I believe, demolished), but he found the service unsatisfactory. He could never say the Creed, because he did not believe in most of it, and he hated some of the Old Testament and the psalms, which were intoned from the pulpit or chanted by the congregation. Passages about dashing out the brains of children caused him particular distress: I recall his response to a reading of Psalm 137, which ends: 'O daughter of Babylon, who art to be destroyed: happy shall he be, that rewardeth thee as thou hast served us. Happy shall he be, that taketh and dasheth thy little ones against the stones.' No, he said, as we walked home down the tree-lined suburban avenue; that was not the way to behave, or the way to talk.

I didn't mind those bits then (I do now) but in St Andrew's I developed a lasting dislike of organ music. To this day the sound of the organ sets my teeth on edge. Just as the cant of Methodist chapels and Sunday schools annoyed my mother and Arnold Bennett, so the windy, droning screech of the organ annoys me. And I didn't like the collection, either. My father would give me a threepenny bit to drop into the nasty, dusty, velvety pouch, which made me feel a hypocrite. It hadn't been mine to give, nor had it been given willingly.

My father escaped from what he saw as the hypocrisies of the Church of England by becoming a Quaker. He was not a Pacifist, as he maintained that the Second World War was a just war and he was right to have served in it, but by and large the enlightened and rational Quaker faith suited him. It did not compel him to say he believed in the impossible, and he liked the emphasis on social service and internationalism. He became involved, as lawyer then as judge, with the Quaker prison reform agenda, about which he felt strongly. He thought it important to try to belong to a community of believers, although he was in many ways a solitary man. I don't know whether or not he believed in God, but he would certainly have liked to have been able to do so, and he behaved as though he did. I have often wished I could have asked him what he made of Hugh Kingsmill's words about the Kingdom of Heaven, which 'cannot be created by charters and constitutions nor established by arms. Those who set out for it alone will reach it together, and those who seek it in company will perish by themselves.' But I didn't discover these moving words until after his death. I was introduced to them by Michael, Kingsmill's biographer, who found them for himself in Maidenhead Public Library, and by the time Michael met my father in Amsterdam in 1982, my father was on his deathbed.

Attending a Quaker school and being exposed to Quaker morality and literature (George Fox, William Penn, John Woolman, John Greenleaf Whittier) had an effect on me, and I have never reacted against the Quaker spirit as I did against the church organ. On the whole, I value it, and I was not surprised to discover that Quaker publishing families had been involved with the early days of juvenile literature and educational toys and puzzles, as well as with anti-slavery tracts. This was all of a piece. The vast output of the Darton family has generated a great deal of bibliographical research; descendant Lawrence Darton devoted many years to producing *The Dartons: An Annotated Check-List of Children's Books Published by Two Publishing Houses 1787–1876* (2004), a volume of 729 pages, and Jill Shefrin has been working on a descriptive bibliography of everything published for children by the Dartons other than books. This is a task that could have been pursued for many decades or, indeed, in perpetuity. The objects are ephemeral, and their survival chancy, and you can never know when you have reached the end of the list. They seem designed for the employment of those who, like Georges Perec, are addicted to the endless pursuit of classification.

Lawrence Darton was the first winner of the Harvey Darton Prize, which is awarded by the Children's Books History Society for a work 'which extends our knowledge of some aspect of British children's literature of the past'. This prize was named after his cousin F. J. Harvey Darton, a man whose career began to intrigue me more and more as I looked into this subject. F. J., or 'Fred', is an interesting character, whose modest, authoritative and kindly authorial tone gives little indication of his troubled life. While dipping into his great work *Children's Books in England*, I had endowed him with a Teas-with-Hovis personality; I assumed he was a kind father, an attentive grandfather, a benevolent Quaker patriarch. My father, the kindest of men, was known as 'Fred' to his family in his youth, and I saw Fred Harvey Darton as a man cast in the same mould, but perhaps a little more austere than my father, who was known to startle the teetotal members of his Quaker Meeting by offering them a gin and tonic on a Sunday morning in his later years when Meeting was held in his Suffolk home.

I could not have been more wrong. Harvey Darton's life surprised me as much as the life of Alison Uttley surprised Auntie Phyl.

I suppose I should have been alerted to Harvey Darton's true character and circumstances by a faint whiff of Grub Street desperation manifested in the length of the catalogue of his published works. He turned his hand to anything – magazine editing, museum guides, monographs, reviews, topographical works – and he also, more revealingly, published two pseudonymous novels, which give a startlingly different picture of the book trade from that portrayed in his enduring magnum opus.

The first of these novels was titled *My Father's Son: A Faithful Record* by 'W. W. Penn', a novel that claims to have been 'prepared for the press by John Harvey' – both Penn and Harvey being deliberately giveaway Quaker names. Published in 1913 by Hodder & Stoughton, it has an attractive, two-tone, blue-canvas jacket with gilt lettering, and a skyline of the towers and spires of the City and the dome of St Paul's – a silhouette of the old publishing world of the Bible and the Book. It is the story of William, the spendthrift offspring of a bankrupt grandfather and a respectable, lower-middle-class, book-trade father. The family business deals in 'moral pamphlets and goody-goody children's tracts', and Will hates and despises it, but makes such a mess of his university career at Oxford and his Civil Service examinations that he is obliged to enter it.

Office life repels him; he hates the smell of paper and disinfectant, the tedium, the impoverished illustrators and engravers, the 'priddy liddle Victorian uglinesses' of the magazine stories, the meanness, the lack of imagination, the rejection of anything original or beautiful. He hates the 'awful chromo-lithographs, with their staring reds and their glossy finish'. But the public like 'finish'; the best way to use flesh or red, maintains his father, is to use 'only a little, but just so that it hits you in the eye'.

Harvey Darton paints a gloomy picture of the dirty London streets and alleys round Ludgate Hill and St Paul's Churchyard, a picture far removed from the romantic antiquarian world that captured many budding bibliophiles. But he writes with more feeling of St Paul's itself, and the 'astonishing exhilaration of seeing London's most glorious monument against the morning sun'.

At Oxford the fictitious William had been encouraged to scout around for up-and-coming children's authors, and had even wondered whether he could 'divert the firm's energies to broader, more humane channels than those of the Church and childhood'. Nothing comes of these dreams and he finds himself musing, 'If only I had control of the business... If my father were no longer alive!' At this very moment in time his father is conveniently killed by a dray horse, but William is already so deep in debt and deceit that he decides to flee the country, and ends up doing quite well growing bananas in British Honduras.

Harvey Darton's second novel, *When: a Record of Transition* (Chapman & Hall, 1929), is credited to 'the late J. L. Pole', and its story is even more darkly illuminating. The novel, in memoir format, is introduced by Pole's old friend Peter Grimstone and 'edited' by his late aunt (conveniently mown down by a fast-moving car 'as she emerged from a tavern into which (no doubt) she had pursued one of the fallen women whom she gloried in rescuing'), who tells us that John Pole, an alcoholic, had died in an institution of an overdose of methylated spirits. Pole's family, like Penn's in the earlier novel, was bookish; they read over meals with a book propped up against a tumbler or a cruet, but they read 'ephemeral stuff', and his father had been a publisher of 'small magazines and cheap books for housemaids'. Pole describes himself sardonically as three persons: 'a general utility "littery-gent", a piety-monger and a licentious novelist', with a weakness for the bottle. His 'wicked' pseudonymous novels (*The Goats of Hell, The Jellied Eels of Purity*) were published under the pen-name of Vincent Snarsgate and were, he says, 'a safety-valve for my natural malice'. He also published under his own name 'sob-stuff' with titles like *Susan's Repentance*.

Pole, like William Penn in the earlier novel, toys with entering the Civil Service after Oxford but he too ends up in Grub Street, reviewing over a thousand novels a year, taking twenty minutes on average over each, and learning all the tricks of the trade. He thinks there must have been some strain of 'literary crime' in his blood, for one of his great-uncles had written what Pole calls 'Christian Dreadfuls'. He gives a vivid account of Grub Street poverty:

The most flippant cynic cannot treat as a humbug a man who, on a cold day, pulls up a dickey and shows you his bare skin underneath and implores you to buy his rubbishy story. The artists were even more painful, in some ways, for the great transition in book and magazine illustration was at its critical point. The wood-block, that even now underrated glory of the sixties, was virtually dead.

Some of these illustrators held their own under the title of Bohemians, while others crept

from office to office, even more shabby, more feeble, some hungrier, some more sodden, until at last an editor would say to a colleague 'Where's old Stickey? He hasn't been in for weeks…' In those days publishing houses possessed, through compassion, a rubbish heap of unusable or forgotten ghosts, bought out of sheer pity. I am told there is less pity now. The publishers are forming combines, and few combines have any bowels for the old.

There's a familiar ring to that complaint.

Pole does not reach old age, and the descriptions of his decline into alcoholism are painfully authentic. He continues to function in 'the same dreary round of aimless soaking and drab administrative efficiency', realizing that he is ruining his health, but also resolving

in my clearer moments, to set down my memories of the War before my memory failed – as it was beginning to fail. I also began research, chiefly at the British Museum, for a large serious work I had long contemplated – a history of relations between the author, the journalist, and the publisher in England, from the earliest times…to today, with its numerous subdivisions and classifications.

I take it that this imaginary work, *The Workshop of Letters* (a precursor of the subject that is now known as the History of the Book?), stands in for the *Children's Books in England*, which Harvey Darton heroically completed, and I also take it that Pole's description of his sudden collapse is autobiographical: 'It was in a tavern, near the B M, just after the Reading Room had closed for the day. I went there with a journalist I knew, with whom I had been discussing some small point of interest, and laid (as I thought) the foundation for a good dinner with a couple of strong whiskies. "At one stride came the dark".'

He wakes from this fit in the mental ward of a London hospital, suffering from delirium tremens, and is taken to Broadwindsor Hall, a private asylum, to which, after various sorties and efforts at recovery, he returns to die.

This is not the private life that, perhaps naively, one would have expected of the master scholar of children's literature, and Harvey Darton's own life mirrored his fictional creation's all too closely. He died of cirrhosis of the liver on 26 July 1936, aged fifty-seven, and his last address was a public house in Dorset. He was buried at Cerne Abbas.

Which was the real Fred, the spendthrift alcoholic, or the tolerant and delighted observer of children's books and games, the connoisseur of woodcuts and half-tones, the amused and amusing recorder of literary taste and 'the struggle between instruction and amusement'? His fictional characters feared some kind of hereditary insanity. Perhaps descent from a clan of high-minded publishers of pretty poems for little people, jigsaws and grammars did not provide an ideal heritage, although it provided him with rich materials.

I searched in vain for a mention of jigsaws in his two novels, but failed to find one. Children play with an abacus and make 'nasty little mats of coloured paper' but they do not assemble Darton and Harvey jigsaws.

And perhaps it is childish to expect that those who devote themselves to children's games and literature should be good citizens or good family members. Some are. Some are not. Some are neurotic and obsessive, and some do not like children at all. Some are perpetual children, which is not always a happy fate.

Auntie Phyl occupied the middle ground.

I feel, from no evidence, that Fred Harvey Darton must have liked children. He was known as a gregarious man with many friends, and a lover of country life and sports. Maybe, like J. L. Pole, he was at least two people: the outdoor man who wrote about Dorset and Kent, and the indoor man who pored over books in the British Museum and drank himself into a stupor in the tavern across the road. And maybe there was a third and disappointed Harvey Darton. His marriage to the daughter of a schoolmaster was annulled on grounds of non-consummation, a piece of information that brings to mind another scholar-eccentric, John Cowper Powys. Powys, too, was a rambler, a reader and a topographer, with strong connections with Dorset and Cerne Abbas. I wonder whether they ever met.

Children's writers and writers about children's writing are not as Goody Two-Shoes or as Little Grey Rabbit as one might expect.

Remarkably, Harvey Darton left a lasting legacy, and his great work, revised and updated, is still handsomely in print, as well as available on the shelves of every reference library. There must have been an inheritance of discipline that enabled him to finish this book. But the sales during his lifetime were a disappointment to him, and he felt he had, in his own modest phrase, 'let his publishers down'. He was not a boastful man. He did not like to advertise his own wares and carried this fastidiousness to an extreme. Writing about his association with the highly profitable *Chatterbox* and *The Prize* in his *Cornhill* article of 1932, 'The Youth of a Children's Magazine', he refrained from naming them because he thought 'it would be improper of me to advertise them against their many rivals by dwelling on their well-established fame.'

This unworldly and outdated reproach is very much a Quaker attitude, and one that was drummed into us at the Mount School. Advertisement is wrong, we were taught. We must not put ourselves forward or boast about our achievements. Self-praise is no praise. It is curious, in the light of this indoctrination, that so many Quakers became such good businessmen, and that so many Quaker family names are so well known as brand names. In York, we were surrounded by Rowntrees and Cadburys and Terrys.

I often think of my father and his Sunday gin and tonic. He was a good Quaker, and I do not think the Friends of Suffolk held his drinking habits against him. He liked a gin and tonic before his Sunday lunch. And so do I.

Auntie Phyl very rarely had a glass of wine or sherry. She wondered 'what we all saw in alcohol'. (Some of us, and I speak for myself, saw what we saw in it all too well.) She kept a half-bottle of whisky 'for medicinal purposes' in her immensely cluttered kitchen, but it stayed on top of the dresser for years. She thought an aspirin was a better pick-me-up than whisky when she felt off-colour, and of course she was right. My mother, who made mock of her primitive faith in aspirin, thought it an old wives' remedy and, to be truthful, so did I. But I was wrong and my mother was wrong. Now I take my aspirin daily, like nearly everybody over sixty, on doctor's orders.

At her eightieth birthday celebration at Jack Straw's Castle in Hampstead, Auntie Phyl accepted a glass of champagne. I have a fine photograph of her, taken by one of her nephews-in-law, looking happy and festive with a glass in her hand. That was a good lunch party. Auntie Phyl's reply to the toasts to her health was a little frisky, but none the worse for that.

Did Joyce ever persuade her to join her in her half a pint of shandy, to accompany the scampi and chips in the village pub? I think not. I think she stuck to lemonade. But I do remember one Hampstead Christmas when I was uncharacteristically tempted to side with Auntie Phyl's disapproval of hard drinking.

An ageing acquaintance of mine, who could without injustice be described as a whisky priest, had been for some years angling for an invitation to join us for a Christmas drink. I had resisted his hints, because I knew how it would turn out. This vicar was notorious both for his heavy drinking and for his intellectual and social pretensions, and he had taken it into his head that a drink with me and my family of an evening during the Christmas holidays would provide him with a memorable feast of literary gossip and highbrow chat. In vain, year after year, had I tried to warn him that it wouldn't be as he expected. He would not take no for an answer. So I gave in, and round he came, in his cassock, and there he discovered my mother, my father and my aunt, all firmly settled into their deep armchairs and unwilling to give. I poured him a whisky, and doubtless poured a stiff one for myself, plus a gin and tonic for my father. My mother may have had a glass of wine or sherry, and my aunt a soft drink. My father probably made some polite small talk, and my mother may have done the same. They could find no common ground of any sort. And Auntie Phyl sat there, like a rock, watching the priest as he dissolved into desperate incoherence, dropping the names of people most of whom we did not know. And if we did by chance happen to know them, or know of them, we despised them. He gaffed on, regardless, and I refilled his glass. It was not a happy hour. I don't know whether he noticed how badly his banter was being received. He was drink hardened.

I thought he would never leave. By the time that I was finally able to thrust him into his great black crow's overcoat and manoeuvre him down the front steps, I was exhausted. I went back into the drawing room, where Auntie Phyl was still sitting, unmoved. Then she produced one of her rare spoken judgements.

'I don't think it's right for a vicar to drink like that,' she said, her face expressing generations of inherited, chapel-going disapproval. And, as I staggered off to cook their supper, I felt that this time I was on her side.

XXXV

A year or two ago I went with my daughter Becky to see some Tibetan monks as they began to make a sand mandala in the heart of London. They piped brightly coloured sands into an elaborate and preordained traditional pattern laid out on a large low table in Asia House in New Cavendish Street. For a week they would slowly and patiently pipe the sands until the image was complete, and then, on the last day, when it was finished, they would blow it away. I would have liked to have seen the Day of Destruction, which surely had a metaphysical significance, but I could not make the date. And I could not comprehend the aesthetic of the mandala. The colours were too bright and garish for my taste. I mentioned this to my daughter, who replied reprovingly, 'Garishness is not a Buddhist concept.'

I connected the idea of the mandala with the jigsaw, and, indeed, that is probably why we went to see it. I was interested in the ephemerality of the object, an object made with its end already in mind. Is not the act of completion of a jigsaw often accompanied by the sense of disappointment that Southey experienced when he had finished pricking a playbill – a 'sort of dissatisfied and damping feeling'? We build sandcastles, knowing that we or the tide will destroy them. Is that too in some way part of the satisfaction?

Jigsaws may be connected with depression. They serve the depressed, and they certainly flourished during the Depression.

Jigsaws, like tatting and netting and knitting and scrimshaw, are time killers, and when technology had advanced sufficiently for the mass production of cheap cardboard puzzles, they became the occupation of the unemployed. They were cheap to buy, cheap to assemble, and they filled in the empty days and empty evenings. Alan Sillitoe, whose family was hard hit by unemployment in the 1930s and sank into near-destitution, records passing time as a ten-year-old with his sisters doing a jigsaw. (His boyhood fascination with maps and codes continues, but he says his interest in jigsaws quickly waned.) And in America, a curious boom in puzzle manufacturing was to follow the stock market crash of October 1929. In the early 1930s, artists and illustrators had, like so much of the population, been suffering from the country's lack of spending power for luxury items. In America, two decades after Harvey Darton's description of the plight of British illustrators, artists had been suffering in much the same manner, until suddenly a reprieve came in the form of a nationwide craze for weekly jigsaws. This curious little story illustrates the randomness of fashion.

According to Chris McCann, author of *Master Pieces: The Art History of Jigsaw Puzzles* (1998), the miracle began in 1931, when

> a customer asked the Einson-Freeman company in Long
> Island, NY, to make a new product, a die-cut puzzle that the
> customer could give away with toothbrushes. The puzzle was
> an outstanding success. Other customers liked the idea, and
> more orders followed. Then, the next year, somebody thought
> people might actually pay money for a cardboard puzzle,
> and began making them for sale. They were distributed one

at a time, once a week. This event marked the beginning of the weekly puzzle, and the puzzle industry was never the same again.

In a similar kind of promotion, mini-jigsaws were given away in England in the mid-1930s to any customer who bought two bars of Knight's Castile soap.

The twentieth-century connection of jigsaws with advertising is in itself a bit of a mystery. The British-born artist Derek Boshier, born in 1937, painted several paintings showing jigsaw-shaped pieces and cut-out paper men during his pop-art phase in the 1960s, and seems to have intended them as a satiric commentary on the power of 'the culture of commodities' – a theme also dear at this period to Perec. *Identi-Kit Man*, in Tate Britain, shows giant toothbrushes and a man whose right arm is composed of a giant tube of red-and-white-striped toothpaste. His body is punched by a jigsaw-piece-shaped hole, and other jigsaw shapes float elsewhere in the frame. The Tate's caption reminds us that the first advertisement ever shown on British TV was for toothpaste – in 1955, for Gibbs SR. The jigsaw shapes are instantly and uncannily recognizable. Do they suggest that we are all composed of nothing but little interlocking blocks of manufactured desire?

Chris McCann claims that the 1930s spin-off jigsaw boom in America created hundreds of new companies and rescued many commercial artists, at least temporarily, from destitution. By early 1933, over $1 million a week was being spent on jigsaws, and a whole new art form of jigsaw art, a new version of calendar art, was in demand. This was the 'Golden Age of Puzzle Art'. McCann presents many highly coloured images, giving the current market price of each (which varies from $5 to $75 and more), and lists brief biographies of the artists. McCann's account of the boom and what he describes as the subsequent 'Great Jigsaw Puzzle Panic' is as highly coloured as the paintings themselves. The panic was caused by excess demand, which resulted in December 1932 in a forty-eight-hour jigsaw 'famine', followed by increased production during which six million puzzles were sold weekly. This hysteria, we are told, came to an abrupt end when Franklin Roosevelt closed the banks for nearly two weeks, and people began to think more seriously about how to spend their money. The lust for puzzles was over, and the jigsaw began to go the way of the Harlequinade and the diabolo.

People suffered during the famine of the Depression without their daily jigsaw fix, just as crossword puzzlers today suffer without a daily crossword. Playwright Ronald Harwood and his wife Natasha do a crossword every day and feel deprived if they can't get hold of one. And there are many who are still addicted to jigsaws. Theatre producer Michael Codron does a jigsaw, or part of a jigsaw, every day. Actor Sir Donald Sinden is proud of his three-dimensional jigsaw version of the Duomo in Florence, constructed while he was working on a film that was set in the Uffizi. The film was never shown, but his puzzle survives. Perhaps the intermittent nature and the time-wasting and hanging about of theatrical employment encourage actors to take up these time-filling pursuits. Maroussia Frank, wife of the late Ian Richardson, is famous throughout the profession for her formidable Green Room skills at Scrabble, and many actors, less competitively, take up crochet or knitting or rug-making. For many years I cherished a circular rug decorated with the signs of the Zodiac pegged for me by a walk-on friend at Stratford-upon-Avon.

It was Michael Codron who disposed of my theory that most adults who do jigsaws were introduced to them by kind aunts in their childhood. He says that one Christmas he bought a jigsaw of Canterbury cathedral in a village shop in Kent as a stocking-filler for a friend, but the friend showed no interest in it, so he took pity on it and did it himself. And thus, already well into middle age, he caught the habit. He did all the cathedrals, one after another, and then embarked on other motifs. Now he says he usually does one a day. When he has finished a jigsaw, he needs somebody to admire his handiwork before he puts it back in its box, and then, after two or three days, it goes up to the attic, where he has thousands stored away. He says he likes making order out of chaos, and he likes the solipsism of living inside the world of the jigsaw. He was full of advice about where to buy puzzles. Some manufacturers I knew, others I had never heard of. At his prompting I have now ordered more jigsaws than I can ever finish.

He is the kind of client who keeps the puzzle manufacturers in business. He makes his way through the catalogues.

XXXVI

The artwork of the American 'Golden Age' of the compulsive 1930s in *Master Pieces* is extraordinary, and some of it is repulsive. It deserves a page or two to itself. The subjects are largely traditional and familiar – hunting scenes, dogs, cottage gardens, ships at sea, life in the American West, children blowing bubbles and clutching kittens. We recognize reproductions from Rubens and Hobbema, Joshua Reynolds and Millais, Rosa Bonheur and Norman Rockwell. Thomas Moran, famous for his vast views of Colorado, is well represented. But many of the paintings are by artists otherwise unknown or little documented. The phrase 'the archives were silent on this illustrator' recurs frequently in the biographical listing, but nevertheless there are some intriguing brief lives here, and Chris McCann, an energetic man of multiple talents (which he has employed variously in management with General Electric, in computing and in community theatre), has clearly enjoyed his detective work.

A few of the artists, like R. Atkinson Fox (1860–1935), now have a committed following of fans and collectors. Fox, who emigrated from Toronto to the United States to pursue a highly successful commercial career, is represented in McCann's book by hunting dogs, a sailing ship, a girl with a pony, a principal-boy-style female pirate with magnificent legs, and a painting in which a maiden in an orange-and-blue Oriental robe stands precariously on a window ledge with a large bowl of chrysanthemums, overlooking a bright-blue lake, some snowy Rocky Mountains and an orange sunrise.

Robert Atkinson Fox's career trajectory is more conventional than that of Abd'el Kader (1852–1940), said to have been born in Germany, the grandson of Husscin Pasha, the Dey of Algiers. He abandoned his life in Europe as an opera singer, signed up with Oscar Hammerstein to sing in America, was injured in a train crash, lost all his money, and ended up 'living free in part of an air-plane hangar at Municipal Airport in Atlantic City, where he painted and gave art lessons for the next eleven years'. His jigsaw work is represented in McCann by two rustic cottage images, one with snow, the other with a small dog and lupins, and a village scene of sheep going to pasture. His signature, we are told, has 'always fascinated and mystified collectors', and, if half of this story is true, one can see why.

Some of the pictures of children are, by today's more fastidious standards, pornographic. Mabel Rollins Harris's *Look Who's Here* shows two small, fat girls, one naked except for shoes and socks, the other wearing shoes, socks and vest, gazing out of a window at two plumply suggestive lovebirds. In her *Dinner for Six* another little girl is lifting her skirt to show her knickers as she feeds a family of ducks. Nothing is known of Mabel Rollins Harris, not even her dates.

The oddest jigsaw in the whole collection is a bizarre work by an English painter, Briton Rivière (1840–1920), titled *Daniel in the Lion's Den*. This shows a white-haired Daniel, dressed in a red, gold-embroidered caftan, looking away from the artist with his hands clasped (and presumably shackled) behind his back, calmly confronting a group of seven orange lions. The lions crouch and snarl and lour at him in a surge of seething orange. Bones litter the foreground. We are not told when it was manufactured as a puzzle, but Rivière died in 1920 so we know he did not live to enjoy the profits of the American Golden Age. The lions may have been pirated, and they are very ill painted, with strange facial expressions, caught between cringe and attack.

It is surprising to learn that Briton Rivière RA was considered one of the finest of nineteenth-century British painters of animals, second in reputation only to Landseer. (His most famous work is a picture of a barefoot Dickensian waif lying by a milestone and clutching a large dog, titled *His Only Friend*. This, too, must once have been made into a jigsaw.) It is unwise to judge the quality of a painting from a reproduction of a photograph of a jigsaw of a painting, and it would be interesting, though perhaps not sufficiently interesting, to try to track down this peculiar and arresting work, to see what it looks like in its original state.

As a jigsaw illustration, *Daniel in the Lion's Den* is both startling and memorable. It is so very orange.

Alan Sillitoe, in his late novel *The Broken Chariot*, invokes the art of Briton Rivière, who goes largely unmentioned these days. His novelist hero, sitting in a cheap rented room in south London, is inspired by a Rivière reproduction from a second-hand album of prints, which shows, curiously, Phoebus Apollo driving the chariot of the sun, which is drawn not by the more customary horses but by a 'sullen pack of lions in long shafts gnashing their teeth'. This reproduction, Sillitoe's hero reflects, provides 'another stitch in the tapestry of his progress'. It would have been better, from the point of view of my thesis on the ubiquity of the jigsaw, if he'd called it 'another piece of the jigsaw puzzle', but it's near enough. Tapestries and jigsaws connect. Rivière studied his lions in the London Zoo, and Sillitoe says he bought the reproduction he describes in his novel from a print-seller in North Kensington.

The phenomenon of the American jigsaw as a collector's item, regardless of its aesthetic merit, is well documented by McCann, who appeals for information about 'America's Ten Most Wanted Puzzle Artists', about whom 'little or nothing is known'. These are listed as J. Adams, Edwin Bolenbaugh, C. B. Colby, Thomas Crane, Anthony Cucchi, Arthur Frahm, Frederick D. Ogden, Irene and Laurette Patten and Hy Whitroy, and their subjects include sporting pictures, children at play, historic monuments, fat babies, comic genre scenes and Santa Claus in an aeroplane – this last a very popular item. (Georges Perec would have loved this list.) Why these are more wanted than some other artists about whom the archives are silent is not immediately evident, but would no doubt become so if one allowed oneself to be led down this path. Are Irene and Laurette Patten sisters? Why not? And is Hy or Henry Whitroy a pseudonym of the prolific R. Atkinson Fox, reserved perhaps for his more ambitious and less vulgar work?

Not all jigsaw artists sign their work, but many do. I had not known this. Nor had I known that Greek and Roman mosaic artists sometimes signed their work. I suppose everybody else in the world knew this, but I didn't. The creator of the magnificent mosaic representing a stag hunt in the House of the Abduction of Helen at Pella in Greece, dating from the late fourth century BC, is signed by someone called Gnosis. *Gnosis epoesen*. 'Gnosis made this.' He wrote his name in white pebbles. That to me is very unlikely, and very poignant.

XXXVII

A non-geographical, quasi-educational apologia for the doing of jigsaws lies in the 'Old Master' theory, which also raises the question of signature and copyright. Jigsaws reproducing famous works of art may now be purchased on line, as well as in many museum and gallery shops. (In the Matisse gallery in Nice in 2005, you could buy a jigsaw of Matisse's *Dance*, although you could not then find a copy of Hilary Spurling's biography of Matisse.) And there is no question but that in 'doing' a famous painting, as Jill Shefrin said in her letter of 23 September 2006, you learn a great deal about it. 'Assembling a puzzle of, say, a Brueghel painting, reveals all sorts of details.'

From jigsaws, you learn about the brush strokes of Van Gogh, the clouds of Constable, the reflections and shadows of Manet, the stripes of Tissot and Rousseau, the brickwork and tiles of the Dutch masters, the flesh tones of Titian, the undulating fabrics and limbs of Botticelli, the business of Bosch and Brueghel. While struggling to re-create Titian's *Venus of Urbino*, you discover that the little dog at her feet is painted in almost exactly the same shades of apricot and russet as the naked Venus herself. According to Julian Mitchell, himself a master puzzle solver, the dog represents her politely concealed pubic hair.

Doing jigsaws stimulates bizarre theories of art history.

The same little dog appears, less suggestively, in Titian's large portrait of the Vendramin family. Everybody had a little dog like that.

I learned more about the appreciation of clouds and of Constable from doing jigsaws of *The Hay Wain* and *Salisbury Cathedral* than I learned from my first encounters with the original paintings. Now, when I see clouds, I see clouds and Constable, not clouds and the shapes of a jigsaw puzzle, but the puzzle was the medium that introduced me, that fixed my attention, that made me pause. This may sound ridiculous, but it is true. I could have learned about clouds at the Courtauld, but I didn't have the opportunity. I learned through Clementoni. The cumulus and the cirrus and the mackerel, the greys and mauves, the sullen purples, the swelling yellow bruises, the cream and sallow swathes, the white crests and mountains, the bright linings, the tints of pink and red – I studied all of these through assembling the pieces of jigsaws. Constable was very good at clouds. They are difficult, for painters and puzzle solvers alike. (And the jigsaw stonework of Constable's *Salisbury Cathedral*, although it looks much easier, was very difficult too; I was pleased to note that Constable himself commented on this 1823 painting in a letter to his friend Archdeacon John Fisher that it was 'the most difficult subject in landscape I ever had on my easel'.)

You become intimate with the painting, like those students who used patiently to copy masterpieces onto canvases on easels in the National Gallery. You rarely see these copy-makers now. Before the age of cheap reproduction, copyists used to work for profit, like Mlle Noémie Nioche in Henry James's *The American*, who is discovered by James's hero Christopher Newman as she works on a copy of Murillo's *Madonna* in the Louvre. The untutored Newman is more taken with the pretty young copyist than with the painting, and prefers the copy of the painting to the original. Unlike David Teniers, Mlle Nioche clearly prefers a lighter, brighter version, and gives her works a high finish. (As noted, some of the reproductions in Linda Hannas's book on jigsaws look more glossily attractive than the originals, and those in McCann's book are dazzling.)

The market for Old Master copies in Europe has more or less vanished, although we are told it still flourishes in China, but, more ephemerally, pavement artists in Europe continue to produce chalk and pastel versions of Botticelli and Vermeer, and to collect small sums in token appreciation from passers-by. Like the Tibetan monks, they work from a pattern. Doing a jigsaw is less arduous and more pointless than making a copy, but it can give you a similar sense of familiarity. Once you have 'done' a painting, you feel a more personal connection with it, for better or worse. Michael Codron told me that you feel you are 'inside the mind of the painter', and this is true. It is an escape from the self and into another mindset.

Most paintings gain from this intimacy, but I began to dislike the *Venus of Urbino* as I struggled with her in jigsaw form. I took against the murky drapes and tapestries in green and dark red and beige and brown, and the background figure on her knees rummaging in a dark coffer, and the dingy slanting repetitive tiles of the floor, and the silly little floppy-eared silky pubic dog. Above all I began to dislike the woman's sprawling, basking, seal-like, solid, self-satisfied figure, her smooth mounds of naked flesh, her hazy pink nipples, her big fat sausage-like fingers. Only as I neared the end did it occur to me that what I was disliking was not Titian's masterpiece, but the poor and fuzzy quality of the jigsaw reproduction, credited to the 'Clementoni Museum Collection – the Art of Art!' If ever I get to the Uffizi again and can face the queues, I must go to pay my respects to the real *Venus*. Clementoni didn't do her justice. Their version of Botticelli's *Primavera*, though it lopped off a few limbs round the edges, had a much better and sharper finish.

I employed an unusual technique when constructing the *Venus*. I did the frame first, of course, but then I imposed upon myself the constraint of finishing all the background before I embarked on her body. The empty unfilled outline of her body looked very striking and strangely meaningful on the dark lacquer table. I wish now I had asked Michael to take a photograph of it in this state. I will never be able to bring myself to repeat the experiment. I don't know what the empty space suggested, but it looked in some way significant. I am sure the Oulipo painters would have had a theory about it.

My Oxford grandchildren, knowing my weakness for this seemingly pointless employment, purchased for me one Christmas a 2,000 piece reproduction of a work titled *The Battle of Valmy* (1792), which clearly says on its box that it is by Jean Baptiste Mauzaisse (d.1844). (I now know exactly where in Oxford they bought this unusual item, thanks to information provided by Michael Codron; he rumbled them.) It is a Falcon Imperial de Luxe Puzzle, and the box credit reads: 'Louvre, Paris/Giraudin/Bridgeman Art Gallery, London'. The painting portrays, in the foreground, a number of mounted officers, several dying horses, and a field hospital full of wounded and dying men. The field hospital has picturesque tiles and woodwork. Further off, in the middle ground, we see the windmill of Valmy and a line of infantry and, beyond the infantry, the cavalry. There are large explosions of shellfire from what I take to be the enemy line, and the high horizon is marked by puffs of smoke. The revolutionary French are apparently about to defeat the Prussians in a famous victory.

My grandchildren did not seem to consider the subject macabre or unsuitable for their Quaker-educated Granny Maggie. 'They all look in the pink to me,' protested Danny, inspecting the wounded officers more closely. It is not a painting before which I would have lingered. I doubt whether, in other circumstances, I would even have noticed it. But I got to know it well.

Some curious coincidences attached themselves to this jigsaw. While I was in the course of labouring over its 2,000 pieces, in the year 2000, the windmill of Valmy, a famous revolutionary land-mark, was blown down in the same violent storm that uprooted many thousands of trees at Versailles. I felt its destruction person-ally. The windmill has now been rebuilt, and in September 2006 it served as the site for far-right Jean-Marie Le Pen's launch of his presidential campaign. There, 'on the glorious ground of Valmy', he unsuccessfully invited the French to follow his nationalist agenda.

The second incident involved a greater act of destruction than the fall of a windmill. On the day after the collapse of the Twin Towers (which began to disintegrate as I was quietly reading *Thus Spake Zarathustra* in the British Library) I went into the National Gallery. I think I went there to reassure myself that it and its paintings were still there, and to my astonishment I beheld, high on the wall above me, a massive version of my jigsaw. I stared at it, unbelieving. What was it doing there? What did it mean? Why was this vast French painting in London? Did it have a message for me? Was I dreaming?

And *The Battle of Valmy* was not alone; three other huge canvases in a similar vein accompanied it, which I subsequently discovered portrayed the battles of Gemappes, Montmirail and Hanau.

Valmy was unmistakable.

One does not forget a jigsaw.

(Danny and Lillie: I am not Auntie Phyl. I loved my Christmas present. I am not Auntie Phyl. I loved it, dying soldiers and all.)

Now, some years later, I can clearly remember the sombre mood in which I had visited the National Gallery that day, a mood of mingled apprehension and defiance. We were afraid, in those immediate days after the Twin Towers, that something similar was about to happen in central London, and therefore we wished to show ourselves to be part of London, to show London that we valued it. So we went out into our city, to prove we were not afraid. And there, in the Gallery, I met this old friend.

Recently, prompted by my new role as jigsaw historian, I went back to see whether those four battle paintings were still there. I had a hunch that they would have vanished, and they had. Nobody I knew had ever noticed them. More mysteriously, the helpful man on the information desk knew nothing of a painter called Mauzaisse. There was nothing in the gallery by a painter of this name and, as far as he could see, there never had been. He looked up *The Battle of Valmy* for me in the National Gallery catalogue, found the image, showed it to me, and told me that it was by a painter called Horace Vernet, and that it, with its three companions, was now hidden away in some storeroom. Was I mistaken about the image, he suggested? Was this another treatment of the same battle?

No, I was not mistaken. I've admitted to a poor visual right-brain memory (though I have, or used to have, a good left-brain word memory) but there was no possibility that this field hospital, these officers, these horses, this heavy cloudy sky, these flashes of gunfire and clouds of smoke that were glimmering at me now from a small screen on the information desk were different from those in my jigsaw. I ordered a print, to prove to myself that I was not mistaken. It cost £10. You can print out any image at the National Gallery. I suspect I am the first person ever to have requested a print of *The Battle of Valmy*.

There was, as I now know, a whole family of painters called Vernet, of whom Horace was the most successful. Baudelaire hated him because Baudelaire hated the army, and Vernet glorified it. Baudelaire also hated Vernet's popularity. Or so we are told.

One does not forget a jigsaw.

The Mauzaisse is a copy of the Vernet, but there is no indication of this on the Falcon box. This raises more questions about jigsaw image copyright. Who gives permission to the puzzle manufacturer? May it be withheld? The American jigsaw artists catalogued by McCann were paid for their original work by the manufacturers, but did they have a copyright agreement?

I became more and more interested in the phenomenon of the art jigsaw, and asked around and about for an explanation of its genesis. When did it become popular, who first thought of it, and what about the question of copyright? Titian's 1,000 piece *Bacchus and Ariadne* is copyright of the Board of Trustees of the National Gallery, 2002, all rights reserved, whereas Claude's 'JR de Luxe', 500-piece *Seaport with the Embarkation of the Queen of Sheba* has no copyright line, though the box tells us that the original of this work also hangs in the National Gallery. Claude has his dates on the box, but not on the puzzle. Brueghel's jumbo 1,500-piece *Spreekwoorden*, or *Proverbs* (mistranslated into French, oddly, as *Scène Religieuse*), is credited not on the box but on a slip of paper within the box: ©1990 by Koninklijke Hausemann en Hötte nv, under Berne and Universal Copyright Conventions. So some puzzle makers take copyright seriously. Not all jigsaws are pirated.

Nobody seemed to know the answer to my query about the origins of museum and art gallery jigsaws until I happened upon a possible solution in a BBC Radio 4 programme by Alan Dein titled *The World's Most Difficult Puzzle*, first broadcast on 27 March 2004. This is an account of the 340-piece puzzle based on Jackson Pollock's *Convergence*, produced in 1964 by Springbok Editions in the United States, and it is an odd and interesting story. In the placid 1950s, the jigsaw industry in the US was at a low ebb; the craze of the Depression was forgotten, and the jigsaw had become unfashionable, stuck at the bottom end of the toy market. The images chosen by manufacturers were of scenic, snow-capped mountains, castles on the Rhine, fields of tulips, rose-wreathed cottages, English hunting scenes, and clippers at sea. Alison Lurie, the American novelist, recalls that during the summer holidays of her childhood there was always a jigsaw laid out on a table, always of traditional genre scenes of this nature – pictures on the Mary Russell Mitford, Helen Allingham, Barbara Trapido sickbed model. (It is well known that jigsaws are good for convalescence, and a Shakespeare scholar of my acquaintance claims that they are also a cure for the hangover.)

Two American enthusiasts and entrepreneurs transformed this tranquil scene. American printing executive Bob Lewin, whose family and office staff had always enjoyed puzzles, was inspired while on a business trip to England in the 1950s to try to revitalize the home industry. He had been in the habit of taking home gifts of circular Waddington puzzles, then still a novelty; now, on a visit to Leeds, he saw a Waddington display in the Queen's Hotel and got in touch with the company. He went back to the United States and, with the help of Waddington's expertise, tried out some upmarket ideas of his own. (John Waddington Ltd was a well-known firm of Leeds-based printers, which in the 1930s had branched out into playing cards and games such as Lexicon and Monopoly. It survived until 1995.)

In 1963, Lewin founded a company called Springbok Editions, with his wife and business partner Katie. They pursued their new agenda: Katie, an art lover, went round the art galleries with 'jigsaw eyes', selecting and commissioning new work. She chose work by Salvador Dali and other celebrated artists, but her most sensational choice was Pollock's *Convergence*, painted in 1952. This represented everything that the snowy mountains and cottages and farmyard scenes had left out: turmoil, controversy, freedom, movement, modernity.

Pollock had been killed in a car accident some seven years earlier, and his name and work were notorious. *Convergence* is one of the key works of Abstract Expressionism, a rich and complex patterning of blues and yellows and reds and oranges and white swirls and drips and squiggles, against a black background. It is a sprawl of primary colours on a large canvas (93½ × 155 inches). The jigsaw version is deeply puzzling and, as American jigsaw historian Anne Williams explains in Alan Dein's radio programme, even the cutting of the pieces was a puzzle. Most mass-produced puzzles are cut on a grid, with rows of repeating shapes, but the Springbok dies were irregularly curved and unpredictable, making the puzzle even more difficult.

Convergence was a great success in its jigsaw format. It rapidly became a conversation piece and a status symbol. Those who completed it were so proud of their efforts that they converted their handiwork into coffee tables and wall plaques. Soon the jigsaw was better known than Pollock's original canvas (which is still to some the object of derision, and always at risk of parody), and visitors went to the gallery in Buffalo in search of the jigsaw, not the painting. It made Springbok prosperous. A replica of a Pollock seemed to evade the philistine suspicion with which the source work was regarded, and the kitsch art of the jigsaw had mysteriously made Abstract Expressionism popular with a middlebrow clientele. *Convergence: The Jigsaw* was featured in Newsweek in December 1964, and Katie Lewin did a jigsaw tour of thirty cities in thirty days, talking about it. This must have been much more fun than a book tour. It became more famous than Pollock himself. It also introduced a vogue for more and more difficult adult puzzles, some of them perversely difficult – all white, all black, all blue, or, like 'Little Red Riding Hood's Hood', all red. A new vogue for difficulty had begun.

The Lewins sold their company to Hallmark in 1967, and it

continued to thrive, but *Convergence* remains the most celebrated of Springbok's products. The original painting still hangs in Buffalo, in the Albright-Knox Gallery, and during the BBC Radio 4 programme we can hear presenter Alan Dein talking to Ken Wayne, the Curator of Modern Art, as he scatters the pieces of the puzzle on the gallery floor in front of it and then attempts to assemble them. Pollock painted with his canvas spread upon the floor, and Dein spread his cardboard pieces before the canvas in homage. ('It's so much bigger than the jigsaw puzzle version,' he says to his microphone, sounding somewhat daunted.) It took him seven hours and forty-six minutes to assemble the puzzle, with a little transatlantic advice and moral support over the phone from expert dissectologist Tom Tyler in Ipswich.

My assembling of this puzzle took far longer than seven hours and forty-six minutes. I think it must have been easier to do it in front of the Real Thing. The image on the puzzle box was not very helpful, as it was not complete, and I kept getting it upside down. This wouldn't have happened to me in Buffalo.

Reproducing the free swirl and squirt and drip of rich oil in little dry hard discrete cardboard pieces is a paradoxical activity, but very satisfying. Why? I keep looking for the answer.

XXXVIII

I don't know whether Springbok's innovative approach to
puzzles was the real starting point for the great leap forward in
the international trade in dissected Old Masters. The story of the
spectacular rise of the museum shop has not yet been told. I love
museum shops, although I slightly despise myself for doing so, and
chide myself for the need to appropriate bits and pieces of culture
instead of relying on the purity of unaided memory. I indulge my
weakness by buying Christmas presents for grandchildren in the
British Museum and the Tate and the Science Museum. I'd just
visited the National Gallery shop and was having a pre-Christmas
lunch with my brother and my sister Helen in a wine bar off
Trafalgar Square, loaded with parcels, when the idea for writing
a book about jigsaws began to take shape. I remember telling
them about it. I thought my little book would make the perfect
stocking-filler. It would surely be as desirable as a Van Gogh calendar or a fake Sumerian necklace or a cardboard build-your-own
dinosaur.

Our need to buy souvenirs and replicas has been profitable to
traders for thousands of years. St Paul railed at the silversmiths of
Ephesus for turning out little silver replicas of the Temple of Diana,

but Christians were not deterred from longing for their own little idols. Relics of saints succeeded little silver temples, and pilgrims, crusaders, curious travellers and rival ecclesiastical institutions purchased the bones and teeth and hair of saints, fragments of the True Cross, scraps from Jacob's coat, and walking sticks made from the rod of Moses. The Holy Vase or Grail was the source of many a legend and fabrication. Canterbury, as Chaucer told us, was a manufactory of sacred objects for commercial purposes, as were all places of artistic and religious pilgrimage. Calvin complained in his Treatise on Relics that there were so many bits of the True Cross scattered around the abbeys of Christendom that if they were gathered together they would make a great shipload, far too heavy for even Jesus to have carried. Mary Magdalen left at least five corpses, but, as her devotees protested, all things were possible to God.

The story of the True Cross is one of the more incomprehensible and incoherent legends of the Middle Ages. It comes from a compilation of saints' lives and ecclesiastical commentary by Jacopo Voragine titled *The Golden Legend*, or the *Legenda Aurea*, which was once immensely popular; it was Caxton's best-selling title. (The story of the Holy Grail, in comparison, is straightforward.) The legend of the True Cross is most famously depicted in the murals of Piero della Francesca in Arezzo, in which we see Seth placing in the mouth of the dead Adam a twig from the tree of Good and Evil, which becomes the wood of the True Cross on which Christ was crucified. Further images show the meeting, centuries later, of the Queen of Sheba and Solomon, as she kneels and prays on a bridge made of the wood; the Dream of Constantine presaging victory in battle; a miracle in which the cross restores a youth to life; the recapture of the cross from the Persians by the Greek emperor Heraclius; and other related or possibly unrelated scenes. I am indebted for this précis (but not for any errors in it) to Helen Langdon's account in her 1984 guide to Italy, where she describes the frescoes as 'hauntingly still and grave', their beauty 'dependent on the masterly arrangement of geometric shapes and cool tones…and on the dramatic power of expression and gesture'. Piero della Francesco's murals are of great dignity, unlike the medieval tourist trade, which thrived on fragments and splinters, but you may purchase them, of course, in irresistible post-card format. And you can buy his *Madonna del Duca da Montefeltro* as a jigsaw.

We love replicas, and replicas of replicas, and we did so long before Jean Baudrillard came up with his theories of a simulacrum society. We like to take something home with us, to prove we have been there, to remind us of what we saw, to keep us in touch with the spirit of the place. We know they are not authentic, but we don't care. Historian Tom Holland writes in *The Author* (Summer 2007) that he treats himself to some antiquities to accompany each work on which he embarks: coins issued by Julius Caesar for research on the Roman Republic, a crusader's ring for the Middle Ages. But, his means being limited, he has also acquired a supplement of tat.

> Mostly, this consists of trinkets that have been flogged to me
> over the years outside a wide variety of archaeological sites.
> In fact, I like knowing they are wholly without value: it makes
> me less nervous about re-arranging them…Among the
> treasures currently on display are a plastic Caesar bought from
> a rip-off merchant outside the Roman Forum; a fridge-magnet
> in the form of a Viking from Uppsala; and a statue of Artemis
> from Ephesus.

He follows in an old tradition. Wealthy tourists taking the Grand Tour in the eighteenth century purchased real antiquities and commissioned original paintings and casts, but they also set in motion a vogue for miniature and easily transported copies of famous sights and objects. From the eighteenth century onwards the Piazza di Spagna in Rome was surrounded by the workshops and studios of artists and craftsmen and mosaicists, making snuff-boxes, jewellery and other 'collectibles' for the tourist trade. As an Italian historian commented, 'Ladies now wear in tiny finger-rings the largest monuments of ancient and Christian Rome.' You could buy brooches decorated with St Peter's or the Coliseum, or a fan showing the tomb of Cecilia Metella, or a ring displaying the Temple of Vespasian, or a perfume bottle of green lava adorned with micromosaic views of ruins and doves.

Goethe in his *Italian Journey* recorded his dislike of the degradation of classical art into 'snuffboxes and bracelets', but the fashion had caught on and continues to flourish. (Goethe's taste in knick-knacks was not impeccable: in 1793 he tried to persuade his mother to buy a toy guillotine for his son August, but the wise woman robustly refused.) As with little pretty pocket books, the miniaturization is part of the attraction. Edith Wharton, whose wealthy American parents did the Grand Tour in the 1840s (and happened to run into a revolution in Paris in 1848) were avid collectors of bric-a-brac, mercilessly described by their daughter. In Wharton's short story, 'The Old Maid', she evokes the rosewood whatnots adorned with tropical shells, with 'feldspar vases, an alabaster model of the Leaning Tower of Pisa, a pair of obelisks made of scraps of porphyry and serpentine picked up by the young couple in the Roman Forum'.

Goethe was seriously and scientifically interested in stones and mineralogy, and on his travels could not resist collecting as he went. Edith Wharton's parents, the Joneses, were more like magpies. Mark Twain was a magpie *malgré lui*; he didn't mean to buy the stuff, but he did. The marketing and the ubiquity of souvenirs overwhelmed his better judgement. In Switzerland he resisted the *Lion of Lucerne* rendered in wood, ivory, ebony, marble, chalk, sugar or chocolate, and grew very tired of looking at wooden quails, chickens and chamois, but he succumbed to buying three wooden clocks, which he thought would be 'pretty enough, no doubt, when I get them home'. This was despite his long-held aversion to the inane, silly and aggravating cuckoo clock. The merchandise was too much for him.

Even Wordsworth, that touchstone of the authentic, was intrigued and half attracted by souvenirs and mechanical toys, by 'imitations fondly made in plain Confession of Man's weakness, and his loves'. He was not above taking note of models of the Firth of Forth and Edinburgh Castle and microscopic views of Rome and Tivoli and the Temple of Sibyl. He saw the parts as parts, but with a feeling of the whole. (That's his own phrase, from *The Prelude*.) He condoned our weaknesses.

Amongst Auntie Phyl's jumble of jewellery and curios are an inch-long Eiffel Tower on a chain and a tiny tortoiseshell book the size of my thumbnail. It's not really a book, and it's probably not really made of tortoiseshell, but it has a spine, and a metal clasp, and into it is set a tiny spyhole not much larger than a pinhead. If you look through this little spyhole, you can see, astonishingly, a large view of the Marine Parade of Margate, complete with Edwardian ladies in hats walking along the promenade. How did they get in there? I never saw this object or this view when I was a child, and maybe Auntie Phyl never knew they were there. Perhaps the little book had belonged to Grandma Bloor. It is sheer chance that I noticed the spyhole, and put it to my eye. The ladies had walked unseen for a century in their hermetic seaside kingdom before I saw them.

I wonder if it was purchased as a souvenir of an outing to Margate. Mablethorpe, not Margate, was the favoured resort of the East Midlands, but I suppose my grandparents could have ventured to Margate. They loved touring with their motorbike and side-car, and they purchased hundreds of postcards to mark their travels through the Lakes and the West Country. They kept them in a large tin toffee box from Doncaster, which accompanied my aunt to the care home in Newark, and is now in the custody of my sister Helen.

Postcard views were, and remain, the cheapest form of memento, and old postcards now have dedicated collectors. Large art jigsaws are more expensive, but the jigsaw has been reinvented as a postcard, and is on sale in this format in many museum shops. You can buy greetings-card-sized jigsaws of Michelangelo and Van Gogh in galleries throughout Europe. In the shop of the Gilbert Collection in Somerset House in London, you can buy a little 'Post-Puzzle' of the collection's famous micromosaic tigress, complete with an envelope for posting, or more elaborate and expensive, wooden, seventy-five-piece jigsaws of the micromosaic 'Ponte Rotto and Tiber Island' or of the design on a Florentine *pietra dura* table top. As micromosaics and *pietra dura* tables are in themselves a kind of jigsaw, involving the fitting of small pieces together to make a larger image, we have here the manufacture of jigsaws of jigsaws. Sir Arthur Gilbert and his wife Rosalinde, the founders of this idiosyncratic collection, were very keen on dissections and resections, on patterns and shapes. The Lewins had jigsaw eyes, and the Gilberts had mosaic eyes.

Charles Saumarez Smith, in an essay on 'The Future of the Museum' (*A Companion to Museum Studies*, 2006), points out that 'shops are becoming more like museums – places for visual and aesthetic display – while museums are becoming more like shops…as shops become more creative, more historical, and more aesthetically suggestive, museums are driven by their financial circumstances to become more aggressively commercial.' It is claimed that more people visit the shop of the Metropolitan

Museum of Art in New York than visit the museum itself. Some gallery shops now sell specially commissioned objects, published by a gallery imprint. The Tate, which in the 1960s enjoyed ever-increasing sales of postcards (particularly of Salvador Dali, always the people's choice), established a new gallery shop in 1972, and in 1995 a new company called Tate Gallery Publishing was set up, owned by Trustees, with the profits covenanted to the gallery. The Science Museum recently opened a retail outlet in Selfridges. Nick Prior, in an essay on 'Postmodern Restructurings' (*A Companion to Museum Studies*, 2006), notes that whereas 'Once upon a time, the stands at museum shops sold postcards and posters, a few books and some table mats', now 'merchandise covers everything from film, opera and poetry to fashionable clothes, catalogues and kitchenware'. He doesn't mention jigsaws, but he could have done.

I once bought a really disappointing jigsaw in a National Trust shop, I think at Stourhead. It's one of the very few I've never finished, and I failed to finish it not because it was too difficult, but because it was too dull. It represented, as I remember, an eighteenth-century painting of some prize specimen of livestock – a large cow, or perhaps a bull, of an ancient breed, with small legs and a large square bulk of body. I thought it would be fun to do, and even mildly educational, but it wasn't. After wasting some time on its enormous flank, I gave up. It was not interesting enough to finish.

This was an instructive experience. I didn't take against the creature, as I took against *Venus of Urbino*, but I didn't think it repaid attention. Maybe it was badly cut. I can't now recall the shape of the pieces. An expert might well have blamed the cut. And maybe it was a pig, not a cow. A huge sow, like the sow at the Home Farm in Blue Anchor. Maybe that is why I took against it.

XXXIX

Jigsaws have now been with us for so long and have become so much a part of our way of thinking that it is hard to know how we did without them. The jigsaw as metaphor and simile is everywhere. It is used as a logo by Microsoft Word and by the online encyclopaedia Wikipedia, and it pops up on the screen of the Barclays Bank Hole in the Wall. Those instantly recognizable little shapes, dubbed in friendly fashion by Perec 'les bonhommes' (the little chaps), 'les croix de Lorraine' (the double crosses) and 'les croix' (the cross-bars), are familiar to us all, although they post-date Spilsbury and belong to the age of the fretsaw and the cardboard punch.

Clothes shops and furniture designers have adopted the word 'jigsaw' as a brand name. I wrote some of this text while wearing a Jigsaw cardigan given to me for Christmas by my son and daughter-in-law. Kiran Desai uses the word as a verb in her novel *The Inheritance of Loss* (2006), where she speaks of jigsawing 'cups, saucers, teapot, milk, sugar, strainer, Marie and Delite biscuits' on a tea tray. (Is there a suggestion here that jigsaws, like Marie biscuits, are part of a threatened and fading Anglophile world? I think not.)

Every day a journalist or broadcaster uses the word in one context or another – in the space of a few weeks we had the avian flu jigsaw, the England cricket team jigsaw, the Ipswich murders jigsaw, the juvenile crime jigsaw, and innumerable other jigsaws, too many to note, too many to quantify. We even had the missing-pieces-of-God jigsaw on 'Thought for the Day'. Open any newspaper any day and you are likely to find a jigsaw. I have stopped counting. The word suggests at once difficulty and comfort – the frustration of the unsolved puzzle, the satisfaction of the possible solution.

The word 'jigsaw' was never patented or enshrined in copyright. It has appeared in many titles. Barbara Cartland's first novel, a Mayfair romance of implausibly resolved misunderstandings, is called *Jig-Saw* (1923). Sybille Bedford's volume of autobiography, which fits together the disparate characters and episodes of her long and international life, is also, more relevantly, called *Jigsaw* (1989). Michael Holroyd's second volume of memoirs, which fits together the missing pieces of family information that emerged after the publication of *Basil Street Blues* in 1999, is called, analogously, *Mosaic*, though it too could have been called *Jigsaw*, for much of the new information revolves round the missing piece (and missing portrait) of his grandfather's mistress Agnes May, the blonde beauty who ruined the Holroyd family fortunes. Vikram Seth at one point thought of calling his memoir of his aunt and uncle *Mosaic*, but Holroyd got there first, and Seth settled on the title of *Two Lives*.

John Fowles, writing in a similar autobiographical mode, worked for a long time on a volume of autobiographical fiction called *Tesserae*, a ghost title that occasionally appears in his bibliography, though it was never published. Fowles said it would have been 'a sort of existentialist mosaic of what it was like in the 1950s to be poor, unfocused, and unpublished', but he did not finish it. He thought of reusing the title for his collected essays and writings, which appeared in 1998 as *Wormholes*, and in the preface to this volume he tells us that 'An early book I tried to write was entitled *Tesserae*; to be of minor relationships, dabs of colour. I always felt then that I was best understood and seen – or felt – as a sequence of very small happenings, little brick squares of opinion and feeling.'

The assembly of squares and fragments: the picture made up, like Queen Adelaide's face, in stitches, or in pixels, or in small blocks, or in dots, or in stipples, or in particles. Virginia Woolf, reflecting in her diary (September 1924) on the heterogeneity of daily life and its mixed tapestry composed of postmen, invitations to Knole, and lectures on the League of Nations, notes: 'All this confirms me in thinking that we're splinters and mosaics; not, as they used to hold, immaculate, monolithic, consistent wholes.' (It's not clear who the 'they' are who used to hold this view of identity – old-fashioned novelists like Arnold Bennett, perhaps?) A fragmented view of personality and consciousness has been widely held since the days of Locke and Berkeley and their successor David Hartley, and neuroscientists today nudge us even further towards the notion that memory, character and consciousness itself are made up of small, discrete, neurological events, events that build up a mosaic, a jigsaw, a pattern, which we may take for a whole. A pointillist self, made up of tesserae.

Experimental novelist Paul Ableman in *the secret of consciousness* (1999) proposed the view that the human mind is fundamentally discontinuous: 'a "person", even though fully material, and indeed biological, is not a stable and continuous entity but rather an inter-mittent and discontinuous one.' We need to make up a linking narrative, but the links may be arbitrary or even false. Identity is no more (or less) than the unique set, or narrative, of sensory data in each individual. The novelist's use of 'interior monologue' is an attempt to mimic both the instant chaos and the archival organization of the mind.

When Paul tried to explain his theory of the mind to me, he seemed to think I might find it in some way threatening, although he argued that it wasn't; he insisted that it didn't imply that we were 'robotic', but he insisted a bit too much. I wasn't sure whether I understood him fully. (He was amused by my lack of grasp of the simple principle of the transistor, which I had always thought was something to do with tiny radios, but which proved to be an important part of his twin-data-stream theory of consciousness.)

To me, the concept of the self as a sequence of very small but discrete happenings is persuasive and attractive, not alarming. It allows for addition, for retrieval, for accretion, and for the retrospective solving of puzzles. If one could only retrieve from long ago that little block of fear, or disgust, or attraction, that sudden flash of recognition or enlightenment, one could hook it into the pattern, one could rebuild and reinterpret the fuller picture.

The Oulipians had a word for language used in small, recognizable blocks, in the verbal equivalent of little brick squares. They called this 'langage cuit', or 'pre-cooked language' or 'canned' language, and in this category they included 'proverbs, clichés, quotations, historical declarations, book and film titles etc.', which became for them the base of many artful substitutions and variations. Auntie Phyl and I, in our daily converse, used a good deal of canned language (just as, during and immediately after the war, we ate a lot of canned food), and I found it a comforting medium of exchange. You knew where you were with canned language. I have used quite a lot of it in this book. Writers spend much time – sometimes too much time – striving for originality of diction. You can communicate perfectly well with many people, indeed often better, if you stick largely to a common canned language, and draw from a common source.

Mary Poppins uses a great deal of canned language, which forms a piquant contrast with her unpredictable behaviour. She is fond of phrases like 'Care killed a cat' and 'I wouldn't half like a cup of tea' and 'You got out of bed the wrong side this morning' and 'Strike me pink!' Children find this reassuring.

Auntie Phyl had a friend, Mr Hubbard, who used to come to sit with her on Sunday afternoons. He was, I think, a neighbouring farmer. He hardly ever said anything, and neither did she. I used to find these silences trying, until it occurred to me to look at them in a different light. These were Long Bennington silences. They were the silences of the tribe, and they had a long history. And the phrases of greeting and parting that they uttered were time-honoured, and the odd scrap of information about a dog, or the weather, or the crop of apples or greengages needed no embellishment. They were what they were. They were complete in themselves.

XL

The explorer Sir Ernest Shackleton gives us an extended description of pack ice as a jigsaw, which poses interesting questions about the nature and source of fabric and pattern, and the interlocking of blocks. As he describes in *South* (1919), on 18 December 1915, his ship *Endurance* found herself

> proceeding amongst large floes with thin ice between them. The leads were few…I had been prepared for evil conditions in the Weddell Sea, but had hoped that in December and January, at any rate, the pack would be loose, even if no open water was to be found. What we were actually encountering was fairly dense pack of a very obstinate character. Pack-ice might be described *as a gigantic and interminable jigsaw puzzle devised by nature.* The parts of the puzzle in loose pack have floated slightly apart and become disarranged; at numerous places they have pressed together again; as the pack gets closer the congested areas grow larger and the parts are jammed harder till finally it becomes 'close pack,' when the whole of the jigsaw puzzle becomes jammed to such an extent that it can with care and labour be traversed in every direction on

foot. Where the parts do not fit closely there is, of course, open water, which freezes over in a few hours after giving off volumes of 'frost-smoke.' In obedience to renewed pressure this young ice 'rafts,' so forming double thicknesses of a toffee-like consistency. Again the opposing edges of heavy floes rear up in slow and almost silent conflict, till high 'hedgerows' are formed round each part of the puzzle. At the junction of several floes chaotic areas of piled-up blocks and masses of ice are formed. Sometimes 5-ft. to 6-ft. piles of evenly shaped blocks of ice are seen so neatly laid that *it seems impossible for them to be Nature's work.* [italics added]

'It seems impossible for them to be Nature's work.' This power-ful passage seems to suggest that the jigsaw is at once a force of nature, a natural phenomenon, and the product or by-product of some supernatural plan. Nature creates its own puzzles, and we imitate them. (Maps demonstrating continental drift and the earth's tectonic plates always look like huge jigsaws; they are the original Spilsburys. It's amazing that tectonic plate theory wasn't formu-lated until the 1960s, and that, once formulated, it was so bitterly resisted. Once you know, it's obvious, but Shackleton didn't know, couldn't have known.)

It also makes one wonder, less philosophically, whether Arctic and Antarctic explorers, like imprisoned passengers on cruise liners or underemployed members-in-waiting of the royal family, used to while away the time with jigsaws when they were not busy working at scrimshaw or fitting ships into bottles. Shackleton's crew seem to have been keener on playing cards, strumming the banjo and singing than on the quieter half-arts, and Shackleton's biographer, Roland Huntford, says that he cannot find any record of his subject's personal application to jigsaws, although the passage above shows that he was familiar with them. Huntford suggests that he may have come across them when an officer on the Union Castle Line. Or perhaps his wife and children may have done them during his long absences? Penelope's weaving was as pointless as a jigsaw, as ephemeral as a sand mandala, and the wives of explorers have much time to kill.

XLI

Jigsaws and maps have always fitted together, and jigsaws and cottage gardens have, as we have seen, a long and soothing association. Jigsaws and detective fiction also have a natural affinity. During the 1930s there was a vogue for publishing simple thrillers with a real jigsaw puzzle offering the solution attached to the back flap in a brown-paper pocket. Walter Eberhardt's *The Jigsaw Puzzle Murder*, published in 1933 by Puzzle Books Ltd of Covent Garden (but set in and printed in the USA), is even more elaborate. It consists of two volumes, one a short narrative of 184 pages, which ends with the arrest of the murderer, but does not give the murderer's identity; the second a book-shaped cardboard box containing a 200-piece cardboard puzzle portraying the scene and the 'solution'. This jigsaw shows a jigsaw within a jigsaw, for the plot, such as it is, revolves around a jigsaw, and it also incorporates several (not very well made) pieces shaped like pistols. The box alerts us: 'Watch Next Month for Another Jig-Saw Puzzle Murder Mystery!' (The red-dressed heroine of this drama, Diana, has just seen the movie, *Cavalcade*.)

In a later and darker world, the tormented victim of detective writer Henning Mankell's *The Return of the Dancing Master*

(Harvill, 2003) is a jigsaw addict who orders his puzzles from a club in Rome:

> Whenever he finished a puzzle, he would burn it and immediately start on a new one. He made sure he always had a good supply of puzzles. It was a bit like a smoker and his cigarettes...He didn't think much of the mechanically produced ones. There was no logic in the way the pieces were cut, and they didn't fit in with the patterns. Just now he was working on a puzzle based on Rembrandt's *The Conspiracy of the Bathavians under Claudius Civilis*. It had 3,000 pieces and had been made by a specialist in Rouen.

Scattered pieces of the jigsaw, naturally, suggest clues to the brutal murder that shortly follows.

The world of jigsaw competitions, or 'the professional US speed puzzle circuit', is the background of the plot of a novel titled *The Missing Piece* by French novelist Antoine Bello, published in 1998. This is a macabre thriller about a serial murderer who polishes off various rivals and competitors, using severed body parts as clues in the deadly puzzle he creates. It was praised as 'Borgesian' when it appeared in English in 2002, and I was expecting to enjoy it, but found it an unpleasant if well-informed exercise in historical pastiche, sadistic fantasy and smart post-modern narrative. One of the characters is a young American called Nicholas Spillsbury, in homage to John Spilsbury, and there is a good deal of knowing discussion about collectors and cutting techniques and solving techniques (both of the morphological and colour-coding variety), but the spirit of the novel contradicts all the virtues that jigsaws traditionally embody. (This is, of course, intentional.) It is all about speed, money, enmity, rivalry and the cutting of throats. The jigsaw is treated as a race, and the tone is macho and ageist, which I suppose is the reason why I didn't find it very entertaining. It promises much, with its pseudo-academic sections on 'The Detective Novel during the Depression' and 'The Puzzle as Metaphor for Police Procedure', and its references to non-fictional scholars such as the American jigsaw historian Anne Williams. But it fails to deliver. This isn't because Bello isn't a clever writer, but because there is an insuperable mismatch between his subject and his plot. It's hard to turn innocent, everyday jigsaw puzzles into a hard-edged, brutal male fantasy about dismemberment.

There are signs that Bello is well aware of this difficulty. He may have been attempting to satirize the corrupting commercial spirit of capitalism in the United States, but if so he chose the wrong vehicle. Dismissive comments about 'the most inoffensive of pastimes, once so beloved of our grandmothers' sit uneasily in his text. In short, he abuses the jigsaw. The jigsaw isn't a metaphor for cutting throats or dismembering legs. It is a different kind of metaphor. It may be a complex metaphor, even a despairing metaphor, as Georges Perec's novel shows, but it is not a violent metaphor.

The jigsaw, like push-pin, is innocent. It is more innocent than poetry.

Jules Verne's Royal Game of the Goose novel is full of American capitalism, ruthless competition, cheating and gambling, but it is a romantic and high-spirited story, from a less brutal age.

Auntie Phyl and I, unlike some of the puzzle solvers mentioned in or cross-questioned for this book, and unlike the eighteenth-century card-playing ladies condemned by Mrs Sherwood, were not at all competitive. We were strictly non-violent. We never came to blows. We sometimes got in one another's light, but we weren't trying to win anything, or break any records. Speed was of no interest to us. It was depressing to me to read a book about jigsaws that concentrated on record breaking and murdering by numbers.

Anthony Brown, one of my most seasoned jigsaw correspondents, admits to 'a competitive spirit', which sometimes upset his puzzle companions. He, his wife and his four sons would sit round the kitchen table with a puzzle each, of about ninety pieces, 'and, ready, steady, go, each would tip out his cylinder and race to finish his puzzle first'.

We weren't like that.

Once I lost my temper with my daughter when we were doing a puzzle together in the country. I accused her of getting in my way. The real problem, as I remember with shame, was my recognition that she was now much better at it than I was, partly because she could see the pieces better than I could, partly because she'd drunk less wine with her dinner. My eyes and wits were failing, and I didn't want to know this.

I was and am turning inexorably into Auntie Phyl.

XLII

The concept of the jigsaw is, as I hope I have shown, deeply embedded in our language, and we use the word so often because it is useful. But it is recent. I often think about Kevin's words in his cab on the way to the Museum of London, when he asked me to consider the phenomenon of the mosaic. He made me think about the history of shapes and patterns, and to wonder whether that was part of my enquiry. The fitting together of small pieces to make larger objects and images is a curious and widespread human activity, common to many (almost certainly to all) cultures, and there is an intrinsic physical pleasure in it, as well as an aesthetic satisfaction. Our responses to pattern – within a culture, across cultures, within a class or a family – are personal and idiosyncratic. Why do some of us like the long-surviving and still-ubiquitous Paisley motif, while others fastidiously recoil from it? And is this motif a teardrop or a flower or a pine cone? Whatever it is, its sinuous outline has spread far beyond the cashmere or Kashmir shawls that brought it to Europe in the eighteenth century, and like a form of algae it has colonized the world. Why?

Why do some of us like tiled floors, or William Morris wallpapers, or minimalist decor, or marquetry, or ogee arches, or

Islamic domes, or the pelta pattern, or the 'line of beauty'? (Mary Russell Mitford believed that the greyhound represented 'the line of beauty in perpetual motion'. She was very fond of her pet greyhound Mayflower, despite the fact that her father lost so much money on the dogs.) Some of us prefer curves, some geometry. Some hate the opulence and artificiality of *pietra dura* table tops, while others (like me) respond to them with rapture. Who knows what genetic combinations these choices reflect, what fragments of DNA they embody, what early-implanted memories they carry?

DNA itself is a puzzle, a zipped and helical puzzle.

I can understand why objects made in *pietra dura* can set the teeth on edge. They are, at various stages in their manufacture, not unlike jagged teeth. But I find it hard to imagine anyone who could remain unresponsive to the beauty of classical mosaics.

The word 'mosaic' is of much more ancient and distinguished provenance than the word 'jigsaw'.

After my brief tour of London with Kevin, I thought I ought to look further into the subject of mosaics, and I went off to inspect a few in the British Museum, where I used to visit them regularly in the days when I worked in the old BM Reading Room. I browsed in books about them in the British Library, and googled them on Google. I talked about mosaic restoration with the head of conservation at the British Museum, and he showed me ways of spotting which bits of a Roman mosaic have been replaced or restored. The fashion now is to restore less, and to leave bald patches to show where the missing pieces would have been; the result is a deliberately unfinished jigsaw. An artist may still sketch in the missing portions, but restorers will not necessarily fill the gaps. I have been told that at the end of a large restoration a bucket or two of leftover tesserae may remain: not so much missing pieces as extra pieces.

At first I was looking for anything that would connect mosaics with games and play and therefore, by analogy, with jigsaws, and I found a passage that suggested something of the sort in a book by Peter Fischer, translated from the German (*Mosaic: History and Technique*, 1969, 1971). He writes:

> The birth of mosaic art can be seen when children press shells and pebbles into the sandy beach and discover that the various hues can be laid out to form patterns or pictures. This happens so naturally that it may be regarded as one of the basic inventions as old as that of cooking. Very early man may have used this simple method to make a firm floor in his cave or hut...When one thinks of existing cave paintings, prehistoric mosaics seem quite conceivable – but of course they would have been washed away by the waters of thousands of years.

This seemed quite promising, as an introduction to mosaic history, but it didn't really lead anywhere, and none of the other mosaic experts seemed interested in the sandcastle aspect of mosaics. They eschewed idle speculation in favour of dating techniques. So, I learned that the earliest surviving mosaics are pebble mosaics, like that of Gnosis at Pella, made of pebbles coloured by nature, not by man. (*Opus signium* are humble floors; they and their name are still current.) I discovered that Sir Arthur Evans found at Knossos a stone box containing fragments of rock crystal, amethyst, beryl, lapis lazuli, and gold, which might or might not have been something to do with mosaics. I found no suggestion anywhere, except in Fischer, that children might have played with pebbles, though of course they must have done.

A classicist whom I met at a philological conference in Montreal sent me some interesting material about Greek and Roman children and games in antiquity, which described games with oyster shells, potsherds, knucklebones and dice, and gave detailed accounts of the Roman board game, 'Ludus Latrunculorum', to which allusion is made in many literary sources, including Ovid and Seneca. He also alerted me to an essay titled 'Games and Playthings' (1932) by bio-mathematician and classicist D'Arcy Wentworth Thompson, which tells us that 'Suetonius wrote a whole book on children's games, just as he did on the cries of animals and on the nightingale's song; but all these pleasant books of his are lost, though we should willingly have given three lives of his grammarians or one life of an emperor in exchange.' D'Arcy Thompson, more famous for his mathematical work on organic growth and form and natural patterns, systematically collected any references he could find to children's play in classical literature and the ancient world, but he gives no hints of a proto-jigsaw. We may never know for certain whether or not Greek and Roman children played at making pictures with pebbles or tesserae, or whether they amused themselves by reassembling broken crockery with ancient resin and mastic. They must have done, but we can't prove it.

Most mosaics were and are made of tesserae, which are little cubes of stone or terracotta or glass, but there is a form of mosaic called *opus sectile*, which uses marbles, tiles and stones pre-cut into shapes and fitted together 'like a jigsaw puzzle into geometric or figural patterns'; these are the antique precursor of Renaissance Florentine hardstone mosaics. The National Museum in Naples has a small collection of early Roman panels in *opus sectile*. In jigsaw terms, modern successors to *opus sectile* mosaics are made by Wentworth Puzzles, which incorporate pieces shaped like dogs or birds or flowers, or other motifs appropriate to the pictured design. These are called whimsies. The more whimsies you order, the more you pay for your puzzle; just as in the old days of Spilsbury, when you had to pay more for maps with the sea. It was Michael Codron who explained whimsies to me. I had never heard of them. We did not have them at Bryn.

In pursuit of mosaics, I found a pleasant little book about how to draw your own Roman mosaics, by an author called Robert Field, who is fascinated by patterns. He has also published books on *Geometric Patterns from Islamic Art and Architecture* (1988) and on patterns from churches and cathedrals and patchwork quilts and tiles and brickwork and mazes. Very laboriously, at his prompting, I drew a Solomon's Knot on graph paper. It took me a long time, but it was, as he had promised, quite satisfying. (Why?) If I were more persistent I could learn to do guilloches and palmettes. The very words of these patterns enchant. The guilloche, the palmette, the scroll, the acanthus, the arabesque, the chevron, the crowstep, the meander, the coffer, the cable, the Greek key...

And I started work on a tapestry cushion, based on a design I adapted from the border of the Orpheus Mosaic at Littlecote in Berkshire, illustrated in Field's booklet. I haven't got very far with that, and wouldn't know what to put in the middle anyway. Orpheus is too hard for me.

I wrote to Mr Field to ask him why he liked patterns so much, but he didn't answer.

I am really bad at sewing. Auntie Phyl used to tick me off for my bad hem stitches, which strode unevenly along the edges of squares of practice handkerchiefs. I am ill placed to criticize those anonymous stitchers who cobbled together Judy Chicago's *Dinner Party*. But tapestry is easy. You don't need finesse or delicacy. You can't go wrong (or not very wrong). You just fill in the grid. It's quite like doing a jigsaw. My father used to do tapestry, and I think it was he who taught me.

At boarding school we were obliged to have a hobby to pursue on wet Wednesday afternoons, and after a few desperate and messy stabs at bookbinding and throwing pots I declared that my hobby was tapestry. I bought a stretched canvas printed with a wreath of so-called Jacobean flowers against a brown background, on which

I worked, year after year. I made very slow progress, because when I was supposed to be sewing, I was secretly reading the novels of Thomas Hardy or the plays of Christopher Marlowe or the Terrible Sonnets of Gerard Manley Hopkins. I remember the expression on the face of the supervising teacher as I displayed, term after term, like Penelope, my unfinished wreath. She smiled a sceptical but complicit smile. She knew quite well what I was up to, down in the boiler room. I think that was when I realized that I was grown up, and could do as I pleased, provided I seemed to obey the rules. Nobody minded. The teacher agreed with me that my time was better spent reading poetry than doing tapestry. She couldn't say so, because of the school rules, but she agreed with me.

The Mount School had produced more distinguished needlework in its earlier years. Isabel Richardson, a student in 1790, had embroidered 'a map of England upon white silk in which the shape of each county was defined with the exactness of outline equal to any work of an engraver. This was done in chenille, whilst the names of the counties and of the chief towns were worked in silk.' This was geography for girls, in silk: a version of Spilsbury.

> Thou shalt not wash dishes, nor yet feed the swine;
> But sit on a cushion and sew a fine seam,
> And feed upon strawberries, sugar and cream.

That nursery rhyme was a promise for nice girls who married well.

My wreath wasn't a contender in this creative league, but I finished it. I am, or used to be, a completer. I still have it, and the chair onto the seat of which it is fitted. It is a little bald and worn now, like me, but it survives. Its crude roses and its strange blue ivy leaves and its little twirls of gold tendril bear witness to years of intermittent toil. The brown background is thinning, and it is uneven in colour and texture: I must have run out of wool, and bought odd batches. My father warned me about that kind of hazard, but not very seriously. He knew there were more things to worry about in life than skeins of unmatched wool.

Literature records bad embroidery and bad tapestry as well as good. Mary Russell Mitford makes fun of the uselessness of school samplers, describing in detail one with a plain pink border, a zigzag green border, a crimson wavy border, and a brown and more complicated zigzag border, all enclosing the alphabet

> great and small, in every colour of the rainbow, followed by a
> row of figures flanked on one side by a flower, name unknown,
> tulip, poppy, lily – something orange and scarlet, or scarlet
> orange; on the other by the more famous rosebud; then divers
> sentences, religious and moral…then, last and finest, the
> landscape in all its glory…In the centre was a house of bright
> scarlet, with yellow windows, a green door, and a blue roof: on
> one side, a man with a dog; on the other, a woman with a cat –
> this is Lucy's information; I should never have guessed, except
> in colour, between the man and the woman, the dog and the
> cat; they were in form, height and size alike to a thread.

And in Arnold Bennett's *The Old Wives' Tale*, the young Constance Baines passes time with what is clearly a very unattractive piece of needlework, destined for a firescreen. When we meet her, in chapter 1, 'The Square', she is at work on the mustard-coloured background of a bunch of roses, having finished the more interesting petals and leaves:

> The whole design was in squares – the gradations of red
> and greens, the curves of the smallest buds – all was contrived
> in squares, with a result that mimicked a fragment of
> uncompromising Axminster carpet. Still, the fine texture of

the wool, the regular and rapid grace of those fingers moving incessantly at back and front of the canvas, the gentle sound of the wool as it passed through the holes, and the intent, youthful earnestness of that lowered gaze, excused…an activity which, on artistic grounds, could not possibly be justified.

Bennett appreciated the tableau of young Constance with her wools, just as Elizabeth Gaskell, in *Sylvia's Lovers*, celebrates the aesthetic and erotic advantages of spinning.

The pretty sound of the buzzing, whirring motion, the attitude of the spinner, foot and hand alike engaged in the business – the bunch of gay coloured ribbon that ties the bundle of flax on the rock – all make it into a picturesque piece of domestic business that may rival harp-playing any day for the amount of softness and grace which it calls out.

Gaskell invokes the round arm, the tapered hand and the little foot on the 'traddle' in its smartly buckled shoe. This spinster knew what she was doing. But I don't think that we, secluded as we were in our girls' boarding school, were aware of the seductive aspects of our craft activities. There was nobody to watch us.

We were, however, well aware of the disastrous implications of a one-off Whitsuntide sporting event, which was, unusually, attended by boys from our brother school. We girls, aged fifteen and sixteen, were made to do gymnastics in the school garden wearing aertex shirts and our regulation navy school knickers. Not even shorts, which would have been bad enough, but knickers. We couldn't believe it, we couldn't understand how our squeamish, ladylike staff could possibly have been so naive as to endorse such an exhibition. We knew it was a bad idea. How the boys gathered and gazed!

I have made dozens of cushions since that first pseudo-Jacobean wreath. The house is uselessly full of them. Most of them are simple geometric patterns, designed by me, though I have done a couple of Ben Nicholsons (transferred to canvas by my son Joe) and a Kaffe Fassett cauliflower. Flowers and wreaths don't come out so well, or not in the gross-point stitch sizes that I deploy. Christopher Fry had a magnificent firescreen showing the house and garden in Bristol where he had lived, beautifully worked by his wife Phyllis, and I thought of trying something along those lines, but it was too difficult for me. I never got beyond the sketch.

I didn't know who Kaffe Fassett was when I bought the cauliflower canvas. I bought it because it was so eccentric. I was stitching away at it on an aeroplane somewhere, I think on the way to the Gothenburg Book Fair, when the stewardess said to me, 'Oh, what a lovely Kaffe Fassett!' I pretended I'd known who he was all along, but for a long time after this incident I thought he was a Scandinavian woman, not a North American man.

You can't easily do embroidery on aeroplanes now. You can't take scissors or needles through security.

Auntie Phyl said to me once, reprovingly, watching my stitching, 'That needle's like a poker.' I was taken aback. I don't think it had then occurred to me that needles came in different sizes. To me, a needle was a needle. With my mother, it was nearly impossible to do anything right; with my aunt, it was quite hard to do anything wrong. But on this occasion, with my selection of a needle, I had managed it.

My father and the Duke of Windsor both did tapestry. They had little else in common. And the Duke of Windsor also did jigsaws. He and Wallis Simpson could be said to have fallen in love over, or at least in the vicinity of, a jigsaw. In January 1932 Wallis Simpson was invited by the prince with her second husband Ernest Simpson to a weekend at Fort Belvedere in Windsor Great Park, as she records in her memoirs, *The Heart has its Reasons* (1956). There she discovered the Prince of Wales (as he then was) surrounded by cairn terriers and at work on a tapestry in gros point. Queen Mary had taught him how to do it, he said, and it was destined to cover a backgammon table. (A tapestry-covered backgammon table is an anomalous concept, rather like a biscuit tin made to look like a leather-bound novel by Walter Scott, but that is what Mrs Simpson said he said.) In the evening, after a dinner of oysters and roast beef, some guests played cards, while others worked on 'an extremely complicated jigsaw puzzle of which the pieces lay scattered on a large table in front of the main window'. It sounds quite like Bryn but on a grander scale.

There is a photograph of the prince, by now King Edward VIII, at work, though not very hard at work, on a large jigsaw on the deck of Lady Yule's yacht, the *Nahlin*, defiantly and adulterously afloat in the Adriatic in the summer of 1936. It is not clear whether the puzzle itself portrays a bathing beauty, or whether a bathing beauty is painted on the table on which the puzzle pieces lie. We at Bryn wouldn't have approved of it either way. We didn't do bathing beauties (though Auntie Phyl did go on a cruise to Norway in the summer of 1951, in a second-class cabin of the M/S *Venus* of the Bergen Steamship Company). Wallis Simpson and Lady Diana Cooper were both of the royal party, but they do not appear in the photograph. We know that after the Abdication the Windsors went on doing jigsaws for the rest of their lives, commissioning hand-made, personal, *opus sectile* jigsaws, many of them incorporating a little dog-shaped piece, a whimsy, for they loved their cairn terriers and their pugs, just as Auntie Phyl loved her Westies, and my father his Staffordshire bull terrier Anna.

Windsor was full of tapestry wool. Henry James's effeminate and wealthy friend the novelist Howard Sturgis lived in a 'chintzy, cosy Victorian house' called Queen's Acre (or Qu'acre) on the edge of

Windsor Great Park, where he was perpetually engaged in needle-point. He would stitch and embroider over cups of tea and cakes and gossip. His literary friends tolerated this, though some of them thought he was too much under the cosy spell of Berlin wool and his lazy dog Misery. I don't know when or why my father took up needlepoint. It certainly wasn't through idleness, as he worked too hard all his life. It was probably to ward off melancholy, to which, like Dr Johnson, he was prey. When he was dying of mesothelioma in the Slotervaart Hospital in Amsterdam, I bought him a canvas of Bargello work, thinking it might help him to pass the time. He didn't start it for days, but then he began to work it, slowly, sadly, patiently.

My father used to complain that Bargello, unlike gros point or petit point, used up too much wool too quickly. It was enjoyable to do, but it was expensive and wasteful. It didn't kill time slowly enough. But even so, he didn't have time to complete this design. He didn't finish it, as Auntie Phyl didn't finish the last Porlock jigsaw. I finished it for him. I have it still.

XLIII

Bargello or Florentine work is geometric. Its stitches are like tesserae, and they work in steps. They do not attempt to reproduce curves. Kaffe Fassett has done geometry, but he has also done more ambitious representational designs, like my cauliflower. Why would one want to reproduce a cauliflower in wool? Or to crochet (as the wife of one of my friends has done) a Full British Breakfast? Or to imitate a marble bust in mosaic grisaille? Or to embroider a portrait of Napoleon? Or to make a biscuit tin look like a straw basket or a bird's nest or a book?

The desire to reproduce one medium in terms of another, or to imitate natural objects in unnatural substances, is a curious, widespread and deep-rooted human need. It may or may not be at the mysterious root of art. The very difficulties of translation are a challenge. Workers in *pietra dura*, mosaicists, micromosaicists and jigsaw-puzzle manufacturers have noted that some subjects reproduce much better than others, and are particularly popular with the commissioning and purchasing public. Jigsaw connoisseurs, when cross-questioned, often confess to a liking not for cottage gardens with hollyhocks (popular though these remain) but for brickwork and architecture. Dutch Old Masters and English cathedrals feature high on their lists. Ships with a lot of rigging seem to offer allied attractions.

The great craftsmen knew both sides of this challenge – the satisfaction of a good reproduction; the difficulty of an unlikely subject. French master goldsmith Louis Siries, the eighteenth-century director of the Grand Ducal Workshops of Florence (the Opificio delle Pietre Dure), proposed various subjects to Ferdinand III of Lorraine to adorn the vastnesses of the Palazzo Pitti, including a cycle of hardstone pictures representing 'ancient buildings', because, he said, 'architecture is the subject that can be represented most perfectly'. The happiest result of this suggestion was a fine stone picture of the Tomb of Cecilia Metella, worked in *pietra dura*, marble, alabaster and gilt bronze, showing the antique tomb, some peasants, two cows and a goat. It was completed in 1795, travelled around a little after the French invasion of Italy, was presented to Pope Pius IX by Leopoldo II in 1857 and is now in the Gilbert Collection, along with several other, less fortunate hardstone pictures.

Reproduction and copying can be dangerous. They may be regarded as appropriation or theft. Goethe, on his *Italian Journey*, fell into difficulties with the authorities at Malcesina for trying to sketch the old tower as a memento of his visit. He gathered what he took at first to be an admiring crowd, but one of the spectators suddenly stepped forward and tore up the drawing on his pad. Soon the *podestà* arrived on the scene, accusing Goethe of breaching military security by making a record of their fortress. He protested that it was not a fortress but a ruin, which drew the response: 'If it were only a ruin, why was it worth noticing?' Goethe was obliged to describe the picturesque beauty of the scene with exaggerated rapture, praising even 'the ivy which had luxuriantly covered the rocks and walls for so many centuries'. Eventually he persuaded the authorities of his innocence, but was left with the reflection, as so many of us have been, that 'man is indeed a strange creature, who, in order to enjoy something which he could perfectly well have enjoyed in peace and comfort and pleasant company, gets himself into trouble and danger because of an absurd desire to appropriate the world and everything it contains in a manner peculiar to himself.'

Mosaic artists have not confined themselves to the geometric and the architectural, to brickwork and ruins, where they have most chance of success. They have also, from antiquity, struggled to imitate and appropriate the organic, and have produced some extraordinarily naturalistic effects, effects far more remarkable and aesthetically pleasing even than a wool cauliflower. The stag hunt at Pella has an animal vitality that bounds through the little, hard, dry, gradated stones that compose it. Perhaps the most celebrated of antique Roman mosaics, known as *The Doves of Pliny* or the *Capitoline Doves*, shows four closely observed doves perching on the lip of and drinking from a round bowl. The realism and artistry of this work created a sensation in 1737 when it was discovered at Hadrian's Villa during the excavations led by Cardinal Furietti. Furietti thought it was the work by Sosus of Pergamon mentioned by Pliny in his *Naturalis Historia* but some scholars believe it to be a copy of the work of Sosus made for Hadrian. Pliny had praised the craftsmanship of the shadow cast by one of the doves upon the water in the drinking bowl. Polymath Pliny, like Goethe, loved stones and minerals.

Copy or original, Pliny's doves from Hadrian's Villa have been copied in many formats – in mosaic, micromosaic and *pietra dura*. I am sure they must have been made into a jigsaw, though I haven't located one yet. The Gilbert Collection in Somerset House contains a fine table top based on this famous dove design, made of porphyry, antique black marble, onyx, branches of coral, and Aquitanian black and white marble.

Doves were popular motifs, but many other birds and fish and animals appear in Greek and Roman mosaics, so realistically portrayed that they can be securely identified. Scholar Antero Tammisto in his weighty illustrated volume *Birds in Mosaics* identifies (albeit with varying degrees of certainty) kingfishers, mallards, teal, geese, partridges, cranes, herons, parrots, peafowl, owls, eagles, pigeons, bee-eaters, quail, swans, storks, cormorants and many other fowl. Cocks fight, a plump mythological boy holds a struggling pigeon, a kingfisher perches ready to dive, long-tailed parakeets share the rim of an ornate vessel with a dove, Egyptian geese spread their wings in the spandrels of a mosaic floor, and an astonishingly realistic partridge tweaks a trinket from a beaded casket. (The bird and the casket are a much-favoured Roman subject.) Antero praises Pliny's doves in these terms: 'This is closest to painting because of the very fine *opus vermiculatum* made with the finest tesserae.' The plumage of the birds, he notes, is executed with stripes resembling brush strokes, and the zip-like setting of the tesserae has 'no equal among the Hellenistic and Romano-Campanian mosaic, not even from Pergamon'.

Mosaic imitates brush work, and the brush imitates nature. Mosaic imitates marble, and hardstones imitate flowers and fruits. Mimesis, mimicry.

The sea creatures in antique mosaics are as remarkable as the birds. Artists delighted in crowding in many different species of shells and squids, eels and rays, skates and jellyfish, mackerel and lobsters, prawns and cuttlefish, sometimes against an abstract background, sometimes displayed as at a dinner or in baskets at a market. These scenes delighted Goethe in Naples. A traveller from northern landlocked Weimar, he rejoiced in the spectacle of the wonders of the deep, alive and gasping in the fishermen's catch on the shore, or captured in eternal stone in Pompeian mosaics. The jacket of the Penguin Classic selection from Pliny's *Natural History* displays a reproduction of a fine array of mosaic marine monsters, surrounding a magnificently tentacled giant squid worthy of Verne's *Twenty Thousand Leagues Under the Sea*.

Sosus, the creator of Pliny's doves, was also famed for the pleasing and curious motif of 'the unswept floor' (*asaratos oikos*), a type of floor mosaic that appears to portray a floor scattered with the debris of a meal: a device that gives a vivid sense of time suspended, a meal just abandoned, a party newly ended. Scholars have looked for allegorical meanings in the 'unswept floor', suggesting a funerary significance, or a statement of overflowing abundance. Of these, the latter seems more plausible, but it is surely not difficult to explain the attraction of this inspired double use of *trompe l'oeil*. It is witty, it is pretty, it gives delight, and it suggests good company.

I have yet to find a jigsaw of a mosaic, though I am sure I shall soon. (Jigsaws of stained glass are popular; Clara Farmer, editor, and one of the first to approve an early version of this project, once devoted wet holiday time to the windows of Chartres cathedral.) Historian Tom Holland tells me that while pursuing his research in Naples he acquired a jigsaw of the celebrated Alexander mosaic from Pompeii. It proved interesting but difficult to assemble, because of the double set of fault lines. The blank spaces were easier, he says, than the pictorial sections. I looked for it when I was recently in the region, but failed to find it, although I saw the real thing on display in the National Museum in Naples, and a copy of it in its original location in Pompeii. It shows the battle of Issus where Alexander defeated Xerxes III and the Persian army, and the little pink ribbons that tie Alexander's breastplate must have been fun to do. I wonder whether the mosaicists saved them till the end, as I saved the little scarlet square in one of my Ben Nicholson tapestries, or whether they did the interesting bits first, like Arnold Bennett's Constance Baines in Bursley. And I wonder whether it is possible that the design of this great work was, as has been plausibly suggested, taken from a painting executed by a woman. We know that Helen, daughter of Timon of Egypt, painted the battle of Issus. Maybe she was responsible for those little pink ribbons.

Italy is full of toyshops, much fuller than England, but the Alexander mosaic jigsaw is not a children's toy. I thought my best bet was the museum shop in Naples, where I dared to enquire of the very young and attractive shopkeeper, who, to my surprise, did not snap at me for my folly; she smiled with unfeigned and friendly delight, and said that indeed this jigsaw existed but she didn't, alas, have it in stock. She'd last seen it in Paestum, where there was a 'bella libreria'. But I really couldn't go traipsing off to the majestic ruins of Paestum in search of a cardboard puzzle. That would have been too foolish.

XLIV

The city of Rome is an immense mosaic. So are all cities, but Rome is more literally a mosaic than most. During the Renaissance, Rome, Florence and Milan all produced notable work of tesserae and *pietra dura*, but the Roman hardstone mosaics contained more archaeological spoils. Florence and Milan drew on the coloured stones and gems of the Alps (which Goethe could not resist pocketing as he journeyed southwards) whereas Rome drew from its past treasury. The reuse of old stones and carvings and the rediscovery of the classical spirit went hand in hand, and it was not until Goethe's day that imitation became suspect.

Goethe, attending a debate on the relative merits of 'Invention and Imitation' at the Academy of the Olympians in Vicenza on 22 September 1786, notes with interest in his *Italian Journey* that those praising 'Imitation' received more applause 'because they voiced what the common herd thinks, so far as it is able to think…they had not felt the force of the many excellent arguments which had been offered in favour of Invention'.

Goethe tended to favour what he considered a more modern concept of originality. Yet he was also at this time deep in his intensely admiring study of the antique. He may have despised the collectors of portable snuffboxes and fake antique curios, but he could not resist purchasing large statues and cumbersome casts of ancient models. The desire for souvenirs and mementoes and copies went very deep in him, as in less serious tourists. He writes with interest rather than with contempt of the new fashion for 'encaustic' art, with which ladies on the Grand Tour occupied their spare time. Women who might in a later age have occupied themselves with jigsaws of ancient Rome would apply themselves to works of art in wax relief, a technique from antiquity rediscovered in the eighteenth century and inspired by the excitement of the recent excavations at Pompeii and Herculaneum. He described it as one of the 'half-arts (*Halbkünste*), calling for manual dexterity and a taste for handicrafts'. This activity was laid on and supervised by tour manager Hofrat Reiffenstein, who

> had long come to realize that people who arrived in Rome
> with no other idea than to see things and amuse themselves
> often suffer from the most awful boredom, because they are
> deprived of the ways in which they usually spend their free
> time…He therefore picked on two activities with which to
> keep them busy: encaustic painting and the imitation of
> antique jewellery in paste.

The women favoured the painting, the men the jewels. He offered so much tactful help that his students were frequently astonished by the beauty of the products of their unsuspected artistic talent.

These secondary artistic pursuits recall the activities of Mary Delany and her circle in England, although Delany herself, as we have seen, was much more inventive than these tourists. Yet it is an irony that Angelica Kauffmann, with whom Goethe spent much time in Italy, and who was one of the few women artists to be taken seriously by him and by her contemporaries, became better known through the endless adaptations and reproductions of her work than for the works themselves. Her designs were so popular that they appeared on snuffboxes, vases, teasets, fans and chocolate cups. They did not appear in jigsaw format, for, although the dissected puzzle was in her lifetime being used to portray subjects other than maps, it had not yet been co-opted by the fine-art market.

Particularly curious is the relationship between Kauffmann's mythological oil paintings and portraits and the 'stippled' versions of them, which attracted (and still attract) many admirers. Stippling, a technique that evolved in the late eighteenth century, is a type of engraving using dots or spots to create shading and gradations of colour and tone, and William Wynne Ryland's works after Angelica Kauffmann were one of its earliest successes. Most of Ryland's engravings were shaped as circles or ovals and were destined for use in schemes of interior decoration. Stippled work was softly attractive and richly coloured, making it especially suited for miniatures and reproduction in fashion magazines. It was also easily adapted for needlework designs. In other words, it had a 'feminized' feel to it, a softness that linked it to fashion, crafts and design as well as to art, thus ironically harnessing Kauffmann's reputation to a womanly sphere that she had in so many ways boldly resisted.

Stippling was a novel technique in the eighteenth century, but encaustic art has an antique lineage. Like the mosaics of Hadrian's Villa, it too had been described by Pliny, who tells us that a famous Greek woman artist called Iaia of Cyzicus excelled at miniature portraits in the medium. She worked in Rome in the first century BC, producing mainly female portraits, which included a large picture on wood titled *Old Woman at Neapolis*, and a self-portrait done with the help of a mirror. She painted fast, and her work fetched high prices. Did encaustic art have a particular attraction for the woman artist? There was a long tradition of women working in encaustic, established long before Goethe's grand tourists learned to dabble in it in Rome.

Some of the most extraordinary works in encaustic that have come down to us from antiquity are images, not by but of women. These funerary portraits, discovered in the nineteenth century at Fayum in Egypt, date from the second century AD, and have a poignant beauty, a vivid living naturalism, that speak to us across two millennia. Were any of them made by women? We do not know, but maybe one day we will. The zipped and helical codes of DNA may yet reveal wonders to us. The past is in the future.

Some years ago the British Museum, which holds some of the best of the Fayum mummy portraits, mounted an exhibition titled 'Ancient Faces'. This made a deep impression on me and on many of those who saw it. I was at that time writing *The Peppered Moth*, which dealt with mitochondrial DNA and the recovery of genetic information, and the faces in the British Museum seemed to have personal messages for me. They looked at me from their dark and lustrous eyes; there was language in their lips, their necks, their noses. Confidently they insisted on resurrection, with the full poly-chrome glow of the fully human. They waited for the morning. They had never died. I wove them into my novel, basing the appearance of Faro, the high-spirited representative of the younger generation in my saga, on these women: she had their large brown almond eyes, their delicate pink and smiling lips, their apricot flesh tones, their golden hoop earrings, their charming hairstyles of bandeaux of small corkscrew ringlets, their fondness for brooches and necklaces, their untiring grace and vivacity. Physically, Faro has inherited a little from the Fayum, a little from my daughter, and a little from my sisters-in-law. The womanly traits live on.

One of the Fayum-related women (a painted woman, not an encaustic portrait) has something of the look of Cherie Blair. She has large eyes made larger with spiked mascara, a wide red mouth, fine bare breasts, corkscrew curls, and hoop earrings threaded with gold beads and pearls. She wears a yellow tunic with a pretty pink-and-green geometric collar, and her sleeves are adorned with the protective green wings of Isis and Nepthys. Her hair is garlanded with rosebuds, through which winds a coiled green stem. She holds a sprig of sage-green leaves in her left hand. She gazes at us so confidently, smiling slightly, with such a pleasantly inviting intimation of immortality. She looks just a touch crazy, as, sometimes, does Cherie Blair.

What she does not look is dead.

Maybe the Egyptians were right: maybe we live on in the body.

These portraits not only preserved the features and personalities of the men and women they commemorated; they also preserved and embodied the great Greek painting tradition. 'Almost all the work in that tradition has been lost to time and the elements, the Mediterranean not sharing the exceptional preservative conditions of the Egyptian desert,' writes Euphrosyne C. Doxiadis in the catalogue (1997) to the exhibition.

> The paintings of the Fayum, sheltered in this way, are a dazzling testament to the sophistication of the Alexandrian school from which they are derived and show us the heights that had been reached in the rendering of nature. It is not until some fifteen centuries later, in the faces painted by Titian or Rembrandt's depiction of his own features, that the same artistry that characterises many of the anonymous artists of the Fayum is witnessed again.

This may be an overstatement, but it is telling.

The Egyptians preserved their dead so carefully because they knew we would need the body in the next life. They took food and utensils and cosmetics and weapons with them to the next world.

The living had a tradition of dining with the dead, and they sat down to banquets with Anubis, the lord of the dead, in little pavilions near the embalmed bodies of their loved ones. Or so the Greeks and Romans told us, and so a papyrus from Oxyrhynchus excavated by Flinders Petrie seems to confirm. Dining with the dead is a challenging concept.

The paintings are alive and beautiful, but the beliefs are disquieting. Preservation and perpetuation may be considered dubious aims.

Not long ago, I had a disquieting dream about Auntie Phyl. It began pleasantly enough, for in my dream she seemed alive and well, and was wearing a familiar and becoming silky rayon dress with a bright blue-and-green geometric pattern that signified festivity – a birthday, or a Christmas gathering. But as the dream unfolded, I realized that she was not really alive at all. She was a robot, a simulacrum, an animated waxwork, summoned up by me for my own dark purposes. At the end of my dream (as at the end of this book) she would depart again into the shades. She had not been able to enjoy the events of the dream or to participate in them. She had not tasted her food, or enjoyed her glass of champagne. She had merely been a helpless dummy, an unwilling and unfeeling participant in a story of my devising. A zombie. She was dead, with no right of redress, and she was not willing to collaborate with me. She had not wanted to walk again.

This dream does not need much interpretation. It is about the way in which writers abuse their subjects. I am trying not to abuse her, but of course I am doing so. As I have abused all the sources of all my work, always. As all writers do, always. The dead may not want to come back to life. It may not be proper to try to resurrect them.

The dream was also about the conditions of life in a care home for the elderly. That is a larger question.

The dry sands of Egypt preserved the mummies and the corpses. I have always been interested in the bog men, accidentally preserved in the peat, and have introduced them into several of my novels. I like amber too, which is a great preservative. Amber necklaces are associated with women novelists, and when somebody pointed this out to me I stopped wearing mine.

The sand, the peat, and the refining fire.

T. S. Eliot invoked the sprouting corpse in the garden. He deplored the practice of childhood reminiscence.

I was much taken with Stevie Davies's detailed descriptions of the process of the reconstruction of the living flesh of a dead face from a seventeenth-century skull in her novel *Impassioned Clay*. (She credits a book titled *Making Faces: Using Forensic and Archaeological Evidence* by John Prag and Richard Neave.) We have all watched these reconstructions on television history programmes – dead pharaohs, Ice Age travellers, Aztec victims, being restored to a semblance of life by twentieth-century expertise.

My father was cremated, as I hope to be. His ashes were scattered beneath one of the trees he planted in his Suffolk garden. I dug them in with a little green tin seaside spade that my mother found in the garage. The tree is felled now, for when the house was sold after my mother's death the garden was built upon. He used to spend a lot of time in that garden.

I dreamed of my father last night. We were walking together along a street (I think near Regent's Park), and he wanted to recite to me a poem about an emerald. 'It's gone out of fashion now,' he said, 'but it's a beautiful poem.' In my dream, I heard the first line of the poem, although I have now forgotten it. But then his recitation faded on me, although the words still came stumbling through, and his voice choked, and I knew, even in my dream, that my sleeping brain did not have the quickness, the ability, to create or record or overhear this poem. So where is this dream poem

now? I heard it. I half heard it. It was somewhere. It existed. It flickered through my neurons, leaving some trace in them. But now it
has gone.

XLV

Goethe may have championed Invention against Imitation, but he was also, on his travels, in search of the authentically antique. He was profoundly moved by the buildings of Palladio, that great imitator of classical architecture. Out of respect for Palladio he bought a copy of the works of Vitruvius. But Galliani's edition of Vitruvius weighed heavy in his luggage and heavy on his brain. 'I skim through the pages or, to be more exact, I read it like a breviary, more from devotion than from instruction,' he noted.

The use of the word 'antique' can be puzzling in its imprecision. Does it just mean 'old', or does it have a more specific meaning? (Baudrillard, in his discussions of 'bygone' objects, has much to say about the real antique, the fake antique, the replica, and the yearning for authenticity. And we have coined new market meanings for the words antique, heritage and vintage – 'vintage', I gather, now applies to the objects I played with as a child in the 1940s and 50s. You can find a wonderful compendium of these in Adam Mars-Jones's 2008 novel, *Pilcrow*.)

Master craftsman Giuseppe Antonio Torricelli (1662–1719), writing of work in the Milanese workshops of the Grand Duke of Tuscany, pleasantly confesses that: 'We use four different sorts of mixed stones and we call them antique because no-one remembers where they were mined. There is a yellow one, called oriental, then red antique, green antique and white and black antique.' Rome, according to Torricelli, is a great heap of old stones, imported and refashioned.

> There are three types of granite and Rome is full of great
> columns and pyramids made from them. One is white and
> black, finely mixed. Another is red and white with a tiny bit
> of black, and another white, black and reddish with larger
> flecks like the other red one. Only the white and the black is
> so much finer. They are all antique and known as Egyptian
> granite. Porphyry and serpentine are also antique granites,
> also thought to be from Egypt.

These quotations from Torricelli confirm that in his lifetime the use of the word 'antique' was already highly flexible, as were the artistic aims of the cutters and commissioners of the products.

I found Torricelli's description in an appendix on 'techniques' in Anna Maria Massinelli's volume describing the hardstones of the Gilbert Collection. This collection displays an extraordinary variety of precious and expensive objects, but the hardstones and micromosaics are perhaps the most curious of all. They are slightly shocking, some in their beauty, some in their opulence, some because they are so kitsch. The Gilberts were fascinated by richly composite artefacts and densely patterned works of art. Many of the Florentine caskets and table tops are of a ravishing beauty, displaying extraordinary botanical detail; the table top of 'The flora of the two Sicilies', commissioned by Tsar Nicholas I, is to my eye one of the most desirable and decorative objects ever made – not that I would want to own it, but I can see how one might long to do so. The waters of the Bay of Naples and Paestum are rendered in exquisitely delicate shades and flecks of iridescent, pearly beauty, and the trees, fruits and flowers rise upwards and inwards with supreme elegance, in green and brown and purple and copper and gold. There must have been joy as well as pride in this fashioning. But other specimens in the collection are of a jigsaw-art crudity, admirable largely in that they have been made at all, and from such expensive, intractable materials. Some of the cabinets look very like children's wooden jigsaws, although they are made of jasper, black marble, green antique marble and lapis lazuli, and are set in gilt bronze, mahogany and ebony.

I went to the Museo dell'Opificio delle Pietre Dure in Florence, in pursuit of the origins and history of the hardstone mosaics that so captivated the Gilberts. This small museum, where the craft is still practised, provides a pleasant refuge from the crowds and queues and chaos that attend the Uffizi, the Pitti, the Accademia, the Palazzo Vecchio. When I visited the *studiolo* of Francesco de Medici in the Palazzo Vecchio, on a 'special guided tour', we were shown around by a man pretending to be some sidekick of Vasari, dressed up like an animated waxwork in Florentine costume, who peppered us with fake-antique parlance, irritating questions and coyly unreliable information. (I should have gone with Martin Randall.) The Opificio is not like that at all. It is calm, scientific and instructive, and the objects are captivating. They range from sixteenth- and seventeenth-century coats of arms and floral panels, through 'stone paintings' of Biblical and classical scenes, to table tops from the late seventeenth, eighteenth and nineteenth centuries showing shell-and-coral motifs, fruits, doves and flowers. One circular table board of black Belgian marble displays in its centre an illusionistic silver tray, on which an absent-minded lady returning from a party appears to have dropped a white camellia, a necklace and a ring. The casual permanence of the frozen moment, like that of the 'swept floors' of Sosus, is charming.

The museum also houses large wall cabinets with examples of the many forms of precious and semi-precious stones used by the workshop's craftsmen: jaspers, chalcedony, fire-marble with fossil shells, mother-of-pearl, lapis lazuli, travertine, cipollino…The very names are poetry. Near Florence, we are told, a river-stone known as 'pietra paesina' may be found on the bed of the Arno; it is especially useful in landscapes (such as one showing Dante and Virgil in the Inferno) for its 'capacity in evocating tortuous ravines and rocky walls sights [*visione di anfratte e pareti rocciose*]'.

The translation of the guidebook has its own poetry, and I was delighted to find that it draws a direct parallel with the art of the puzzle.

> The kind of processing which was mainly perfectioned in Florence, and to which the fame of the Granducal manufacturing was entrusted, was the one of mosaics or 'commessi', as they were defined in order to indicate they were semi-precious stones mosaic works, which were cutting those stones in different shape sections that, later, were so precisely assembled together that the contact zones between each section practically resulted as invisible. That sort of creations, which could be utilized as wall pictures, table, chess-boards, cabinets, caskets of jewel boxes as well as the various pieces of furniture, were poetically defined as 'stone paintings', while nowadays we could call them puzzles, using a quicker but immediately understandable term [*noi oggi, con termino più sbrigativo ma immediatamente comprehensibile, le chiameremmo 'puzzles'*].

'Termino più sbrigativo ma immediatamente comprehensibile' is good. The word 'puzzle' does good service here.

Arthur Gilbert's eye was drawn to mosaics and micromosaics by a less orthodox route than a visit to the Opificio in Florence. It is an odd story. The first two micromosaics that he purchased were of a particularly dubious aesthetic quality. When he bought them at an auction house in Los Angeles in 1965, he thought they were cracked paintings, and presumably it was as cracked paintings that he first admired them. They were made in Rome c.1875, at a period when nearly a hundred commercial mosaicists were working in the city, selling to connoisseurs and gullible amateurs. Each painting shows a cavalier and a lady, but the costumes, hairstyles and furnishings are incongruous and from incompatible historical periods, and the artistic effect would have been dismissed by Mary Russell Mitford and Arnold Bennett as unacceptable. They are calendar art, jigsaw art, but they have been assembled with enormous labour.

Nevertheless, there is something fascinating about the spectacle of so much labour devoted to such secondary products, and most of the objects in the Gilbert Collection are aesthetically more satisfactory. Gilbert, a dedicated collector, trained his own eye, and he trained it well. Reproductive effort reaches a dignified apotheosis in Antonio Testa's *Panorama of Rome*, a huge view from the Janiculum on which the artist worked for twenty years. It was taken and adapted from a 1765 etching by Giuseppe Vasi, and it is of great delicacy. This was a labour of love and a way of life: *La Vie: Mode d'Emploi*. The thought of the patient fitting together of so many tesserae over so many years into so useless but so beautiful an imitative object is curiously moving.

Imitation, appropriation, copyright, authenticity: the doves of Sosus, perhaps themselves a copy, have been copied endlessly, and the mosaic tigress in the Gilbert Collection's 'Tigress Lying Below Rocks' was taken from an engraving of the Stubbs oil painting of 1769, which hangs in Blenheim Palace. (This is also available, as noted, in a charming small jigsaw, which cannot, however, do justice to the extraordinarily tactile rendering of the feathery fur of this mosaic beast's striped chest; the little hard grains of mosaic uncannily mimic a velvety softness that the hand longs to reach out to stroke.) Mosaicists copied works by Caravaggio, Salvator Rosa, Reni and Raphael, and the workshops of the Vatican produced mosaic copies of sacred masterpieces that took several years to produce. Some artists were attracted by the idea of their work being made more durable in stone painting. Others would perhaps have been appalled by it.

Arthur Gilbert, like the dukes of Tuscany before him, had an eye for riches and colour, although he had not been brought up in luxurious surroundings. He was born in Dalston in 1913, the son of a Polish Jewish immigrant who became a furrier in Aldersgate. Gilbert's wife Rosalinde, whom he married in 1934, was a designer with whom he set up a successful wholesale dressmaking business, selling ball gowns and wedding dresses. They prospered, in ball gowns and in property. His life as a collector took off when they moved to Beverly Hills and began to furnish their 'Italian-Greco-Jewish Villa' with a theatrical and eclectic assortment of antiques. He made himself into a scholar and the world expert on 'micro-mosaic' art, coining the word to describe the objects of his passion, and until recently we could all see them for a small entrance fee in Somerset House. We were even able to dine amongst them, if we had the corporate money to do so. And the less well-off amongst us can continue to buy the jigsaws.

XLVI

I too have a liking for opulence, despite my Quaker schooling. I like the look of opulence. I like red and gold. I was taught to suspect any form of opulence as vulgar bad taste, but when I first went to Italy, at the age of seventeen, I realized I had been falsely indoctrinated. Plainness is not the only virtue.

Many decades ago, my mother-in-law gave me a tiny hand mirror with a little handle, an ornate gilt frame, and a French, eighteenth-century-style, faux-shepherdess painting on the back. It wasn't valuable, it was just a trinket, a stocking-filler gift, but I loved it. (My Jewish in-laws didn't do stockings and Christmas, as such, but they did presents in a very big way.) My sister, when she saw this small gift, eyed it with a mixture of censure and envy, and said, 'We don't give one another pretty things like that in our family, do we?'

No, we didn't. We weren't very good at gifts of any sort.

I still have the mirror, but the painting has come unstuck and mislaid itself.

I occasionally bought what I thought were pretty gifts for my mother-in-law, in reciprocity. It was a pleasure to do so, and I wish I had dared to buy her more. I once bought her a beautiful silver serving spoon embossed with fruit from Shrubsole's famous shop in Museum Street. And a Venetian lace handkerchief in Venice. These were ceremonial objects, expensive and delightful.

Opulence moves me. When I started to leaf through a book on the restoration of Federico da Montefeltro's *studiolo* in Gubbio, I was astonished to find tears starting to my eyes. There I sat, in Humanities Two at the British Library, weeping. My quest for jigsaws and mosaics had by now meandered to a search for marquetry images of cabinets within cabinets, for *trompe l'oeil* bookshelves, for benches and cupboards, for intricate geometry and perspectives, for cunning woodwork. And they are all there, in the Gubbio *studiolo*, in abundance – fictive niches of illusionistic intarsia, musical scores and instruments, birds in birdcages, lecterns and books, hunting horns and candlesticks, some of them so convincingly three-dimensional that the eye cannot persuade itself that it is seeing a flat surface.

But what brought the tears of joy to my eyes was a photograph of a coffered ceiling.

The Gubbio Studiolo and its Conservation shows photographs of the main ceiling and of a ceiling in a window niche of the Gubbio *studiolo*, and ceilings from the Palazzo Vecchio and the Chapel of the Palazzo Medici in Florence. These ceilings, with their glorious symmetries of gold, scarlet, silver and azure, with their mix of patterned surface and rich embossed depth, are astonishing works of art, which satisfy something profound in our desire for ornamentation and control, for exuberance and majestic regularity. Lowered as I was by ill health, and by a journey on the underground, and by the habitual stress of negotiating what was then the building site of King's Cross station, with its steps and its barriers and its ever-changing grey congeries of exits and entrances, I was overcome by this small vision of ordered polychrome splendour on my library desk. These were only photographs in a book, but they made me weep.

Had I ever seen any of these ceilings, had I ever bothered to look upwards? I'd been to Florence, I'd been to Gubbio, but I couldn't recall that I had noticed any ceilings. (The Gubbio ceilings are now in New York, but I haven't seen them there, either, and as I'm very unlikely to go to New York again, I never will.) The designs of palmettes and acanthus leaves, of five-petalled gilded flowers and flower buds, of octagons and trapezoids, of panels painted to resemble green, red and purple porphyry, seem to unite the natural and the unnatural, the organic and the mathematical, in the great artifice of eternity. These ceilings are the starry vaults of the heavens themselves, re-created upon earth.

Are the Gubbio ceilings still the Gubbio ceilings, now that they have been relocated and restored in America? This is not an idle question. They were purchased in Italy in 1937 by the international dealer Adolph Loewi, who found them not in Gubbio but in the Villa Lancellotti in Frascati, whither they had been transported during the 1870s. Loewi bought them from their (disputed) owner Prince Lancellotti, and shipped them to America for their better health in 1939, along with all the marquetry panelling of the *studiolo*. They arrived in their crates in New York on 15 May 1939, were purchased by and eventually delivered to the Metropolitan Museum of Art on 30 November, and the restored *studiolo* was unveiled on the first floor of the museum in January 1941, amidst much wonder and acclaim, and learned reference to the hyper-realist and surrealist spirit of the marquetry. Then, in 1966, the *studiolo* disappeared once more from public view, this time for thirty years, to re-appear after a second and much longer process of restoration and conservation (1987–96) in May 1996. And there, in the Metropolitan, the *studiolo* remains. It is of Gubbio, and not of Gubbio. It is even less likely than the Elgin marbles to make its way home.

You can't buy it in jigsaw format in the Met Store, which is a pity, but you can buy a reproduction wood-inlay copy of one of the panels for $125, including hanging hardware.

America, like the British Museum, is full of expatriated treasures.

Would it be a good idea to try to repatriate at vast expense the cloister of Saint Michel de Cuxa from the Cloisters of Fort Tryon Park in New York to its original site in the Abbey of Saint Michel de Cuxa in the French Pyrenees? Baudrillard thought not, arguing in *Simulacra and Simulation* that

> if the exportation of the cornices was in effect an arbitrary act, if the Cloisters in New York are an artificial mosaic of all cultures (following the logic of the capitalist centralization of value), their reimportation to the original site is even more artificial: it is a total simulacrum that links up with 'reality' through a complete circumvention. The cloister should have stayed in New York in its simulated environment, which at least fooled no one.

I see what he means, which, with Baudrillard, is not always the case. But I think I am happier with the concept of second-hand representations than he is. I can burst into tears over a picture or a photograph in a book. I can do a Clementoni jigsaw of Botticelli's *Primavera* and feel that I am paying homage to the painting rather than insulting it. I am quite humble in that way. Goethe might have agreed with Baudrillard. But then again, he might not.

When I was first in Florence, aged seventeen, encouraged by a sophisticated young man called Geoffrey who said it was 'all right' to do this, I bought a cheap reproduction of the head of Flora from the *Primavera*. It was painted on wood, with a gilt edging, and I thought it was beautiful. It can't have cost more than a few shillings, because that was all I would have had to spend in those days. It had a very 'antique' look to it, and I was pleased on my way home when the Customs Officer at Dover detained me to look at it quite carefully. I kept it for years, but I always thought of it as a cheap copy, and I must have thrown it away when I sold the house in Hampstead. *How could I have done that?* My daughter now tells me that it was in her Hampstead bedroom for years when she was a child. I wish she had told me to hang on to it. I wish I had hung on to a lot of the things that I took to Oxfam.

The original transportation of the cloister of Saint Michel de Cuxa from France to America did not go unremarked. Englishman Alfred Emberson, in an English guidebook to the fashionable spa of Vernet-les-Bains (*All about Vernet-les-Bains*, 1913), commented on the threatened appropriation with indignation. He wrote, in 1913, just before its removal:

> One experiences a sort of shock when one reads in all the papers of the efforts of an American sculptor to capture and carry off to his own country the ruins of the ancient Abbaye of Saint Michel de Cuxa, near Prades…The incident recalls the alarm I experienced when a charming American and his wife and daughter, who were staying here, quietly announced at lunch how disappointed they were that they had not been able to buy the quaint old church bell at Casteil to take home with them.
>
> It always impresses me…how regardless our cousins from across the Atlantic are of the terrors of 'extra luggage'…
>
> It would require a Shakespeare to adequately describe the sensations – if they could only 'sensate' – of these mediaeval stone-built structures, which withstood not only the raids of the Visigoths, Moors and Romans, but more wonderfully still the ravages of Time, when they find themselves helpless before the power of Money and the relentless disregard of their feelings of Modern Barbarity.

The French government tried but failed to save the cloisters for France. Thirty-seven capitals, nineteen abaci, seven arches and various bits of parapet and doorway were bought, transported and eventually re-erected in New York. I have seen them there. Other fragments made their way to the Louvre, to Boston, to Philadelphia and to Eze-Village on the Riviera. Some have now made their way home to Prades, but yet more are no doubt standing as ornaments in private gardens or serving humbly and unrecognized as doorstops or cattle troughs all over the department of Roussillon. Perhaps on the Day of Judgement they will all rush together again, at vast destructive speed, like a disaster movie being played backwards.

Rediviva saxa.

The cloisters and the *studiolo* went to New York, but the horse-shoes of Scarrington stayed at home, saved from American purchasers by a preservation order and Nottinghamshire County Council.

The American novelist Booth Tarkington wrote an amusing parody of American collectors titled *The Collector's Whatnot* (1923), in which he satirizes the habit of acquiring frying pans and sow scrapers and hooked rugs and camping stools and bits of wood full of wormholes, as well as the practice of hanging agricultural implements as decorations on restaurant walls. There is a chapter on how to avoid being cheated in Europe, which makes it clear that the antique dealers usually have the upper hand.

XLVII

I have strayed far from my plan, which was to write a brief
illustrated history of the jigsaw puzzle. I find myself with a
bucket full of leftover tesserae, some with jagged and uneven edges
encrusted with old mastic and resin, which do not fit into my
original design. Nick Tucker wrote to me that one of the lessons of
the jigsaw is that 'order is always attainable in the end so long as
one works hard for it', but of course I have made things difficult for
myself by straying out of my frame and finding new pieces as I go
along. This is not the book I meant to write.

I think I have been trying to write about authenticity and family and folk memory, and how these concepts affect our view of
the idyll of the *Cider with Rosie*, Teas-with-Hovis, Golden Legend
past. I have been trying to recapture my aunt and my childhood. I
have been trying to use simpler shapes and brighter colours than
I have used in my work of late. I have been trying to fit the simple
building blocks together. Bryn stands for the house the child
draws, the simple solid village house on a main thoroughfare in the
middle of England.

I have long been uneasy about the Uttley-style fetishization of
the past. I was wary of it long before I read Raphael Samuel,

Georges Perec and Jean Baudrillard. (I don't think any of them would have read Alison Uttley, though one can never be sure with Perec.) They articulated my sense of the overlay and appropriation of 'real' objects by fashion and nostalgia, and the concomitant fear of 'inauthenticity'. A fear, one might posit, of horse brasses and crinoline ladies embroidered on tablecloths. This is akin to the more solemn and political *mauvaise foi*, which exercised us in the 1960s, but it is more object-based, more materialistic. It is more concerned with 'Things'.

Let me return to the warming-pan from Bryn. It has a very dark wooden handle, thirty-four inches long. Its circular copper pan has a diameter of just under a foot and is about three inches deep. The copper cover is engraved – one might say scratched – with a very simple and basic design of five leaves and five sprays of flowers. I cannot see any manufacturer's name on it and I do not know how old it is. It was not made as a replica, and it was certainly not a *unicum*, so there may be many almost-identical objects surviving in Britain. It is, in this sense, the real thing, and was once filled with hot coals to warm damp beds.

I do not think it was given to my grandmother as part of her brass collection. When it came 'into the family' I do not know, nor do I know how it came to me rather than to anyone else in the family. Maybe I appropriated it, maybe nobody else wanted it, maybe Joyce rescued it for me and made me take it away before it got lost or was put in the house sale (into which, to my regret, the grandfather clock vanished). Now it stands, ornamentally, decoratively, non-functionally, in my study, inside the brass fender of the tiled fireplace in my husband's house in North Kensington. The fireplace may or may not be an original feature of this London house. The copper has a soft, yellow-gold, burnished glow.

What does this object mean? It has come to me, for better or worse, but it is not very intimately connected with my evenings playing Belisha or pegging rugs or making spills and lavender bags or going to bed in the apple loft by the Kelly light. The Kelly light and the Campbell tile from Stoke-on-Trent have much more powerful associations for me. The warming-pan was as decorative and non-functional at Bryn as it is now in London. But it is durable, and too good to throw away.

My mother discovered electric blankets. I was converted to them for a while, but began some twenty or thirty years ago to consider them a fire risk. They heated the bed, fine, but what if you fell asleep on top of all that unreliable and prickly wiring? And I didn't like the fuzzy, felted texture of the covering. So I returned to the safety, the traditional comfort, of the hot-water bottle. You really can't do yourself much damage with a hot-water bottle, apart from mottling yourself with red blotches, and the fact that they are still so widely available means that others agree with me. You'd have thought they might have gone out of production by now, but they haven't.

My mother wanted to be modern. She hated coal fires, because they were dirty and reminded her of the South Yorkshire where she was born, and from which she had always longed to escape. She liked central heating and electric blankets and her electric kettle and her Teasmade. My daughter wrote a fine poem invoking that Teasmade.

I suppose it is just possible that my grandparents bought the warming-pan as a non-functioning item of decor that would help to authenticate their removal from the coal belt of Mexborough to the clean air, flat fields, mild beasts and marching pylons of Lincolnshire. I have explained that they had no hereditary stake in that agricultural Midlands county; their forebears were from industrial Leeds, the horrors of which were chronicled in the 1850s by Engels and Elizabeth Gaskell, and from the Five Towns, which had to wait until Arnold Bennett for their scribe. What, then, was the source of their feeling for their Teas-with-Hovis home, and, two generations later, to what kind of legitimate connection with it could I make a claim?

John Clare, the poet of the local, loved his native Midlands. In middle life, suffering from a form of dementia, he was taken south to an asylum at High Beech (now High Beach) in Epping, whence after a few years he absconded. He walked his penniless way back up the Great North Road (or, as he sometimes called it, the Great York Road) to Helpton, guided at one point by gypsies, and sleeping rough for several nights in trusses of clover, or sheltering from the wind beneath a row of elms or in a dyke bottom. On the third day, he writes, 'I satisfied my hunger by eating the grass by the roadside which seemed to taste something like bread I was hungry and eat heartily and in fact the meal seemed to do me good.'

Clare in his madness had delusions of grandeur, and thought at times he was Robert Burns or Byron or Ben Caunt the prize fighter. (Some of his lyrics are more than worthy of Burns, and his pastiche of Byron is brilliant.) But he was at the same time realistically aware both of his own declining fame and status and (as Jonathan Bate has convincingly argued) of the falling sales of poetry in general, lamenting in his poem 'Decay', 'O Poesy is on the wane / For fancys vision all unfitting…' And yet he went on writing, not only at High Beech, but after his brief return to Helpton, and also through most of the years he spent in Northampton General Asylum. He could not cease to be a poet. The poetry poured from him; as another poet once said, 'there was no stopping it'. His first-hand observations of the natural world and his faultless ear did not fail him, even when there was hardly anybody left to read or to listen.

We do not know how much a sense of failure and the drifting away of powerful friends contributed to his madness. Like many peasant and ploughmen poets, he had both profited and suffered from the dislocation of being taken up by publishers, aristocratic admirers and established literati. The gap between the world of the village and the world of literary London was almost unbridgeable, although at times he had seemed to have succeeded in crossing it. His instinct was to walk back to his birthplace, in a hope of finding himself and a way out of 'this sad non-identity'. But when he got there, he was not there.

Writers are often and rightly accused of self-absorption and egoism, but many have a very fragile hold on the self. (These states are not incompatible.) At times I am not at all sure that I am a writer, although I have published more than twenty books and have earned what I consider a good living at the trade. I clearly remember an occasion years ago when I set off to deliver the typescript of a new novel (I think it was my fourth, *Jerusalem the Golden*) to my publishers, Weidenfeld and Nicolson, whose offices were then in Bond Street. I was walking along cheerfully with my package, not quite able to visualize the building that was my destination, although I had visited it on one or two occasions. But I was confident that I had the correct street number and that it would materialize. However, when I reached 20 Bond Street, it wasn't Weidenfeld and Nicolson at all, but a dress shop. I stood there in the street, astonished. And my first reaction was shocking. Instead of assuming that I had made a mistake in the address, I knew, suddenly, in a thunderbolt of awareness, that I had been deluding myself for years, and had madly fancied myself a writer, when I was nothing of the sort. I had been living in a fantasy, and I had better get on the bus, go home to Highbury and adjust to reality. It was a bad moment, but I swallowed humbly and prepared to confront the madhouse that might await me.

In a matter of seconds, I worked out that either the publishers had moved, or that I was in the wrong bit of Bond Street. And I was, of course, in Bond Street, instead of at 20 New Bond Street where I should have been. It was a simple mistake and easily rectified. I just walked down the road. But I was shaken by my first response. It wasn't even as though I had longed all my life (as some do) to become a writer. I hadn't. I had no lofty sense of destiny, I didn't suffer from that form of hubris. I had wanted to be an actress, but my stage career hadn't worked out as I'd hoped. Being a writer was a second choice for me. I had settled into 'being a writer', for better or worse, because I was (and am) no good at doing nothing, but I hadn't sunk my whole identity into the occupation. I now think that at that moment in Bond Street I was confronting the other life I might have led. Time might have split, as in an H. G. Wells or Borges story, and I might have rejoined the real world in which I might have lived, and rediscovered another and perhaps happier identity.

I don't mean that I didn't value reading and books and literature when I was young. I valued them as highly as did my mother and Dr Leavis, and perhaps, therefore, too highly. (My mother had been taught at Cambridge by Dr Leavis.) But I didn't see myself as a contender.

Whereas John Clare's poetry was his destiny. There was no avoiding it. And yet it alienated him from the very roots and source of his inspiration. This was a hard lot. He belonged to his home country and therefore he was wedded to loss. And yet, in his verse, the happy spring continues to sing and flow, as the poetry continued to flow, even when nobody would publish it, even when its burden took the form of a lament. Nothing could permanently dam it up or divert it. Of the little brook he wrote 'Go on, thou little happy thing, Amid the strife of men...' It is heartbreaking, this little brave metrical resurgence.

XLVIII

Bryn, to me, was rural England and, although it didn't belong to me nor I to it, I had known it all my life. I had been taken there in the womb before I was born, before the outbreak of the war. Its images were deeply imprinted. It was Clare country, and I think maybe that is one of the reasons why he means so much to me.

I've tried to trace some of the ways in which images of rural life perpetuate themselves in jigsaws and calendars and tea caddies and card games and embroidery patterns and children's books and tea towels, long after the originals have disappeared. The maypole, the village green, the duck pond, the horse-drawn plough, the farmyard and the cottage garden live on in the memory of the race. Or that's one way of looking at it. It's as though we believe we could put England back together again, if we could forge enough copies of it. But it's not just a longing for real antiques like warming-pans or for fake antiques like carriage clocks. It's not just nostalgia.

And this hankering after a rural past isn't exclusively English, though we associate it with Wordsworth's sublimated sense of the transcendence of landscape. We tend to think of landscape in connection with the English Romantics, and of sex in association with the French. But the French do landscape and nostalgia, too, in their plastic copies of the board game of the Royal Game of the Goose, in biscuit tins and cheese labels and promotional blotters and curtain fabrics.

In the omnium gatherum of Perec's Paris apartment novel we find a strange hymn to a small market town in the department of Indre, which successful businesswoman Madame Moreau, now eighty-three years old, has been forced by accumulating wealth and the growth of her machine-tool business to abandon. (Indre is a real department, but I'm not sure whether Saint-Mouezy-sur-Eon is a real town.) She hates Paris, where she lives in reclusive comfort with her school friend Madame Trévins, giving the occasional smart and stylish promotional dinner party for clients. But she hankers after Saint-Mouezy.

> She'd have done better to sell up and go back to the farm
> where she'd been born. Rabbits and chickens, some tomato
> plants, and a couple of beds for lettuces and cabbages – what
> more did she need? She would have sat by her fireside amongst
> the placid cats, listening to the clock ticking, to the rain falling
> on the zinc drain pipes, and the seven o'clock bus passing by
> in the far distance; she'd have carried on warming her bed with
> a warming pan before getting into it, warming her face in the
> sun on her stone bench, cutting recipes out of *La Nouvelle
> République* and sticking them into her big kitchen book.

And she does go back to the village from time to time with Madame Trévins, snatching a few hours and a night there whenever she can. But her parents' old farm has gone to ruin; it is damp; the wallpaper is peeling from the walls, and the orchard has ceased to bear fruit, and she can't get a gardener – not even a part-time local man, because Saint-Mouezy has become a second-home village, 'empty all week and chock full on Saturdays and Sundays', when it buzzes to the sound of townsfolk brandishing their Moreau tools as they lay bare old beams and old stone, and hang coach lamps, and convert barns.

Long Bennington hasn't got to that stage yet, although Joyce's neighbour reported to us with some amusement when I was last there that he'd heard a Tesco van delivering in Church Street at nine-thirty at night. I don't know why we all found that so funny, but we did.

If Madame Moreau was eighty-three in 1975, she was only a decade or so older than Auntie Phyl, and very much younger than my grandmother, who may or may not have used the warming-pan to warm her bed.

Grandma Bloor was bad at making beds, an unfortunate defect in someone running a bed and breakfast. She was teased for this by her daughters. No hospital corners for her; the sheets wrinkled and bunched and drooped and fought you damply in the night. The hair mattresses of her beds sagged in the middle, in deep hollows and permanent declivities. I have no idea how old those mattresses were. Some of them probably dated from 1905.

Grandma Bloor occasionally accused her paying guests – although luckily not to their faces – of wetting the bed. And maybe some of them did. 'They *said* the sheet fell into the chamber pot,' she would snort, indignantly, as she surveyed the damage. '*That's* a likely story.' I was frightened of wetting the bed, although I was not a habitual bed-wetter. I was frightened of her scorn. Stammering was my childhood weakness, not enuresis.

Grandma kept rabbits and chickens at Bryn, though not in my day. She inherited a kitchen garden from her predecessors, which produced potatoes and carrots and beans and peas and giant woody trees of sprouts. It had once produced asparagus, but Grandma couldn't be bothered with that. It was too much trouble. The little green curled heads, like bluebells or bracken, poked their way up randomly and in vain, recalling another more skilled and patient epoch. In Mexborough, in the dank backyard in Bank Street with the outside lavatory, there was no space for vegetables, so she can have had no knowledge of how to cultivate them. Unless such skill was bred in the bone and the blood and remembered through folk history.

As a small child, I was enchanted by the very tiny new potatoes which I could unearth when nobody was looking. They were so small, and so white, and so shining, so doll-like and diminutive. They were like little marbles, or pearls, or jewels. We used them for pretend dinner parties.

There is a public house a few miles from Long Bennington, in the Vale of Belvoir, which still gives me a shudder of authenticity. It is far from any urban centre, though not very far from what was once the Great North Road, and only a mile from the 'three-shires bush' where the three counties of Nottinghamshire, Leicestershire and Lincolnshire meet. It is not, however, very easy to find; it is even advertised as a 'hidden place of England'. It is a pleasant, old, seventeenth-century, brick building, not unlike Bryn, and when I last saw it, it had not been over-restored. The food was modern, of course – scampi, chips and peas, fish and chips, lasagne – but the walls were old, and sepia agricultural photographs, together with a family tree of the people who gave their name to the inn, hung on them. My interest in the family is minimal but my interest in the building is almost painful. Unlike the Ram Jam, it makes me feel slightly vertiginous, as though I were in some uncertain patch of time from which I might quite easily disappear. That could be considered a whimsical, Mary Poppins, Alison Uttley kind of sensation, and I am not particularly proud of it.

Unlike the Ram Jam, this inn is not a roadhouse. It was not built to cater for passing trade. Its place in the landscape would have been recognized by John Clare, George Morland, Oliver Goldsmith, William Cobbett or Anthony Trollope.

I know that my feeling for Bryn and the landscapes around it is vulnerable to accusations of romanticism and inauthenticity. And yet these places work on in my memory and my imagination, representing something, as the fragments of the True Cross represented something to those who purchased them, even though they must have suspected that they were not very true.

XLIX

Archaeologist Matthew Johnson, in *Ideas of Landscape* (2007), provides an interesting and at times worrying analysis of what he calls W. G. Hoskins' romantic view of the past, 'in which emotive kinship and empathy with the people of the past is primary'. He argues that the sense of being linked in feeling with the past, in a Wordsworthian continuity, may seriously mislead us when we try to interpret archaeological evidence. He sees this sense as a form of pathetic fallacy, a fallacy of empathy both with landscapes and with the dead. He writes:

> There is no *a priori* reason why medieval peasants are any
> more or less 'linked in feeling' to the modern world than
> prehistoric settlers. To suppose that they were, one would have
> to posit some extremely simplistic form of evolutionary theory
> in which the mentality of human groups becomes 'more
> like us' the closer to the modern world one gets. This might
> just be a sustainable position, but it is not an argument that I
> have seen made anywhere in the work of the English landscape
> tradition.

The men, women and children who lived in prehistoric sites at Standon Hill and Grimspound, Johnson maintains, had 'feelings that were quite different from ours'.

So much for my fanciful musings in the flint mines of Grimes Graves or in the Iron Age fort of Bats Castle; so much for my sensitive response to Cleeve Abbey; so much for my communion with John Clare in the ditch bottom at Bryn.

Maybe I could invoke Jung and a concept of the collective unconscious here, to rescue me from the cruel chronology of history. This surely is what Hoskins wished to call upon when he wrote in *The Making of the English Landscape* (1955) of sitting beside a wide estuary

> as the light thickens on a winter evening, dissolving all the irrelevant human details of the scene, leaving nothing but the shining water, the sky, and the darkening hills, and the immemorial sound of curlews whistling over the mud and fading river-beaches. This, we feel, is exactly as the first men saw it…for a moment or two we succeed in entering into the minds of the dead.

Except, of course, as Matthew Johnson reminds us, the dead didn't have minds like ours, or eyes like ours. We might as well try to identify with amoeba or bees or bats. The race has no memory. There is no way back to that place. We invent our own family tree, we construct our own ancestry, we collect our own fragments, we ignore the pieces that don't fit, we deny the stories we don't like. We make up our own Golden Legend. We throw the extra pieces into a bucket, and pretend they belong to some other design, some other puzzle.

Bryn was nothing more than a house that my Bloor grandparents happened to buy. And the house belongs once more to strangers.

L

Auntie Phyl's last months in the care home were extra pieces. They were unnecessary. Age is unnecessary. Some of us, like my mother, are fortunate enough to die swiftly and suddenly, in full possession of our faculties and our fate, but more and more of us will be condemned to linger, at the mercy of anxious or indifferent relatives, careless strangers, unwanted medical interventions, increasing debility, incontinence, memory loss. We live too long, but, like the sibyl hanging in her basket in the cave at Cumae, we find it hard to die.

I do not like to think of Auntie Phyl, as her solid body stubbornly resisted death. She had a powerful constitution that did not surrender easily. She struggled. Her GP had told her some years earlier, on one of her annual visits to the village surgery, that she could guarantee her good health up to the age of ninety but couldn't promise anything much after that. This prediction had proved uncannily accurate, although she was already in the home on her ninetieth birthday, where she deteriorated rapidly, as people do.

Her character was such a strange mixture of stoicism and complaint that we found it hard to tell how she was feeling in her last days at Bryn, before she and Joyce decided she couldn't cope on her own any more. She used to get very cross with us if we didn't ring at the usual time on a Sunday, which made me cross, because it wasn't always possible to stick to the appointed hour, and I felt I was doing my best. I thought she was just being difficult, and only later did I realize that she was now finding it physically so hard to get from the front room to the telephone a few feet away in the hall that she would go and sit in the hall and wait there for the phone to ring. Of course she was cross if she had to sit there in the cold and narrow gloom for half an hour or more. This problem could have been resolved by moving the telephone, but somehow this never happened, partly because she didn't make the situation clear to us. She didn't like to ask for help.

The last few occasions on which I visited her in Newark were a horror to me and I do not think they gave much pleasure to her. But I continued to make the old Belisha journey up the Great North Road and to comfort myself with a night in the Ram Jam, listening to the slipstream. What else could I do? I did not want her to think we had forgotten her, and I wanted to see for myself that she was not being neglected, although we hoped Joyce would have let us know if anything seriously bad was happening. Though Joyce, too, is a stoic and doesn't like to complain.

The subject of ageing has been addressed by many writers, and I do not know whether I ought to add to the volume. Accounts that lodge uncomfortably in my mind include Simone de Beauvoir's book about the death of her mother, Blake Morrison's book about the death of his father, John Bayley's painfully frank descriptions of how his wife Iris Murdoch succumbed to Alzheimer's, and Polly Toynbee's matter-of-fact chapter in *Hard Work* on the experience of working in a home for the elderly. And I also remember stories by friends who have looked after dying relatives, and stories by friends who have since died. One of these friends, in her last illness, after many strokes and various kidney malfunctions, told me that it was strangely comic to be congratulated by the nursing staff for wetting the bed. 'Well done!' the nurses would cry, when they discovered that she had peed into the mattress. This is second childhood, when we are praised for actions that were forbidden when we were young. And it takes a brave woman to find that amusing, and she was nothing if not brave. Ann was an oak of a woman, rather like Auntie Phyl.

Visits to Auntie Phyl in Newark initiated me into care home ways. I learned that gifts of flowers were a nuisance to the staff, and would be left to rot in vases of greening and slimy water. I learned that many old women of her age were called Phyllis. (I have since learned the meaning of that name: it means 'leaf', a concept too light for Auntie Phyl's robust physique.) I learned that objects used to disappear into the communal storehouse. While she was interned there I bought her as a birthday or Christmas gift a black, Oriental, kimono-style, silky dressing gown with a pattern of pink and red butterflies, which she seemed to like very much. I'd chosen it with care because it reminded me of some of the clothes she'd worn in the 1930s. It vanished after a week or two and she rang me to complain. I in turn complained to the staff, who said they knew nothing about it. So I trailed heavy-footed, back into Oxford Street and bought her another, not quite but almost identical, and took it up to her on my next visit. This persistence was greeted with what I can only describe as cynical incredulity, not by her but by everybody around her. Why on earth had I bothered to replace a garment that would probably vanish like its predecessor? And what did an old woman at death's door want with a pretty dressing gown?

What indeed?

But it stayed in her room, a tribute to her honest indignation and my resistance to the system. When she died I took it home with me and wore it for a while before I gave it to Oxfam. I gave it away because it was depressing me.

Another object that stayed in her room till the end was a little jar of brandy butter I made and took up for her at Christmas. I thought she could have some on a mince pie. But I don't think she understood what it was, and I don't suppose anyone offered her any, so it sat there, week after week, month after month, on the shelf. I just let it be there. I'd lost the will to intervene.

The activities in the home did not appeal to her much. She did not play bingo and she stopped watching the television because the channels were always going wrong and the faces of the presenters were bright orange. Sitting in a circle of old women whom she did not even know and throwing a ball around struck her as deeply pointless. What was it for? To keep the fingers moving. What for? To be able to eat more easily. What for? To stay alive. What for? No answer.

Playing fivestones as a child is fun, but throwing and catching a ball as an old woman is silly.

She had been distressed some thirty years earlier by the old age of her Aunt Thyrza, always the favourite of that generation of aunts. Thyrza had been a kind, plain-faced, dignified woman, famed within the family for her beautiful embroidery, which was much finer than Auntie Phyl's or Grandma's. She often went to stay at Bryn, and my mother liked her well enough to invite her to stay with us. (We rarely had guests.) But in old age she suffered a personality change, according to Auntie Phyl, and became malicious and resentful and maybe even worse. Auntie Phyl found this very upsetting. She knew that such things happened, and that it wasn't anyone's fault, but nevertheless she thought it was very unfair that it had happened to such a good person. And she was also annoyed to discover that Aunt Thyrza, in her care home, had been bullied into doing sewing as a form of occupational therapy. Angry child's sewing, with a big needle, when she had sewn the finest seam of all. It was a bitter ending to a good life.

Auntie Phyl worried that she herself might 'turn nasty'. I think that may have been the phrase she used. But she didn't. She had often been grumpy and rude when younger, but her manners didn't deteriorate, and when she was grumpy in old age she had good reason to be so.

She was confronting, as I was through her, the pointlessness of survival, the uselessness of all the little strategies by which we manage to stay alive and fill our time and get through our days – gardening, playing patience, doing jigsaws or crosswords, embroidering, watching snooker, reading, trying to learn a new language, listening to *The Archers*, collecting little bits of scholarship about the history of games and pastimes.

She wasn't really one for self-deception. And she didn't like *The Archers*. She didn't like it when people assumed that she listened to it, just because she lived in a village. She thought it was inauthentic.

On one of my earlier visits to the Oaks, I took with me a ball of cheerful scarlet wool and a crochet hook and asked her to teach me how to crochet. I had never mastered this art when I was a child. I could knit, once upon a time, very badly, but never managed to make any object or garment that was useful or wearable. (My gros point cushions and rugs are, as I have indicated, more satisfactory, indeed almost pleasing.) Auntie Phyl used to crochet a good deal, and I still have and wear several of the scarves she made for me. Surely, I thought, I could learn to crochet, even though I was in my sixties. I wanted to learn, and she wanted to teach me. But I simply couldn't get the hang of it. She began to get annoyed with me, as I sat there by her institutional bed, and I began to get annoyed with myself. She was still a good teacher, but I had become a bad learner. I was too old to learn a new trick. I gave up, promising her I'd try to practise by myself when I got home. But I didn't bother.

I wish now that I had persevered. It might have been good for my bad thumb, might even have prevented it from getting so bad in the first place. The thumb joint of my left hand is now afflicted by De Quervain's tenosynovitis, sometimes known as washer-woman's thumb. It's annoying. No worse than annoying, but annoying. I don't know who De Quervain was. My doctor tells me that she doesn't approve of naming maladies after dead men.

LI

Michael, who was very ill when I started to write this book and is now not so ill, claims from time to time that he is the new Auntie Phyl. In this role he has taken to watching *The Antiques Roadshow*, and has been known to watch the same episode more than once. He likes the soothing repetition. Like Auntie Phyl, he has allowed himself to be bullied into employing people who knock casually at the door and demand to be allowed to resurface the front steps or clean the windows. The mixture of menace and pathos with which they present themselves on his doorstep gets him down, and he lets them do things that don't really need doing. He is sorry for them. They always do their work very badly and demand to be paid in cash.

And I am going that way myself. The young mercenary from Rupert Murdoch's army who jumped around recently like an ibex all over my roof at Porlock, adjusting the dish to stop it speaking Welsh, said he wanted to be paid in cash. Luckily I hadn't got enough on me, and the nearest bank is many miles away, so he had to accept an old-fashioned cheque. (I did tip him £20, in conciliation. He had been up there for hours.) The week after, I weakly agreed to pay hundreds of pounds in advance for someone to come and inspect my electrical installations – not to fix them, just to inspect them – because I couldn't work out how to get out of the transaction, once my enquiry had been set in motion. I've forgotten how to say, bugger off, I'm not paying something for nothing, do you think I'm a fool? As we grow older, we become more vulnerable to these pressures. The salesman or the antique dealer or the itinerant cowboy builder or the utilities company smells weakness, scents blood, goes for the kill. The victim kneels, bows the neck and surrenders. It is easier to surrender than to struggle.

I won't mention the pseudo-leather jackets purchased from a con man on a motorway service station forecourt, or the excessive supplies of ironing board covers and yellow dusters and unsatisfactory tea towels and strangely textured absorbent cloths that pile up in the utility room. I forget they are there, and recently went out to purchase an ironing board cover from a shop (which is not easy), forgetting that I'd bought enough from Gary to last me until death.

No, I don't think I want to write much more about ageing. Telling horror stories is too easy. My worst memories of events surrounding Auntie Phyl's last days still have the power to make me very angry, and I don't want to write out of anger. The avoidance of anger has been my self-imposed Oulipean constraint while writing this. It has not been as difficult as trying to avoid the letter E, but it has been taxing. There may be one or two little splinters and signifiers of anger remaining in my text, but they are so deeply buried and coded that not even I can be sure of finding them. I'm still angry with my mother, of course, that's obvious, but that doesn't count any more. It is past cure, past hope, and almost past regret. Doris Lessing wrote recently that she hated her mother, a comment that was perceived as shocking. I didn't hate mine. She filled me with pity and fear as well as anger. But never with hatred.

Jigsaws are a useful antidote to anger.

LII

I ask myself: do I believe in the jigsaw model of the universe, or do I believe in the open ending, the ever evolving and ever undetermined future, the future with pieces that even the physicists cannot number, although the physicists say they cannot be infinite? If I could claim anything as grand as a world-view, towards which of these two would I look? I thought that by writing this book I might find the answer.

I used to think I had a teleological sense of life, in which we moved towards a fore-ordained, apocalyptic illumination. All the lost and buried tesserae of memory would rush together to form part of a bright and dazzling pattern, a complete picture, which would explain, perhaps at the very moment of death, everything that had gone before, if not everything that was to come. I did not believe in an afterlife, merely in an enlightenment. The fragments of the True Cross would at last be united, and all the whispers, rumours and muddled legends of history would be made plain, transforming themselves into the Golden Legend. They would come together, the Stone Age children playing with coloured pebbles on the cave floor, the Greek children with their knuckle-bones, the children of Brueghel and Long Bennington and East

Hardwick School, little Tom Malkin who died at the age of six, and the village children playing ducks and drakes and fishing with a pin. Not one of them would be lost, for all would equally be part of the grand design.

This hope, I suppose, represents the religious strain that I inherited from my father. 'If with all your hearts ye truly seek me, ye shall ever surely find me.' He liked those words from *Elijah*, and used to chant them a little tunelessly as he walked round his Suffolk garden in the cool of the evening. None of us could sing.

As I watched my aunt nearing death, it was more the meaningless dignity and indignity of endurance that impressed me. She stuck it out to the end. She was not a believer.

The concept of life as a journey, a pilgrimage, a quest, a ladder, or a spiral track may be attractive to some, but to me the notion of a goal is not. The very word 'goal' has unpleasing associations. Board games, unlike jigsaw puzzles, necessarily admit elements of competition and victory, and the notion of winners and losers, sheep and goats, the saved and the damned. Whereas the Greek *telos* can mean an end, an aim, an ultimate purpose, a final cause, and need not embrace the concept of competition. In the larger pattern, all the solitary journeys combine, and we arrive together.

The jigsaw, with its frame, is a simulacrum of meaning, order and design. As Nick Tucker said, if you try hard enough, you can complete it. That galactic scatter of inert and inept fragments of wood or cardboard will come together and make a picture.

Books, too, have beginnings and endings, and they attempt to impose a pattern, to make a shape. We aim, by writing them, to make order from chaos. We fail. The admission of failure is the best that we can do. It is a form of progress.

NOTES ON QUOTATIONS

pp. xv,   *'for it would have...distressed him so often'*
73   James Boswell's *Life of Samuel Johnson*, vol. 1, 1709–1765, p. 317, Oxford edition, 1934, edited by G. B. Hill, rev. L. F. Powell

p. 29   *'What is dying . . . There she comes'*
This quotation from Bishop C. H. Brent was sent to me at my request by the Reverend Tony Pick. I have not been able to trace it further.

p. 50   *'Everything shone...for two hundred years'*
Alison Uttley, *The Country Child*, Faber and Faber, 1931

p. 52   *'tiny metallic sounds' 'pursed-up button mouths'*
Alison Uttley, *The Button-Box and other essays*, ch. 14, Faber and Faber, 1968

p. 53   *'and that is why...autobiographical notes'*
This quotation is from a short autobiographical sketch by P. L. Travers in *The Junior Books of Authors*, ed. S. J. Kunitz and H. Haycraft (H. H. Wilson, 1951).

p. 71   *'I choose to mention...favourite amusements'*
James Boswell's *Life of Samuel Johnson*, op. cit., vol. 5, *Tour to the Hebrides 1773*, p. 16

p. 71   *'loved indeed the very act...and on despising no accommodations'*

Hester Lynch Piozzi, *Anecdotes of the late Dr Samuel Johnson* (1786)

pp. 82, 84   '*the organisation of the collection is itself a substitute for time*'
For Jean Baudrillard's essay on 'The Non-Functional System of Objects' see *Revenge of the Crystal: Selected Writings on the Modern Object and its Destiny* (ed. and trans. Paul Foss and Julian Pefanis, Pluto, 1990.)

p. 90   '*I have seen little Girls ... more useful to them*'
John Locke, *Some Thoughts Concerning Education*, 1693, 1695

p. 117   '*in the same way ... has become "atlantique".*'
Georges Perec, from *Penser/Classer* (*Think/Classify*) (*Le Genre Humain*, 1982), an essay which appears in *Species of Spaces and Other Pieces*, ed. and trans. by John Sturrock (Penguin, 1997)

p. 128   '*I should recommend ... a perfect Whole.*'
William Cowper to William Unwin, letter dated 7 September 1780, *The Letters and Prose Writings of William Cowper*, vol. 1, 1750–1781, edited by James King and Charles Ryskamp (Clarendon Press, 1979)

p. 131   '*a playful visualisation ... bosom and rump*'
Diana Donald, *The Age of Caricature* (New Haven, 1996)

p. 132   '*Whoever has watched children ... slow, but sure, and wins the day*'
Maria Edgeworth, *Practical Education*, vol. 1 (vol. 11 of Complete Works; 1798)

p. 139   '*he works very hard all day ... or anything else*'
Stella Tillyard, ch. 3, 'Homes, Education and Adultery', *Aristocrats* (Chatto & Windus, 1994)

p 141   '*The Queen thanked [Lady Carteret] ... that I drew the pattern*'
Autobiography and Correspondence of Mary Granville, vol. 1, 1861: a letter dated 4 March 1728/9

p. 141   '*Indian figures and flowers ... painting on glass*'
Autobiography and Correspondence of Mary Granville, vol. 3, 1861: a letter dated 11 June 1751

p. 142   '*Now I know you smile…banish the spleen*'
Ruth Hayden, *Mrs Delany: Her Life and Her Flowers*, p. 143

p. 143   '*a knife, sizsars, pencle, rule, compass, bodkin*'
Ruth Hayden, *Mrs Delany: Her Life and Her Flowers*, p. 155

p. 147   '*national magnificence… carry into effect*'
The Journal of Elizabeth Lady Holland (1791–1811), published
by Longmans, Green and Co., 1908 (vol. 11, p. 195)

p. 169   '*the lamps from London Bridge…town hall for Swanage in 1881*'
Raphael Samuel's *Theatres of Memory*, 1994. See also *Swanage
Past* by David Lewer and Dennis Smale, Phillimore and Co.,
1994.
'*an overwhelmingly undisciplined example of the City of London
style*'
John Newman and Nikolaus Pevsner, *The Buildings of England:
Dorset* (Penguin, 1972, 1975)

p. 171   '*creep, / Wretch, under a comfort…dies with sleep*'
G. M. Hopkins, untitled poem, 'No worst, there is none'

p. 174   '*Tristes desirs, vivez donques contents… que j'endure*'
Joachim du Bellay, Sonnet VII of his sequence *Antiquitez de
Rome*, 1558

p. 182   '*the belt buckle of a uniform … the chandelier*'
Georges Perec, *Life: A User's Manual* (1978), translated by
David Bellos

p. 188   '*I dine, I play backgammon…with my friends*'
David Hume, Conclusion of Book I, *A Treatise of Human
Nature*, 1739
'*very cheerful, and even elegant…to my Honour*'
E. C. Mossner, *The Life of David Hume*, ch. 37, 'Autumnal
Serenity'

p. 189   '*A peasant and a philosopher…consciousness with a philosopher*'
James Boswell, op. cit., vol. 2, 1766–1776

'*Prejudice apart ... always asserted of poetry*'
Jeremy Bentham, *Rationale of Reward*, Book 3, Chapter 1, 1830

p. 192   '*I am not so great an enemy to cards ... for that purpose*'
Ruth Hayden, op. cit., p. 95

'*I can't help when I play deep ... don't feel pleasant at it*'
Stella Tillyard, op.cit.

p. 193   '*poor little ugly she-mouse ... not being in the house*'
John Hervey, *Memoirs of the Reign of George II*, first published 1848, ed. J. W. Croker

'*Read to the Queen ... provoke one's understanding*'
Flora Fraser, *Princesses*, p. 200 (Harcourt Mss, Elizabeth to Elizabeth Lady Harcourt, 23 July 1802)

p. 194   '*always played ... females in a certain class*'
F. J. Harvey Darton, *The Life and Times of Mrs Sherwood*, 1910

p. 209   '*The house itself ... compose a third*'
Thomas de Quincey, 'Southey, Wordsworth and Coleridge', first published in *Tait's Edinburgh Magazine* in August 1839 and reprinted in *Reminiscences of the English Lake Poets* (also known as *Recollections of the Lake Poets*)

p. 210   '*a house is never said to be properly furnished ... a kitten rising three weeks*'
Robert Southey, *The Doctor*, 1834. The story of Goldilocks is also to be found in this publication.

p. 215   '*Princess Elizabeth is a lovely little fat ... for the purpose*'
Flora Fraser, ch. 2, 'Growing Up', *Princesses*

p. 231   '*cannot be created by charters ... perish by themselves*'
Hugh Kingsmill, *The Poisoned Crown*, Eyre and Spottiswoode, 1944

p. 262   '*hauntingly still and grave ... expression and gesture*'
Helen Langdon, *Travellers' Art Guide to Italy*, Mitchell Beazley, 1984

p. 264   *'imitations fondly made . . . weakness, and his loves'*
William Wordsworth, *The Prelude*, Book 7, 'Residence in London'

p. 268,   *'a sort of existentialist mosaic . . . and unpublished'*

p. 269   *'An early book I tried to write . . . squares of opinion and feeling'*
John Fowles, *Wormholes*, Jonathan Cape, 1988, pp. 367, xi of Preface

p. 284   *'a map of England . . . towns were worked in silk'*
H. Winifred Sturge and Theodora Clark, *The Mount School, York*, J. M. Dent and Sons Ltd, 1931

p. 319   *'I satisfied my hunger . . . seemed to do me good'*
The Prose of John Clare, ed. J. W. and Anne Tibble, Routledge and Kegan Paul, 1951

ACKNOWLEDGEMENTS

Many people helped me, some wittingly and some unwittingly, with this book. Some talked or wrote to me about jigsaws and some recommended further reading.

Amongst my correspondents I thank Peter Barber, Xavier Bray, Anthony Brown, Linda Cameron, William Chislett, Beverley Cook, Alan Dein, Sebastian Edwards, Irving Finkel, Juliet Gardener, Pat Garrett, Daniel Hahn, Howard Hardiman, Roland Huntford, Toph Marshall, Simon Mason, Julian Mitchell, Charles Saumarez Smith, Jill Shefrin, Donald Sinden, Gillian Sutherland and Colin Thubron. Nicholas Tucker was helpful and encouraging in more ways than one. Michael Berry found rare books for me, and Michael Codron submitted to an interview about his jigsaw addiction, an interest to which I was alerted by Michael Frayn.

Julia Hoffbrand of the Museum of London showed me some very early dissected maps and puzzles, and directed me to Alan Dein's BBC Radio 4 programme about the Jackson Pollock *Convergence* jigsaw.

Treasured jigsaws were given to me by Julia Blackburn, Sindamani Bridglal, Carmen Callil, Donald and Shirley Gee, Julian Mitchell, Richard Rowson, Augusta Skidelsky, and various Swift children and grandchildren. Helen Langdon and Susan Haskins talked to me about aspects of art history, and Kenneth Uprichard of the British Museum about mosaic restoration. Hilary Dickinson, Judith Landry and Julian Mitchell listened to me patiently and came up with comments over a wide and random spectrum of interests. Ronald and Natasha Harwood described to me the pleasure of crosswords, and Valda Ondaatje the pleasure of playing bridge. Jeremy Rosenblatt and Ian Blatchford spotted news items and metaphors, and David Millett explained jigsaws and fretsaws.

Kevin Copley opened my eyes to a whole new area of speculation when he mentioned mosaics, and Tom Holland sent me off on a search for a jigsaw of the Alexander mosaic at Naples, which I never found. Alan Sillitoe talked to me about his fondness for maps, and Doris Lessing about the therapeutic uses of jigsaws. Mia Beaumont and Bernadine Bishop also offered very useful comments in this area. Simon Mason alerted me to Georges Perec's novel, *Life: A User's Manual*, which was the starting point for many further quests.

Joyce Bainbridge, who, with her late husband Eddie, was a lifelong friend of my aunt Phyllis Bloor, has been immensely helpful with this book. She has many memories of my grandparents' house, Bryn, and of Long Bennington, the village where they lived. She is a custodian of village history and our visits to her keep the past alive. She has treasured photographs and stories that would otherwise have been lost or forgotten.

I thank all my family for their support. My daughter Becky has shown a keen interest in doing jigsaws with me, and some of her friends have helped to assemble impossible puzzles in my absence. I would never have finished the Jackson Pollock without them. (Paula Smith has a particularly good eye.) Michael Holroyd, who has no personal interest whatsoever in this curious pastime, has watched over me tolerantly, and taken some bizarrely revealing photographs of my works in progress.

I also thank my editor Toby Mundy, for publishing this eccentric book and for sending it off in new directions during various stages of its composition, and Caroline Knight, for her encouragement and help with the text. My thanks also to my agents, Michael Sissons and the late Pat Kavanagh, who looked after me, supported me and encouraged me over many years.

An essay called 'A Day Out in Kew', which incorporates and enlarges on an episode in my research for this book, appears in *Jane Austen Sings the Blues* (ed. Nora Stovel, University of Alberta, 2009), which is a Festschrift in honour of Austen scholar Bruce Stovel.

BIBLIOGRAPHY

This book, as I explain in the foreword, began as a book about jigsaws, and I read widely if randomly round this subject and the subject of children's games and literature. The most important single source was *The English Jigsaw-Puzzle 1760–1890* by Linda Hannas (Wayland Publishers, 1972), a pioneer text that led me to F. R. B. Whitehouse's *Table Games of Georgian and Victorian Days* (Priory Press, 1951) and Chris McCann's *Master Pieces: The Art History of Jigsaw Puzzles* (Collector's Press, Inc., Portland, Oregon, 1998). Jill Shefrin's work in this field – 'Make it a Pleasure not a Task', *Princeton University Library Chronicle*, LX: 2 (Winter, 1999) and *Such Constant Affectionate Care: Lady Charlotte Finch, Royal Governess and the Children of George III* (Los Angeles, Cotsen Family Foundation, 2003) – has been invaluable. Shefrin's *The Dartons: Publishers of Educational Aids, Pastimes & Juvenile Ephemera, 1787–1876. A Bibliographic Checklist. Together with a description of the Darton Archive as held by the Cotsen Children's Library, Princeton University Library & a brief history of printed teaching aids* (Cotsen Occasional Press) will be published in 2009. Peter Haining's *Movable Books: An Illustrated History* (New English Library, 1979) colourfully illustrates an adjacent area.

The specialist literature on children's literature in English is extensive, and the key text for me was F. J. Harvey Darton's *Children's Books in England* (1932; third enlarged and revised edition, ed. Brian Alderson, Cambridge University Press, 1982), which in turn introduced me to his edition of *The Life and Times of Mrs Sherwood* (Wells Gardner, Darton, 1910) and his pseudonymous novels *My Father's Son: A Faithful Record* (Hodder and Stoughton, 1913) by 'W. W. Penn', and *When: A Record of Transition* (Chapman & Hall, 1929) by 'the late J. L. Pole'. Marjorie Moon's *John Harris's Books for Youth 1801–1843* (Five Owls Press Limited, 1976) was also useful, as was *The Oxford Companion to Children's Literature* (Oxford University Press, 1984) by Humphrey Carpenter and Mari Prichard. The new *Oxford Dictionary of National Biography* (Oxford University Press, 2004) is a storehouse of well-researched lesser lives, including those of the Spilsbury family. The account of Robert Southey's childhood is from the first volume of *The Life and Correspondence of Robert Southey*, ed. C. C. Southey, 6 vols. (Longman, Brown, Green and Longmans, 1849). Information about Lindley Murray is from *The Mount School, York* by H. Winifred Sturge and Theodora Clark (J. M. Dent and Sons Ltd, 1931).

Lists of games and pastimes may be found in Rabelais and in Robert Burton's *Anatomy of Melancholy* (1621); and there are early descriptions of card games in Henry Peacham's *The Complete Gentleman* (1622). Joseph Strutt published a classic compendium titled *The Sports and Pastimes of the People of England* in 1801. William Hughes Willshire produced a *Descriptive Catalogue of Playing and Other Cards: Playing Cards in the British Museum* (1876). Catherine Perry Hargrave's *A History of Playing Cards* (Dover Publications Inc., 1930, 1966) is a history of playing cards and their origins. Thomas Fuller's *A Pisgah-Sight of Palestine* (1650) is full of engaging maps, while Victor Morgan's 'The cartographic image of "the country" in Early Modern England' (*Transactions of the Royal Historical Society*, 5th series, vol. 29, 1979) explores adjacent territory. Anke te Heesen's *The World in a Box: The Story of an Eighteenth Century Picture Encyclopedia* (1997; trans. 2002, Chicago Press) records a singular experiment employing picture cards. Willard Fiske's *Chess in Iceland* (1905) is full of arcane gamesmanship.

John Locke and Maria Edgeworth wrote extensively on the use of play in education, and influenced succeeding generations of pedagogues. Johan Huizinga's *Homo Ludens: A Study of the Play Element in Culture* (published in German in Switzerland 1944, trans. R. F. C. Hull, Routledge and Kegan Paul Ltd, 1949) addressed the meaning of play, but it was the publication of *L'Enfant et la vie familiale sous L'Ancien Régime* by Philippe Ariès in 1960 (published in translation by Jonathan Cape in 1962 as *Centuries of Childhood: A Social History of Family Life*) that sparked a new interest in childhood as a subject, which expressed itself in works such as J. H. Plumb's article, 'Children in eighteenth-century England' (*Past and Present*, May 1975), and Lawrence Stone's *The Family, Sex and Marriage in England 1500–1800* (Weidenfeld and Nicolson, 1977). Many biographies of eighteenth-century figures and families now cover childhood and education in more detail than they used to do: of particular relevance to me here were Flora Fraser's *Princesses: The Six Daughters of George III* (John Murray, 2004) and Stella Tillyard's *Aristocrats* (Chatto & Windus, 1994). The most poignant memoir of this epoch remains Benjamin Heath Malkin's *A Father's Memoirs of His Child* (London, printed for Longman by T. Bensley, 1806), a work illustrated by William Blake, which reminds us of Blake's role in the invention of infancy. Vic Gatrell's *City of Laughter: Sex and Satire in Eighteenth Century London* (Atlantic Books, 2006) offers a contrasting and more robust panorama of London life at this period and James Boswell's *Life of Samuel Johnson* (1791) and Ernest Campbell Mossner's *The Life of David Hume* (Thomas Nelson, 1954; Clarendon Press, 1980) provide a valuable backdrop. Germaine Greer's *The Obstacle Race* (1979) is a treasure house of information about women's lives and art.

A detour into art history via a jigsaw puzzle of Brueghel's *Kinderspieler* (*Children's Games*) revealed a world of theory and speculation, which included Edward Snow's sympathetic and revealing *Inside Brueghel* (North Point Press, 1997), Simon Schama's *The Embarrassment of Riches* (Collins, 1987), and Mary Frances Durantini's *The Child in 17th Century Dutch Painting* (Bowker, 1983). *Hanging the Head: Portraiture and Social Formation in Eighteenth Century England* (New Haven, 1993) by Marcia Pointon was also useful in this context.

Jigsaws took me by a different route to the works of Georges Perec and another cluster of texts. I am indebted to Simon Mason for mentioning Perec in the early days of my research, for otherwise I might never have come across Perec's jigsaw masterpiece, *Life: A User's Manual* (Collins Harvill, 1978), translated by David Bellos. Bellos's full and impressive life of Perec, *Georges Perec: A Life in Words*, was published by Harvill in 1993. Other sources include Perec's novel *Things* (1965; trans. Bellos, Harvill, 1990) and Perec's collection of essays, *Species of Spaces and Other Pieces*, edited and translated by John Sturrock (Penguin, 1997); the *Oulipo Compendium*, edited by Harry Mathews and Alastair Brotchie (Atlas Press, 1998, 2005); various works by Jean Baudrillard, of which the principal are *Simulacra and Simulation* (1981; trans. Sheila Faria Glaser, University of Michigan Press, 1994) and *Revenge of the Crystal* (trans. P. Foss and J. Pefanis, Pluto, 1990).

Mosaics, suggested to me as a sideline by Kevin Copley in a taxi between the British Library and the Museum of London, have a literature of their own, as well as their own collections and museums. Works consulted include *The Art of Mosaics* (Los Angeles

County Museum of Art, 1982); Katherine Dunabin, *Mosaics of the Greek and Roman World* (Cambridge University Press, 1999); Peter Fischer, *Mosaic: History and Technique* (Thames and Hudson, 1969, 1971); Maria Fabricius Hansen, *The Eloquence of Appropriation: A Prolegomena to an Understanding of Spolia in Early Christian Rome* (Rome, L'Erma di Bretschneider, 2003); Anna Maria Massinelli, *The Gilbert Collection: Hardstones* (2000); Antero Tammisto, *Birds in Mosaics: A Study on the Representation of Birds in Hellenistic and Romano-Campanian Tessellated Mosaics to the Early Augustan Age* (Rome, 1997). Both Pliny the Elder and Goethe were captivated by and wrote about mosaics; for the former, I consulted both a *Natural History: A Selection* (Penguin, 1991), translated by John F. Healy, and Philemon Holland's earlier version of 1601. For Goethe's *Italian Journey* I have used throughout the translation by W. H. Auden and Elizabeth Mayer (Collins, 1962; Penguin, 1970). Ruth Hayden's *Mrs Delany: Her Life and Her Flowers* (British Museum Press, 1980, 1982) describes Mary Delany's floral mosaics, and Olga Raggio's description of ceilings is to be found in *The Gubbio Studiolo and its Conservation* (vol. 1, published by the Metropolitan Museum of Art, New York, 1999).

The sources of the landscape jigsaw are multiple, and include classic works by W. G. Hoskins (including *The Making of the English Landscape*, Hodder and Stoughton, 1955), Raymond Williams, John Berger and John Barrell. I found particularly eloquent John Barrell's *The dark side of the landscape* (Cambridge University Press, 1980). Matthew Johnson's somewhat revisionist *Ideas of Landscape* (Blackwell, 2007) was also very stimulating. The works of John Clare have long been important to me, and Jonathan Bate's fine *John Clare: A biography* (Picador, 2003) shed further light on the reasons for my interest. Clare's vision of a pastoral childhood connects with rereadings of Georgian poets, the scattered autobiographical writings of Alison Uttley, the strangely disturbing biography of Uttley by Denis Judd (*Alison Uttley: The life of a country child*, Joseph, 1986). Uttley's principal work in this context is *The Country Child* (Faber and Faber, 1931). *Childhood and Cultural Despair: A Theme and Variations in Seventeenth-Century Literature* by Leah Sinanoglou Marcus (Pittsburgh, 1978) is a compelling study reflecting on childhood and the pastoral. Raphael Samuel, in *Theatre of Memory* (Verso, 1994), writes about nostalgia, heritage and the reproduction industry, and Susan Stewart explores some of these themes in *On Longing: Narratives of the Miniature, the Gigantic, the Souvenir, the Collection* (Johns Hopkins University Press, 1984). The psychology of collecting led me to William James (*The Principles of Psychology*, vol. 2, Macmillan, 1890) and the novels of Henry James and Balzac, both of whom were fascinated by it. *La Vie Étrange des Objets* (1959, translated as *Art on the Market*, Weidenfeld and Nicolson, 1961) by Maurice Rheims deals with some similar material. Lady Charlotte Schreiber (1812–95), better known to many as Charlotte Guest, editor of the *Mabinogion*, was a celebrated collector of porcelain, glass, enamels, earthenware, playing cards and fans; she bequeathed her collections to the Victoria and Albert Museum and the British Museum. *Biscuit Tins: The Art of Decorative Packaging* (New Cavendish, 1979) by Michael J. Franklin, the biscuit tin expert, was one of the most colourful of the collectors' manuals in which I browsed. *A Companion to Museum Studies*, ed. Sharon Macdonald (2006), has much useful information about the changing role of the museum, and includes the essays by Charles Saumarez Smith and Nick Prior from which I quote.

I have cited various mentions of jigsaws in fiction, but was unable to find a home for some I discovered or that were offered to me. I particularly regret a reference in Israeli novelist David Grossman's novel, *Someone to Run With* (2000; Bloomsbury, 2003), in which a young man in Jerusalem buys a 10,000-piece puzzle of the Swiss Alps for his family during the Gulf War, 'to try to ease the tension of the evening hours between the shelter siren and the All Clear'. The mother gives up after three days, saying she prefers Saddam's missiles to Swiss torture, and the others drop out over the weeks, suffering from snow blindness, but the youngest member of the family, aged seven, works on it till it is finished, a week after the war ends. This seemed to say something to me, but I never found out what it was. At least it illustrates that the assembling of jigsaws is not an exclusively English preoccupation.

David Grossman's son was killed in the Israel–Lebanon conflict in 2006, but that is part of another puzzle, and I don't know what that one is either.

JEU DE LA RÉV[OLUTION]

REGLE QUE L'ON DO[IT]

Il faut premierement convenir de ce que l'on veut jouer et de ce que l'on doit paye[r]
nombre, gagne le jeu, mais en rencontre bien des empêchements avant d'arriver au [...]
On joue avec deux Dez, on tire au sort a qui commencera, celui qui a le plus haut p[...]
suite en observant que chaque joueur ait une marque differente, il faut observer que si l[...]
en trouve plus mais celui qui auroit plus de points qu'il n'en faudroit pour arriver au nombr[e]
une Oye il recommenceroit a compter toujours en retrogradant. Si en commencant le [...]
et 4 et 6 et 3 iroit juste au nombre 63 attendu qu'il se trouve des oyes de 9 en 9, ainsi [...]
nombre 63.

REGLE DU JEU DE LA RÉVOLUTION FRANÇAISE.

Qui sera 6 ou est le Pont payera le prix convenu et ira au nombre 12 : Qui ira a[u]
Caveau payera le prix convenu et se reposera tandis que chacun jouera deux fois [...]
31 ou est le Puits payera le prix convenu y restera jusqu'à ce qu'un autre le relev[e]
a la place de celui qui l'aura relevé. Qui ira au nombre 42 ou est Labyrinte ou le Cha[...]
payera le prix convenu et ira au nombre 30.

Qui ira au nombre 52 ou est la Prison de l'Abbaye payera le prix convenu et [...]
y restera jusqu'à ce qu'un autre l'en retire.

Qui ira au nombre 58 ou est la mort de Foulon &c. payera le prix
convenu et recommencera de nouveau.

Qui sera rencontré par un des joueurs payera le prix convenu
et ira a sa place.

Prise de la Bastille.   Reunion des trois ordres.